MW00439650

Advance Praise for Developmental Politics

Developmental Politics is essential reading for those who are concerned about the dysfunctional condition of America's democracy. McIntosh's application of integral philosophy to the daunting problem of hyperpolarization shows how we can effectively grow out of our gridlocked politics. I highly recommend this groundbreaking and important book.

> — **John Mackey,** CEO of Whole Foods Markets, and coauthor of *Conscious Capitalism*

Is there a world beyond polarization! Indeed there is. In this inspired and brilliant work Steve McIntosh presents a richly conceived integral agenda and evolutionary strategy for the development of culture and consciousness, one that gives substance and reality to the unread vision of the higher dream for this Earth and time.

> — **Jean Houston,** Ph.D., Chancellor of Meridian University and author of many books on human development

Steve McIntosh is an incredibly deep and clear thinker who shows how people with very different worldviews can find a way to communicate, cooperate, and connect. *Developmental Politics* lays out a step-by-step approach to overcoming the wicked problem of hyper-polarization. This book is just what we need at this troubled time in history.

> — **Tony Schwartz,** bestselling author of *The Way We're Working Isn't Working* and *The Power of Full Engagement*, and CEO of The Energy Project

If I could prescribe one book for every Democrat or Progressive candidate and campaign to read (ASAP!), along with every environmental and climate activist and every advocate for racial justice, LGBTQ and gender equality, education reform, and economic equity, it would be Steve McIntosh's *Developmental Politics*. It's brilliant, well-written, and, I believe, just what the doctor ordered for our ailing body politic.

> — **Brian D. McLaren,** author of *The Great Spiritual Migration,* and *A New Kind of Christianity*

Steve McIntosh's latest book, *Developmental Politics*, explores how America can escape political polarization. McIntosh provides an insightful account of the emergence of postmodernism from modernity, showing how culture evolves through the development of values. He persuasively argues that an enlarged understanding of cultural evolution can help us reclaim our collective aspirations for social "progress." This important study is a must read!

— **Michael E. Zimmerman,** Ph.D., Emeritus Professor of Philosophy, University of Colorado at Boulder and coauthor of *Integral Ecology*

This is the right book for what's next in our politics, both nationally and personally. I found McIntosh's description of the practice of values integration to be instantly indispensable. And I loved his description of how a renaissance of virtue is a tonic for the cynicism of our age. Upon finishing *Developmental Politics*, it was as if I had been ushered into a more virtuous world. Here, to my surprise, I felt humbled and grateful for our unfolding American story, as wild and wooly as it is. After reading this book I can now see exciting possibilities for our next historical chapters. Also unexpectedly, the book has deepened my appreciation for my own story, and for the people and circumstances of my life.

— **Jeff Salzman,** Host of the Daily Evolver Podcast

Everyone feels it—our politics are broken and something must be done! But too many approaches to solving political polarization assume the solution. They are good ideas that could only be implemented in a less polarized environment. *Developmental Politics* cuts the Gordian knot by going right to the heart of this entrenched, complex issue—addressing the cultural battlegrounds that underlie our poisoned politics. McIntosh's timely book presents a powerful way to evolve both our country and ourselves. With a steady stream of clear, unfolding insight, it will make you believe again in the promise of our beautiful, troubled democracy.

— **Carter Phipps,** author of *Evolutionaries*

The divisiveness of our current politics is not sustainable. A new approach is needed to understand and then reconcile the conflicts we see today. In applying integral theory to this problem, Steve McIntosh's new book, *Developmental Politics*, offers such an approach—one that is fascinating and optimistically energizing.

— **Alexander McCobin,** CEO of Conscious Capitalism, Inc.

Developmental
Politics

*How America Can Grow Into
a Better Version of Itself*

Developmental Politics

*How America Can Grow Into
a Better Version of Itself*

Steve McIntosh

PARAGON HOUSE

First Edition 2020

Published in the United States by
Paragon House
St. Paul, Minnesota
www.paragonhouse.com

E-book edition ISBN: 978-1-61083-123-9

Library of Congress Cataloging-in-Publication Data

>Names: McIntosh, Steve, 1960- author.
>Title: Developmental politics : how America can grow into a better version of itself / Steve McIntosh.
>Description: First edition. | St. Paul, MN : Paragon House, 2020. | Includes bibliographical references and index. | Summary: "Developmental Politics describes a new political philosophy of progress that builds on the integration of traditional values and post-modern values. Hyper-partisan political polarization is a cultural problem that requires a cultural solution. This book employs integral theory to demonstrate a method of "values integration" through which citizens from across the political spectrum can reach new levels of consensus and cooperation using integral consciousness"-- Provided by publisher.
>Identifiers: LCCN 2019046814 | ISBN 9781557789426 (paperback) | ISBN 9781610831239 (ebook)
>Subjects: LCSH: Political culture--United States. | Political ethics--United States.
>Classification: LCC JK1726 .M3995 2020 | DDC 306.20973--dc23
>LC record available at https://lccn.loc.gov/2019046814

The paper used in this publication meets the minimum requirements of American National Standard for Information Sciences—Permanence of Paper for Printed Library Materials, ANSI standard Z39.48-1992.

Manufactured in the United States of America

10 9 8 7 6 5 4 3 2 1

Dedicated to

my beloved partner

Tehya McIntosh

CONTENTS

PART I
TOWARD A POLITICS OF CULTURE

1

2

3

4

PART II
TOWARD A NEW POLITICAL PHILOSOPHY
OF PURPOSE AND PROGRESS

5

6

7

8

9

APPENDIX A

APPENDIX B

PREFACE

I'm a first-generation American. My parents immigrated from England and Australia in the early 1950s because it seemed to them that America was the center of the world, and they wanted to be part of it. So I was taught from a young age to be grateful for my American citizenship and to not lose sight of the importance of this unique nation. Although my patriotism is now more nuanced than that of my parents, who were ardently allegiant to their adopted county, I still care deeply about the fortunes of American democracy.

Although America is plagued with abundant problems and challenges, most of these problems have pragmatic solutions that are within our power to implement. Almost none of these solutions, however, can be realized within our current political environment. Our frustrated, stymied, stalemated, and hyperpolarized political process is stuck in its tracks, and this gridlocked condition is now beginning to cause our social regression. Hyperpolarization is really the mother of all our problems because very few of the serious challenges we face can be adequately addressed until we ameliorate the fractious and frozen state of our body politic.

As we will consider in the pages ahead, hyperpolarization is not a problem that can be solved under our current cultural conditions. The only way to ameliorate this "wicked problem" is to effectively grow out of it. This book accordingly explores the broadened perspectives and emerging methods that can help American culture evolve into the next phase of its historical development. The good news is that the daunting problem of our dysfunctional democracy is creating the developmental pressure we need to "think anew and act anew," as Lincoln famously said. Although further regression is certainly a real possibility, the fractured state of American society also has the potential to catalyze a cultural renewal that can lead to a new era of political cooperation and progress. In other words, the difficult work of overcoming hyperpolarization can actually lead to a renaissance in American culture.

Throughout my life I've been fascinated with the times in world history that witnessed renaissances—periods of cultural florescence that brought about more advanced forms of civilization. My careful study of these renaissances eventually led me to an emerging perspective on cultural evolution known as *integral philosophy*.[1] Since the year 2000 integral philosophy has been the primary focus of my working life. This innovative body of thought sheds new light on the intersection of science and spirituality, and the three previous books I've written in the integral genre have concentrated mostly on the spiritual side of this philosophy. But in addition to its illumination of spiritual questions, integral philosophy is also highly relevant to politics.

Recognizing the political potential of this new philosophy, I felt moved to try to use its insights to help improve America's broken democratic process. Beginning in 2012 I joined with some colleagues in the integral movement to found a think tank dedicated to applying this emerging "developmental" perspective to America's political challenges. This think tank, named the Institute for Cultural Evolution, focuses on political problems that are either being caused or exacerbated by America's ongoing culture war. As will become clear as we proceed, the think tank's integral perspective attempts to position itself "outside and above" America's existing partisan factions, which means that its political stance is neither left, nor right, nor centrist. Besides myself, the leaders of the Institute for Cultural Evolution now include: Whole Foods founder and coauthor of *Conscious Capitalism*, John Mackey; education entrepreneur and host of The Daily Evolver podcast, Jeff Salzman; journalist and author of *Evolutionaries*, Carter Phipps; serial tech entrepreneur John Street; and philosophy professor and coauthor of *Integral Ecology*, Michael Zimmerman.

Initially, the Institute focused on the problem of global warming. By 2012 climate change had become a highly partisan and deeply divisive issue in American politics, so this seemed like a good place to start. But after working on the cultural dimensions of climate change for close to two years, it became evident that America's failure to address global warming was actually the result of another wicked problem—the problem of hyperpolarization. And this problem has been the main focus of the think tank ever since.

Between 2014 and 2016 the Institute convened a series of small invitational conclaves on hyperpolarization which brought together influential thought leaders on both the left and the right. The participants in these conclaves included prominent luminaries such as social psychologist Jonathan Haidt, political scientists Thomas Mann and Norman Ornstein, controversial scholar Charles Murray, The Breakthrough Institute's Ted Nordhaus, PBS's *Firing Line* host Margaret Hoover, *Reason* magazine's Nick Gillespie, MoveOn.

org founder Joan Blades, Log Cabin Republicans founder Rich Tafel, and Daily Beast editor-in-chief John Avlon, to name a few.

In addition to convening conclaves, we also gave lectures, wrote scholarly papers, published op-eds, received philanthropic grants, and gained recognition in numerous mainstream media outlets. Yet by the summer of 2016 my colleagues and I realized that we needed a substantial book that would explain our developmental perspective and demonstrate its potential to help ameliorate America's dysfunctional political condition. The writing of this book has accordingly been my full-time job for most of the last three years. *Developmental Politics* distills our learning and describes the new approach to politics and culture we have worked out over the course of this past decade.

The purpose of this book, as well as the larger movement for developmental politics overall, is to help American culture evolve beyond its hyperpolarized condition. While this goal may at first seem unrealistic or overly idealistic, all of my arguments and observations are made with a pragmatic focus in mind. As Otto von Bismarck famously observed, "politics is the art of the possible, the attainable—the art of the next best." As I will argue, under our contemporary political circumstances, achieving the "next best" involves expanding the scope of what we can value and thereby coming to view our political opponents more sympathetically. In other words, because our political problems are being caused primarily by the larger cultural discord that currently plagues our society, working to overcome this discord by evolving our culture is actually the most pragmatic thing we can do.

The work of evolving American culture begins by shining a fresh light on the bedrock values that are at the root of our political problems. While this concentration on values is necessarily philosophical, under our hyperpolarized conditions few things could be more practical than an improved philosophy of cultural evolution. Improving our theory of change is crucial because, as Einstein famously observed, it is your theory that determines what you can see.

The pragmatic applications of developmental politics are accordingly woven together with its philosophy of cultural evolution. In order to make this philosophy accessible to the general reader, the book is divided into two parts. Part I describes a new "politics of culture" that looks beyond the confines of Washington D.C. in an effort to better understand the conflicting worldviews that are behind our contemporary culture war. After analyzing the values-based worldviews that are driving cultural change, Part I concludes by introducing a method for overcoming hyperpolarization. This novel method promises to make progress where previous attempts at political mediation have failed.

In my discussion of the political philosophy of developmental politics, I will provide examples, but I won't spend much time discussing political personalities or offering detailed solutions to specific issues. Such an approach would only leave us bogged down in the stalemated duopoly we need to escape. Almost every current political issue is already so highly polarized that it is nearly impossible to even discuss these issues without appearing to come from either the left or the right. The polar forces that are pulling us apart have become so strong that finding a stable political "center" is like trying to find the center of a strong magnet—the opposing magnetic forces inevitably pull us to one side or the other. This is why we need a perspective that doesn't try to position itself in the middle of a perceived linear continuum between left and right. In order to grow beyond our contemporary political impasse we need an expanded perspective that is effectively positioned outside and above our contemporary cultural battleground.

Part II then goes deeper into the political philosophy that provides the ideational foundation of developmental politics. This philosophy offers a broad and inspiring vision for our collective way forward by reframing the idea of progress, and by advancing a new approach to generating positive political will. Although it is inadequately appreciated, political philosophy has in fact played an indispensible role throughout the history of American democracy. In order to function properly, all democracies need a vibrant and discerning political philosophy that can keep them in touch with their founding values and serve as a moral compass in their ongoing attempts to maintain justice and promote social progress. And given the extent to which American politics have gone off track, the dysfunctional state of our political process itself points to the need to update our political philosophy to account for the radical social changes that have occurred in America over the last fifty years. It is thus my sincere hope that the philosophy of developmental politics can make a useful contribution to the contemporary body of mainstream political thought.

Most Americans continue to love their country and care deeply about its future. But under our current political conditions, many of us feel powerless to effect meaningful change. In response to this dilemma, this book promises to show how we can evolve beyond the hyper-partisanship that is pulling our country apart. As we will see, the evolution we require must include both the personal growth of a critical mass of our citizens, as well as the collective maturation of our culture as a whole. Fostering positive growth at both of these levels simultaneously is thus the mission of developmental politics.

Steve McIntosh
Summer, 2019
Boulder, Colorado

PART I

TOWARD A POLITICS OF CULTURE

1

America's Existential Dilemma

AMERICA'S POLITICS ARE BADLY BROKEN. And they've been broken for so long that many now see this dysfunctional situation as the inevitable status quo for American government in the twenty-first century. For the last twenty-five years, ever since Newt Gingrich became Speaker of the House in 1994, with the exception of a brief reprieve after the tragedy of 9/11, America's political system has been effectively gridlocked.

Prior to the election of Donald Trump, most political experts argued that even though Washington D.C. was severely polarized, ordinary Americans actually agreed on most issues. These commentators and analysts argued that Americans had been "sorted" into artificially polarized camps by the Democratic and Republican parties. But after the 2016 election, even the most ardent centrists now recognize that our stark political divisions are actually a symptom of a larger rift in the cultural fabric of American society overall.

Every human polity is, of course, characterized by divisions. These natural differences of opinion arise from the fact that some people are focused primarily on improving what's wrong, while others are more focused on preserving what's right. There is even research indicating that the left-right polarity we consistently find in almost every form of politics is heritable—that people are born with brains that find one side or the other more congenial, although life experiences can still influence where they end up.

When these natural political differences are contained within a larger encompassing agreement about a common good—such as the good of the country, or our common interests as Americans—competition between opposing sides can generate authentic value and make political progress. But when the binding element of a common goal is lost, centrifugal political forces can cause opposing positions to fly apart, preventing any agreement whatsoever.

Democratic forms of government are almost always messy, but the contemporary condition of American politics has deteriorated to near the point of unsustainability. As Francis Fukuyama observed in his 2014 book, *Political Order and Political Decay*, America's government has become a "vetocracy" wherein our system of checks and balances has devolved to the point where each party has an effective veto on the positive programs of the other. And within our nation's evenly balanced, highly competitive two party system, this has produced the impasse that now paralyzes our government.

As is now becoming evident, the problem of a bitterly divided electorate is arising upstream from Washington politics. It's a *cultural problem* that requires a cultural solution. Although Americans have contested their cultural differences in the political arena since the founding of the Republic, over the last fifty years cultural concerns have come to play an increasingly important role in American political life.

Beginning in the 1960s, America's "culture war" effectively dissolved the political consensus that had prevailed since the end of the Second World War. This tentative postwar cultural truce was shattered as major portions of the population became disillusioned and began to question the moral authority of America's government. Although the disgrace of Richard Nixon and the defeat in Vietnam were triggering events that aroused the nation's suspicions, the deeper social changes that marked the Sixties were actually the beginning of a larger tectonic shift in America's overall cultural landscape.

Sociologists and political scientists interpreting the data from decades-long values surveys have smoothly identified this shift as the move from "allegiance values" to "assertive values."[1] These researchers describe a seamless continuum of political maturation wherein increasing education and wealth have naturally resulted in a more expressive and demanding electorate. But what these data-driven observers of social development fail to adequately recognize or account for is the dialectical pattern of struggle and opposition through which new forms of culture come into being.[2]

COMPETITION BETWEEN ALTERNATIVE MORAL SYSTEMS

I was born in 1960, and throughout my life American culture has been undergoing an unprecedented transition from one moral framework to another. Over this period, traditional forms of morality have lost much of their authority and old social norms have decayed as a significant number of Americans have come to embrace progressive values. For many Americans, especially the young, progressive morality feels more inclusive and liberating—more compassionate and emancipative—than the traditional moral values that guided their ancestors.

Through the influence of this progressive moral framework or system, large segments of the American electorate have become increasingly concerned about social justice and the urgent need to protect the environment. Moreover, progressive values have awakened Americans to the importance of diversity, and these values are gradually supplanting ethnocentric forms of morality with more worldcentric conceptions of those worthy of moral consideration.

This new system of progressive values, which I describe in detail in the pages ahead, now presents itself as a more enlightened and inclusive alternative to traditional values. And while this is undoubtedly true in many respects, as I will argue, this progressive moral system is not able to bear the full weight of America's cultural and political challenges. Although there are certainly many features of this new system of progressive values that represent welcome and needed advances, in their struggle to gain cultural ascendancy, progressives have effectively discarded or erased crucial elements of the traditional moral system upon which the sustainability of American society ultimately depends. Decency, honesty, humility, fair play, and respect for the institutions of marriage and family—these are just some of the crucial traditional values that serve as an indispensable foundation of American culture.

And perhaps most crucial of all, a basic sense of national patriotism, which is rooted in traditional values, is indispensable for the continuing viability of our democracy. However, as the social foundations of traditional patriotic values have been eroded, America's national sense of civic solidarity has become difficult to maintain. A democracy is a fragile institution that depends on some degree of positive national identity for its sustainability. Yet such a form of popular government can only be maintained when its citizens have confidence that despite the messiness and inefficiency, democracy is preferable to alternative forms of nondemocratic government. While most progressives affirm democracy in principle, their faith in the moral standing of Western civilization in general, and the American nation in particular, is increasingly called into question. In their otherwise commendable attempt to atone for

America's past crimes and abuses, progressives frequently go too far by characterizing American history as something akin to a sinister criminal enterprise.

But even though Americans do well to counterbalance traditional pride for their nation's accomplishments with a degree of progressive shame for its historical misdeeds, if we fail to adequately value America's achievements—together with the achievements of the modern world as a whole—we imperil our society's future.

A NEW POLITICS OF CULTURE

What's wrong is not simple. Our political dilemma cannot be attributed to a single factor. Again, we have a cultural problem that requires a cultural solution—the kind of solution that can only come from a more complex and refined understanding of the development of culture itself. America has largely outgrown its traditional moral system, but the apparent alternative of the progressive moral system is not yet mature enough to serve as a replacement. While we would perhaps like to have the best of both, these competing moral systems seem to be wholly incompatible. As America's intensifying culture war attests, traditional values and progressive values seem to be engaged in a ferocious winner-take-all struggle for the moral soul of America.[3]

"Think of the problems we could solve if we could only agree about the best solutions."

This bitter conflict, however, cannot be resolved by conventional political methods. In order to address the deep divisions that plague American society, we need a better understanding of how the evolution of values and worldviews has led to our current situation. And ultimately, we need new methods for building agreement and forging political consensus.

Think of the problems we could solve if we could only agree about the best solutions. Given the requisite political will, we could decrease carbon emissions while sustaining economic vitality. We could reduce income inequality while safeguarding economic freedom. We could end homelessness while preserving our collective expectations for self-reliance. And we could even create an effective healthcare system that ordinary Americans could actually afford. We could accomplish all of these political goals, and many more like them, if we could only overcome the cultural divisions that prevent one half of the country from agreeing with the other.

In response to this challenge, the chapters ahead will explore the exciting potential for *a new politics of culture*—a fresh form of political advocacy and activism known as developmental politics. This emerging approach to politics promises to help us grow out of the seemingly intractable dilemma of a deeply divided society by more clearly revealing the value disagreements that divide us in the present, together with the potential forms of new agreement that can unite us in the future. In other words, the goal of developmental politics is to foster the further cultural maturation of American society. Although this goal will certainly be difficult to achieve, the project of fostering meaningful political renewal is now becoming realistically practicable as a result of recent breakthroughs in the understanding of cultural evolution.

WORLDVIEWS—THE BASIC UNITS OF CULTURE

Human culture is, of course, highly complex; it can't be framed or mapped by a single model. Gaining a deeper understanding of culture involves examining this multifaceted subject from a variety of different conceptual angles. This need for multiple perspectives stems from the fact that the roots of culture extend into every level of human relations. Culture arises from the bonds formed by geographic region, by race, by class, by religion, by nationality, and increasingly by exchanges at a global level.

For example, as described in the 2012 book, *American Nations*, culture is closely tied to historical geography. Even where the ethnicity of the original settlers has been replaced by newcomers, regional political orientations continue to persist across generations. Yet while fascinating and well-documented, this regional explanation of America's cultural differences tells only a small part of the story. And even if we combine this regional view with other perspectives on cultural relations, we will still not have a clear picture because in order to adequately appreciate human culture we need to see it as a developmental process. In short, like life itself, culture is an evolutionary phenomenon.

However, the proposition that culture evolves remains controversial. In the wake of the horrific history of the twentieth century, the naïve Victorian notion that civilization is gradually progressing toward utopia has been thoroughly discredited. While culture evidently changes, the idea that it is evolving is difficult for many to accept in light of the fact that the advent of our modern world has brought about unprecedented global threats. But notwithstanding the new problems and pathologies that result from cultural development, as I will argue throughout this book, the only way to effectively overcome America's contemporary political dysfunction is to foster the further evolution of our culture.

Culture does not evolve in a straightforwardly linear way, but neither is its development merely cyclical, as the authors of the notorious *Fourth Turning* theory have argued. There are indeed numerous theoretical explanations of sociocultural development, and most of them have a piece of the truth. But after studying this subject for over two decades, I have come to the conclusion that among all the distinct ways that the development of culture can be analyzed or described, the most promising (albeit still partial) approach involves interpreting cultural evolution through the concept of *worldviews*.

A worldview, as I define it, is a coherent set of values and ideals that persists across multiple generations. Worldviews are large-scale cultural agreements about what is good, true, and beautiful. They give meaning to reality and help us understand the world. In fact, worldviews are arguably the basic units of cultural analysis and interpretation—the most fundamental structures of cultural evolution. These large-scale value systems are more than mere ideologies; they include numerous competing factions and exhibit internal contradictions. Even though our contemporary social milieu includes hundreds of discrete political perspectives which might be identified as distinct "worldviews" in their own right, the worldviews we will be exploring in this book are the historically significant cultural structures that continue to define the values and provide a sense of identity for major segments of American society.

Although the concept of a worldview inevitably rests on generalizations, there is plenty of evidence for the existence of these macro cultural structures. The social and political influence of worldviews is well recognized in the fields of sociology, psychology, and political science. Indeed, the new politics of culture being advanced by developmental politics places a lot of theoretical weight on this concept of worldviews. So in Part II we will explore the philosophical implications of this idea in greater depth. But for purposes of Part I's more pragmatic focus, the initial definition above will suffice. Simply put, recognizing worldviews is crucial for a politics of culture because when we ponder what our modern world actually is—when we inquire about the essential nature of "modernity"—the best answer is that *modernity is a worldview*.

Because the worldview of modernity (which I will also refer to as "modernism") continues to serve as the dominant cultural structure in American society, it cannot be easily described or defined without resorting to stereotypes or overly narrow caricatures. Modernity, of course, stands for progress, prosperity, individual liberty, and scientific rationality, but it can't be adequately described through a simple list of familiar values. In order to fathom the worldview of modernism, which envelops us like the water around the proverbial fish, we need to appreciate how its core values have been shaped by the larger currents of history through which it originally emerged. That is, modernity can only be accurately understood and appreciated by seeing it in the context of the traditional worldview that preceded it in history, and the progressive worldview that is now attempting to transcend modernist culture altogether.

"The culture war that is roiling American politics has three sides."

As explained at length in the next chapter, like the worldview of modernity, the competing moral systems I referred to above as "traditional values" and "progressive values" are also best understood as worldview structures. Although modernity's values overlap and interact with both the traditional worldview and the progressive worldview, in the timeline of historical development, the modernist worldview stands *in between* these other two cultural systems. And this is why we can accurately refer to traditional values as "premodern" and progressive values as "postmodern."

When lamenting the cultural divisions that have led to America's political dysfunction, mainstream commentators most often frame the problem as a division between "red states" and "blue states." We've all seen the map of election results depicted according to this red-blue color scheme. This simplistic bipolar framing is understandable given that our national politics continue to be dominated by a two-party system. But this historically engrained conception of left and right, which is habitually used to characterize our contemporary political condition as a two-way contest taking place along a horizontal continuum, is woefully inadequate to our present situation. America's political dysfunction is not simply the result of an exacerbated divide between the Democratic and Republican parties. Rather, we are now engaged in a *three-way struggle* between America's three major cultural worldviews: the modernist worldview, the traditional worldview, and what can best be described as the "progressive postmodern worldview." Simply put, the culture war that is roiling American politics has three sides.

So here lies the dilemma: the worldview of modernity has been spectacularly successful; its central value of progress has transformed the American nation from an agrarian society governed by traditional values to an increasingly urban society where progressive postmodern conceptions of morality are ascendant. Yet as a result of the rapidity of modernity's own progress (historically speaking), the abrupt social changes it has brought about are now disrupting the cultural solidarity necessary for a functional national polity. American culture has been "stretched out" to the point where it no longer coheres as a governable political entity, and we have consequently lost our sense of common cause. Stated otherwise, our collective sense of national solidarity has been "dis-integrated" by our own development.

Even though mainstream American culture remains centered within the modernist worldview, significant portions of the American population are losing faith in the project of liberal modernity overall. And because modernity's fundamental political problem of a bitterly divided electorate has arisen as a result of its own success at producing economic and social progress, this is a problem that cannot be solved at the same level of thinking that created it. America's deeply estranged and increasingly ungovernable social condition can therefore be recognized as an *existential problem* whose solution can only be found outside the confines of the modernist worldview. But despite the existential nature of this difficult dilemma, as we will see, this political crisis actually presents a golden opportunity for American society to evolve into a better version of itself—a more mature form of civilization.

2

The Momentous Emergence of the Modernist Worldview

THE RESULTS OF THE 2016 ELECTION demonstrated that America's deeply divided electorate is creating an existential dilemma for our nation. As I argued in the last chapter, the hyperpolarized state of our national politics is a cultural problem that has been brought about by our own rapid development. And because our political dysfunction is resulting from deep divisions within our culture, we cannot solve this problem through "politics as usual." Indeed, the cultural discord that plagues American society is not merely a matter of differences in political opinion; the animosity is rooted in a deeper contest about values and identity. In short, our hyperpolarization stems from a clash of worldviews.

The previous chapter also introduced the idea that American culture is now divided among three major worldviews: the mainstream modernist worldview, the socially conservative traditional worldview, and what developmental politics identifies as the progressive postmodern worldview (or simply "postmodernism"). This framing of America's three major cultures was, however, only asserted. So in this chapter and the next I will justify this framing by describing how these three cultures came about. Although we will be analyzing the characteristics and aims of these worldview structures throughout this book, the expanded cultural perspective of developmental politics is grounded in an evolutionary account of the genesis of modernism and postmodernism, to which we now turn.

THE STANDARD NARRATIVE OF MODERNITY'S EMERGENCE

Most readers are familiar with the standard narrative of the emergence of the modern world. According to this telling, what we now call modernity started in Renaissance Europe, which began to rediscover the lost wisdom of the ancient Greco-Roman world during the fifteenth century. This was followed by the Reformation of Christianity, which encouraged individualism and helped people to think for themselves. Then in the seventeenth century, geniuses such as Rene Descartes and Isaac Newton ushered in a new era of scientific discovery and rational thinking. And as this new rationality was applied to politics by thinkers like John Locke and Voltaire, the ideal of democracy began to seem achievable, which eventually brought about the American and French revolutions. These positive developments are now, of course, known as the Age of Enlightenment.

According to this standard narrative, the same methods of rational inquiry and innovative thinking that gave birth to science and democracy were also applied to commerce and human enterprise, which produced a fantastic outpouring of creative mechanical inventions. As innovations such as the steam engine began to be applied within many different fields of human endeavor, this resulted in an industrial revolution, which greatly expanded the commercial and military power of Europe and America in the nineteenth century.

And it was around this point in the historical timeline of modernity's emergence—the height of the industrial revolution—that things started to go wrong. The astonishing progress of Western civilization that had begun in the Renaissance, flowered in the Enlightenment, and culminated in the unprecedented material and scientific civilization of the nineteenth century, began to turn back on itself. The Western world had achieved immense power over a relatively short period of history. But because of its corresponding lack of cultural and ethical maturity, it was perhaps inevitable that the West would be corrupted by its own power.

"The moral failures of Western civilization have become the main point of the story."

The misdeeds of the West—the crimes of modernity—are also now part of the standard narrative. Indeed, within America's education establishment the moral failures of Western civilization have become the main point of the story. The oppression of slavery and colonialism, the destruction of indigenous peoples, the exploitation of workers and the degradation of the environment;

growing cognizance of these tragedies has now largely eclipsed the immense progress that modernity has managed to achieve, at least within the opinion of a politically significant number of Americans.

MODERNISM AND TRADITIONALISM

There are, of course, different flavors of the modernist worldview. It is not a rigid ideology or strict doctrine. Japanese modernism, for example, can be distinguished from Danish modernism. Some sociologists even argue for multiple modernities. However, I reject this conclusion. There are indeed multiple versions of the traditional worldview—Christian, Muslim, Hindu, Buddhist, to name a few—with each based on a specific form of religious teaching. But while traditional worldviews look to scripture as their foundational truth, modernity's truth is based primarily on science. Science does not vary between countries or religions; authentic science is universal. And in the same way that the international institution of science (having arisen with modernism) strives to be objective and universal, the values of the modernist worldview likewise attempt to claim the mantle of universal reason.

Even though the various traditional worldviews that continue to persist in American culture are not unified by the universal character of scientific truth, as is modernism, these divergent religious groups nevertheless exhibit remarkable and predictable consistency in their political positions and interests. Within the realm of politics, the ascendency of modernism has created the cultural pressure that has helped consolidate most of America's divergent religious outlooks into a coherent political block that often stands in opposition to modernity. This loosely affiliated cultural segment of American society embraces many religious communities, including Evangelical Protestants, Conservative Catholics, Mormons, Orthodox Jews, and many similar subcultures. But despite their diversity, these socially conservative groups do generally coalesce into the politically significant worldview most often referred to as "traditionalism." Members of these groups have been able to recognize each other as sharing the same basic traditional worldview as a result of the growing cultural power of their common modernist opponent. In short, the cultural ascendency of modernity over the last two-hundred and fifty years has brought about the relative political unification of otherwise diverse religious sects.

The cultural divide between traditionalism and modernism is not, of course, unbridgeable. Despite their partially opposing frames of reality there is significant overlap between the values of these respective worldviews, and it is certainly possible for the same person to hold different values in different circumstances—for example, by identifying as a traditionalist on Sunday and as a modernist on Monday. From its beginnings in the Enlightenment, modernity has both conflicted and cooperated with traditionalism. And where these two worldviews have cooperated, many common values can be identified.

But notwithstanding the presence of overlapping values, most people do exhibit a general center of cultural gravity that situates their loyalties primarily within the orbit of a single worldview. Again, when it comes to existential questions about what is real and true, modernism recognizes the authority of science, and traditionalism places its trust in scripture. And when faced with a stark choice between these sources of truth, people usually side with one worldview or the other—either science trumps scripture, or scripture trumps science.

Although it takes a degree of generalization and abstraction to identify these worldview structures, in order to understand the cultural forces that are roiling American politics it is necessary to recognize how these distinct frames of reality constitute real cultural entities. These large-scale systems of agreement are not just contrived classifications. As will become increasingly clear as we proceed, worldviews are the basic units of culture. However, while worldviews are real entities, they cannot be used accurately to simplistically typify individuals. Despite the "gravitational pull" of these discrete forms of identity, they are not entirely culturally determinative. While some people perfectly exemplify these cultural categories, others defy categorization. These worldviews are best understood not as types of people, but as *types of consciousness within people*. And for most Americans, these forms of cultural consciousness sound more in chords than in single notes.

The proposition that worldviews are actual cultural entities, and not just convenient but contrived analytical categories, constitutes the theoretical foundation of developmental politics. But while many readers may readily recognize and accept this proposition, for those who remain skeptical, I can point to the mainstream consensus that the distinct worldviews of modernism and traditionalism are evident social facts. It is beyond dispute that much of the world remains divided between the globalizing culture of modernity, and the premodern religious cultures that continue to prevail in large parts of the developing world.

Even within skeptical academic discourse, the contradistinction between premodern and modern outlooks is now widely accepted. Moreover, this academic consensus has been extended into popular culture through books such as Thomas Friedman's *The Lexus and the Olive Tree,* or Samuel Huntington's controversial *Clash of Civilizations,* which have described the differences between modernism and traditionalism in the international arena. And more recently, the clear divide between modernism and traditionalism has also been explored at the national level through books such as Tara Westover's *Educated,* J.D. Vance's *Hillbilly Elegy,* and Charles Murray's *Coming Apart.*

MODERNITY'S NEW CULTURAL OPPONENT: THE PROGRESSIVE POSTMODERN WORLDVIEW

Although I could argue the point further, I trust most readers will agree that the distinct worldviews of modernism and traditionalism are apparent features of America's contemporary political landscape. However, America's third major cultural block—the progressive postmodern worldview—remains only vaguely understood. In fact, part of the reason why political polarization remains a seemingly intractable problem in the minds of most political observers is that they fail to adequately recognize how postmodernism has become separated into a third major culture of its own over the last fifty years of American history. While progressive interests such as environmentalism and social justice are plainly obvious to the larger culture, the postmodern worldview as a distinct system of values is usually not adequately recognized or appreciated by establishment commentators. Most mainstream thought leaders continue to conceive of America's polarized culture war as simply a two-party contest between traditionalism and modernism.

For example, in his acclaimed 2017 book, *American Covenant,* Yale sociologist Phillip Gorski frames political polarization as a dueling clash between religious values and secular values, calling for a return to the "vital center" in order to "recover the civil religious tradition on which the republic was founded." But while Gorski correctly identifies the continuing struggle over values between traditionalism and modernism, he fails to see how this ongoing clash has now become further complicated by a similar but distinct opposition.

Since the 1960s modernity has had to contend increasingly with a new cultural opponent. Within the philosophy of developmental politics, this third major worldview is most frequently called "postmodernism," although other terms such as the "cultural creatives" or the "green meme" are also sometimes used. Even though the term "postmodern" is itself a battleground of meaning, this word is very useful (and worth fighting for) because it well describes the modernist worldview's cultural successor. Modernist critics of postmodernism attempt to define it narrowly by equating it with the critical theory of philosophers such as Michel Foucault and Jacques Derrida. Controversial psychologist Jordan Peterson, for instance, characterizes postmodernism as "cultural Marxism." From Peterson's perspective, postmodernism is not a new worldview but merely a virulent ideology that has hijacked academia.

"Postmodernism has become separated into a third major culture of its own in the last fifty years."

Yet while academic critical theory is certainly a feature of postmodern culture, it is only a relatively small part of this larger worldview, and not all postmodernists agree with its tenets. As with modernism and traditionalism, the worldview of postmodernism is not a monolithic belief system. It is a cultural structure of progressive values that contains its own internal contradictions and debates. But as will become increasingly apparent as our discussion unfolds, postmodernism must be recognized, not merely as a critical branch of academia, but as a third major worldview in its own right. Progressive congresswoman Alexandria Ocasio-Cortez, for example, epitomizes this cultural worldview, which seeks to right the wrongs of modernity overall.

While postmodernism includes a wide diversity of outlooks and beliefs, its status as a historically significant worldview in its own right is demonstrated by the many similarities it shares with the other major worldviews that have preceded it. Like modernism and traditionalism, the postmodern worldview provides its adherents with a sense of identity and accordingly creates strong loyalties to its perspectives. And following the pattern of the rise of previous worldviews, postmodern values stand in antithesis to the values of the existing culture from which they emerged. With the rise of postmodern values comes a rejection of what are seen as the stale materialistic values of modernism and the chauvinistic and oppressive values of traditionalism.

The three major worldviews of traditionalism, modernism, and postmodernism are each large-scale cultural systems that cannot be statically defined with precision. Yet these three distinct forms of culture can be illustrated by examples, as shown in figure 2.1 below. In the pages ahead we will carefully consider both the positive and negative features of these major worldviews, so figure 2.1 only provides an initial starting point for their description. But notwithstanding this simplified chart, it is important to continuously emphasize that these cultural structures are exceedingly subtle and complex. And again, it is possible for the same person to make meaning using more than one worldview, depending on the circumstances.

In terms of current demographic size, as of this writing modernism remains the majority worldview in America, holding the allegiance of approximately 50 percent of the population, followed by traditionalism with approximately 30 percent, and then by postmodernism with perhaps as much as 20 percent. These rough estimates are illustrated by figure 2.2, which shows the approximate demographic size of these respective worldviews in the order of their historical emergence.

These demographic estimates have been arrived at through research on both the psychology of individuals and the sociology of large groups.[1] The most extensive and empirically valid evidence for the evolution of values comes from the World Values Survey, a large-scale, multi-decade research project begun in the 1980s by Ronald Inglehart of the University of Michigan. Data from the World Values Survey clearly points to the existence of traditional religious values, secular-rational values, and what Inglehart terms "post-material values." But while their research confirms the existence of post-material or postmodern values within large demographic segments of the developed world, the academic researchers responsible for the World Values Survey fail to clearly recognize how these postmodern values now comprise a distinct worldview that repudiates many of the secular-rational values of modernity.

Even the mainstream political observers who do recognize that the postmodern worldview has become a third major culture in America usually fail to appreciate the upsides of postmodernism. While the immaturities and pathologies of postmodernity are apparent to them, they can't seem to see why millions of Americans would choose to identify with this system of values.

	Examples of the Traditional Worldview	Examples of the Modernist Worldview	Examples of the Postmodern Worldview
The Good	Faith, family, and country Self-sacrifice for the good of the whole Duty and honor Law and order God's will	Economic and scientific progress Liberty and the rule of law Personal achievement, prosperity and wealth Social status and higher education	Social and environmental justice Diversity and Multiculturalism Natural lifestyle and localism Planetary healing
The True	Scripture Rules and norms of the religious community Directives of rightful authority	Science Reason and objectivity Facts, evidence, & proof Literature & philosophy	Subjective perspectives, 'whatever is true for you' 'Woke' sensibilities The unmasking of power structures
The Beautiful	Children and family Artistic representations of wholesome and historical themes Country, Gospel, Classical, and patriotic music	Fashionable symbols of power and prestige Glamour and sophisticated style Jazz, Pop, Blues, Rock, and Classical music	Nature Indigenous art, conceptual art, performance art, etc. Techno, World, New Age, Reggae and Sixties music
Some of Their Heroes	Ronald Reagan Winston Churchill Edmund Burke Pope John Paul II Billy Graham William Buckley Phyllis Schlafly Antonin Scalia	Thomas Jefferson John F. Kennedy Franklin D. Roosevelt Albert Einstein Thomas Edison Adam Smith, Carl Sagan Milton Friedman Frank Lloyd Wright	Martin Luther King Jr. Mahatma Gandhi John Muir Margaret Mead Oprah Winfrey Betty Friedan John Lennon Joan Baez
Contemporary Figures	Ross Douthat Patrick Deneen Rod Dreher Rick Warren Tucker Carlson	Hillary Clinton Steven Pinker Thomas Friedman Bill Gates Sheryl Sandberg	Bernie Sanders Naomi Klein Ta-Nehisi Coates Bill McKibben Deepak Chopra

Figure 2.1. Examples of America's three major worldviews

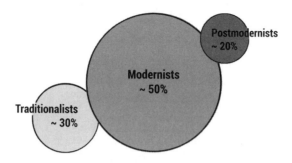

Figure 2.2. Rough estimates of each major worldview's percentage of the American population

The near-success of Bernie Sanders' 2016 bid to become the presidential candidate of the Democratic Party represents more than merely a resurgence of socialist politics, his popularity points to the rise of a larger mass movement in American culture. Beyond democratic socialism, the values of the postmodern worldview can also be seen in the environmental movement, the racial justice movement, and the ongoing struggle for women's rights, LGBTQ rights, and animal rights. Moreover, the influence of postmodern values can also be recognized in nonpolitical segments of American culture such as progressive spirituality, the natural foods movement, alternative medicine, multicultural sensitivity, and egalitarianism in general. Evidence for the proposition that the diverse trends listed above do in fact cohere as a distinct cultural worldview can be readily found by speaking with people who personally identify with postmodern culture. Indeed, most postmodernists will affirm that these diverse cultural characteristics fit together and constitute a larger whole. Yet among all of the defining features of postmodern culture, the most significant binding element is postmodernism's general opposition to modernity. And it is this resistance to modernity that makes this progressive set of values literally "post-modern."

Therefore, if developmental politics is to achieve its goal of more clearly revealing the cultural dynamics that drive American politics, it must help modernists and traditionalists to better recognize the enduring political significance of the progressive postmodern worldview. And again, to understand postmodernism we need to see it as a whole—as a historically consequential worldview that includes beneficial upsides as well as threatening downsides.

In furtherance of this goal, the next chapter will examine the history of postmodernism to see why and how it began in the nineteenth century as a countercurrent within modernity, but did not become clearly separated from modernism until the 1960s. Recounting the recent emergence of the postmodern worldview will thus help explain why it is not yet fully evident to modernists or traditionalists.

But before tracing the origins of postmodernity, we first need to reexamine the standard account of modernity's origins to see how its momentous emergence came about primarily through the appearance of new values. This understanding of the value foundations of modernism will in turn help explain and clarify the countervailing values of postmodernism.

MODERNITY CAME ABOUT PRIMARILY AS A RESULT OF THE EMERGENCE OF NEW VALUES

Contrary to the standard narrative of modernity's emergence, which gives pride of place to the role of science and technology, the rise of the modernist worldview in the eighteenth century was accomplished primarily through the advent of a powerful set of new liberal values. Although the term *liberal* is now used in America primarily as a label for center-left Democrats, the original meaning of liberalism (now called classical liberalism) entailed a new conception of justice that focused on the natural rights and liberties of each individual citizen. *Liberalism*, in the words of author Christopher Lasch, was "the most attractive product of the Enlightenment and the carrier of its best hopes."[2]

The liberal values championed by early modernists established a sphere of personal sovereignty for each individual—a domain of freedom from interference by the dictates of the collective. These liberal freedoms included the legal right to think for oneself and speak one's mind in public, the right to gather with others and organize for a cause, the right to believe any religion or no religion, and the right to a fair judicial process prior to being deprived of one's property or liberty by the government. And in addition to these familiar constitutional freedoms, the advent of modernity instituted what is arguably the most powerful freedom of all—economic freedom. The right to own property, to trade freely with others, and even to own and control "the means of production"; more than any other factor, it was the establishment and protection of relatively free markets that propelled the ascendency of modernity.

According to political scientist John Tomasi, "The institutions of the early American republic emphasized private property, commercial exchange, and guarantees of formal legal equality. Justice, in that social world, was understood primarily as a property of individuals. Justice is distribution to each according to his talent or desert. A society that provided formal protection to the natural rights of citizens could yield something new in the history of the world: a genuinely free and classless society. Or so many Americans of that era believed."[3]

Although the advent of scientific medicine is arguably the achievement of modernity that has benefited humanity the most, modernism's greatest social impact has come about as a result of what economic historian Deidre McCloskey calls "the Great Enrichment." For thousands of years the vast majority of humanity had subsisted on the contemporary equivalent of less than $3 a day. But as the rights and values of economic freedom became established in early modern societies, the average person was enriched by an astonishing and unprecedented degree—close to 5,000 percent.[4] As a result of this Great Enrichment, citizens of the developed world now live on an average of $130 a day. And this profound growth in material prosperity was facilitated and underwritten by the emergence of modernity's new emphasis on individual liberty.

As McCloskey argues convincingly in her trilogy of books extolling the power of bourgeois virtues, more than any other factor, the Great Enrichment was brought about by a change in ideas and ideals—the emergence of a new worldview. The unprecedented prosperity that modernity brings to the societies that have managed to adopt its culture cannot be explained by materialist economics, or by the geographical determinism of "guns, germs, and steel." Rather, this prosperity is the product of a significantly enhanced *valuation* of innovation and entrepreneurial initiative. That is, as McCloskey's historical analysis demonstrates, it was the emergent values of modernity, which honored and esteemed invention, innovation, and commercial enterprise like never before, that inspired average people to "have a go" at creating something new.

Although the individualistic values of modernity continue to be challenged by traditionalism on one side and now by postmodernism on the other, people in the developing, premodern world are nevertheless continuing to strive for both the prosperity and the personal liberty that are the fruits of modernism. And here in the developed world, the incredible technology and connectivity, the scientific medicine, the arts and music, the beneficial institutions, the ease of transportation, the quality and variety of food and clothing, as well as the countless other benefits of modernity, have now become familiar features of our everyday lives that most of us take for granted.

Even before many of modernism's most desirable features were fully realized, the larger social benefits that stem from prosperity were recognized as early as 1917 by journalist H.L. Mencken, who wrote, "with the rise from want to security, from fear to ease, comes an awakening of the finer perceptions, a widening of the sympathies, a gradual unfolding of the delicate flower called personality, an increased capacity for loving and living."[5]

For those who reside in functional modernist societies, it is the problems created by modernity that are naturally most concerning. Yet if we pull back for a moment to take a wider historical view, we may come to recognize how the rise of modernity is the largest social advance in the history of humanity—even more significant than the original domestication of agriculture twelve thousand years ago! Notwithstanding modernity's daunting challenges and abiding shortcomings, few of us would be willing to return to the conditions of the premodern world.

MODERNITY DEPENDS ON THE BORROWED SOCIAL CAPITAL OF TRADITIONALISM

Although modernity originally made its advance by breaking out of the stifling social conformity demanded by the traditional worldview, all forms of modernism rely on and continue to use traditionalism's previous value accomplishments. Even though modernity has improved the human condition immensely, producing more cultural evolution than any worldview before or since, it is nonetheless important to recognize that modernism is not a complete or free-standing value system in its own right. In order to effectively use modernist values to achieve the freedom and prosperity that are the fruits of modernity, people need to have been previously socialized by traditionalism to obey the rule of law, to be honest and reasonably fair, and to continue to acknowledge the needs of the collective to at least some degree.

Without an underlying foundation of functional traditional morality, modernism is unsustainable and indeed dangerous. Again quoting Lasch: "liberal democracy has lived off the borrowed capital of moral and religious traditions antedating the rise of liberalism."[6]

Evidence for this point can be found in societies where modernism has failed to take root, despite sustained governmental efforts and extensive foreign aid. Where traditional culture is itself dysfunctional—where it has been disrupted by colonialism or torn apart by internecine warfare—traditionalism's moral authority is not strong enough to sufficiently deter the corruption and self-dealing cronyism that thwart the development of modernist economies and their accompanying liberal freedoms.

Despite being focused primarily on the rights and liberties of individual citizens, modernity's values nevertheless provide a common identity for millions worldwide. Yet the functionality of this frame of values is ultimately predicated on the existence of an attendant moral system that modernity alone is not capable of supplying. Moral systems are the product of collective agreements enforced through social norms, peer pressure, and the expectations of the larger community. And the effectiveness of these cultural agreements depends on a *communitarian ethos*—a binding sense of solidarity that emphasizes the sacrifice of the self for the sake of the larger group.

This communitarian ethos or ethic is strongly present in both the traditional worldview and the postmodern worldview, which is why each of these worldviews give rise to strong moral systems of their own. Conversely, the absence of a strong communal ethos within modernity helps explain why the modernist worldview, with its contrasting individualistic ethos emphasizing the sovereign expression of the self, cannot supply the communitarian expectations and compelling group norms that are necessary for the functioning of a robust moral system.

Modernity's lack of a communitarian ethos, however, should not be viewed as a regrettable pathology. Rather, by embracing an individualistic ethos and championing the rights of each citizen, modernity was pursuing the main opportunity for cultural evolution that was open to it at the time of its original emergence. From its ancient beginnings, the traditional worldview fostered societies based on the strong bonds of a common religion. But by the time of the Enlightenment, the traditional worldview had accomplished most of the social progress that was possible within its communitarian form of civilization. The way forward was accordingly found in a dialectical pendulum swing toward an ethos of individualism. And now that modernity in the developed world has likewise attained most of the social progress that it is capable of achieving, this has opened the way for a new form of communitarianism, which postmodernism is attempting to define and deliver.

THE DEVELOPMENTAL LOGIC OF CULTURAL EVOLUTION

The philosophy behind developmental politics (discussed at length in Part II) recognizes how the evolution of human culture unfolds through a dialectical process wherein new worldviews emerge by pushing off against the shortcomings and pathologies of previous worldviews. This understanding of worldview development, however, does not rely on deterministic "laws of history," nor does it contend that culture evolves through a series of universal stages toward a single destination. Developmental politics is not a revamped version of Victorian evolutionism. But this developmental view of America's contemporary political circumstances does firmly contend that the emergence modernity itself demonstrates the cultural significance of worldviews, and that this extraordinary emergence constitutes an undeniable step in human history.

"Modernity's achievements have opened the way for a new form of communitarianism which postmodernism is attempting to define and deliver."

Newly emerging worldviews are inevitably defined by their opposition to the limitations of the previously prevailing culture. And this evolutionary process of cultural differentiation creates a pattern of development wherein each new worldview seeks to advance in a countervailing direction that distinguishes it from the status quo. This dialectical course of development can be compared to a sailboat tacking against the wind, or to a river meandering in a floodplain. As communitarian-oriented worldviews attain the maximum social progress that their values can supply, further progress can only be achieved by tacking in the opposite direction by reemphasizing individualism. This is then eventually followed by another turn toward the direction of the communitarian needs of the larger society, and so on.

As illustrated in figure 2.3, over the last four hundred years the leading edge of development of Western civilization has moved from the communitarian worldview of traditionalism, to the individualistic worldview of modernism, and now increasingly toward postmodernism's fresh expression of communitarian solidarity.

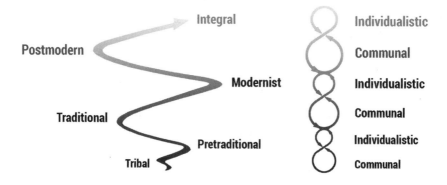

Figure 2.3. A highly simplified illustration of how cultural worldviews develop by dialectical steps, which alternate between communitarian orientations and individualistic orientations[7]

Yet even though every new worldview attempts to transcend the worldview that precedes it in history, each emerging worldview also relies on and necessarily includes the accomplishments of its predecessors. Although cultural evolution cannot be conflated with biological evolution, practically all forms of evolution achieve developmental progress by building on what has come before. That is, evolution always grows from within itself, transcending yet including previous levels of development. This dialectical pattern of transcendence and inclusion is clearly evident in the evolution of human culture. As discussed above, successful forms of modernism necessarily build on the previous successes of traditionalism, relying on the preexisting moral systems of the religious societies that predate modernity. And just as modernity borrows the moral capital of traditionalism, postmodern culture similarly depends on the previous value accomplishments of modernity. Postmodern culture can only fully emerge and take root within societies that are both relatively wealthy and free—conditions created by the success of modernism. Stated otherwise, without the collective prosperity and personal liberties afforded by modernity, postmodernism is culturally unsustainable.

At this point in the discussion I want to pull back for a moment to acknowledged the limitations of this "thirty-thousand foot view" of cultural history. Although it obviously leaves out important counter examples and social nuances, this generalized overview allows us to see how two seemingly contradictory propositions can both be true at the same time: The first truth is that modernism emerged by breaking out of the societal constraints imposed by traditionalism, repudiating many traditional values in the process. And the second truth is that modernity also built upon the civilizing achievements of traditional society, and continues to rely on the functioning of traditional values, even though the religious authority that is the source of these values has now been politically subordinated and culturally transcended.

Although postmodern academics usually dismiss big picture accounts of cultural evolution, the lack of such a wider view of historical development can blind us to the solutions to our political dysfunction. Again, even though recognizing these large-scale structures of development requires us to use "orienting generalizations," this sequential pattern of cultural evolution is very real. It thus bears repeating that in order to foster the development required to overcome America's sclerotic social stagnation—in order to grow out of our cultural and political gridlock—we need a better understanding of cultural development itself. And this is why an overarching thirty-thousand foot perspective is required.

It is also important in this context to include a further disclaimer regarding stage theories of development. Developmental politics acknowledges that cultural growth exhibits many varied characteristics. Viewed from certain perspectives this growth appears not as a sequential trajectory of stepwise advance, but rather as a "sprawling bush" of development that includes numerous branches, contradictory countercurrents, and even forces of decay that work against positive development or pervert it into trends that result in social regression. But notwithstanding the chaotic and contingent nature of cultural evolution, the historical record clearly shows how both modernism and postmodernism have emerged in opposition to what came before. So even though the developmental trajectory of human culture is not linear and can't be neatly pigeon-holed into a series of static stages, the dialectical process through which new worldviews emerge does mark the course of history with a structural sequence of emergence that unfolds in clearly identifiable steps. And these discrete steps of worldview development can be accurately identified as "stages," albeit in a very loose and general way. This dialectical sequence of worldview emergence accordingly demonstrates the "developmental logic" of cultural evolution.[8]

Returning to our evolutionary overview, after breaking with traditionalism during the Enlightenment—after the upheavals of the French Revolution and the eventual ascendency of democracy in Europe—modernity entered a period of relative peace with traditionalism. Although cultural conflicts between modernism and traditionalism continued to occasionally erupt, up until the 1960s religion was generally accommodated and accepted by most citizens as a seemingly natural and permanent feature of the modern world. Traditionalism had been tamed and contained within modernist society through a tacit cultural truce wherein religion could continue to supply the underpinning morality of modernism as long as it stayed mostly out of politics.

> "Traditionalism was contained through a tacit cultural truce wherein religion could continue to supply the morality of modernism as long as it stayed mostly out of politics."

This cultural truce, however, could not last. In the process of establishing its social dominance over traditionalism, modernity had largely delegitimized religious truth claims. And eventually, as more and more leading modernists came to embrace strong scientific materialism and mild philosophical nihilism, the inherent contradictions between science and religion acted as a destabilizing influence. At first, only intellectuals and artists were troubled by the inconsistencies. But as modernity reached the apogee of its cultural maturation in America after World War II, it could no longer credibly claim the sanction of traditional morality. As a result of modernity's "legitimation crisis," increasing numbers of Americans began to sense that the shaky alliance between modernism and traditionalism could no longer be justified.

By the mid-1960s the social complex formed by the relative cultural détente between the modernist and traditionalist value systems had come to be seen by many (especially America's youth) as the corrupt "establishment," which needed to be seriously questioned, and perhaps even overthrown entirely. As modernity's pathologies became increasingly evident, its perceived complicity with the ethnocentric shortcomings of traditionalism only served to magnify the resentment felt toward both value systems. It was this growing discontent with the social status quo that catalyzed the emergence of postmodernism as a countercultural, anti-modernist, anti-traditionalist worldview of its own.

In the next chapter we will examine why modernity, although arguably the most beneficial cultural emergence in human history, is nevertheless intolerable to so many of its best and brightest citizens.

3

Tracing the Development of the Progressive Postmodern Worldview

A S DISCUSSED IN THE LAST CHAPTER, mainstream political commentators and social scientists do not have a viable strategy for ameliorating America's gridlocked politics because they fail to fully grasp how or why the disruptive culture of postmodernism has become so powerful. Like all historically significant worldviews, postmodernism is attempting to remedy the shortcomings and pathologies of the worldview that preceded it, which in this case is modernism. The postmodern worldview has thus been instinctively striving from its beginnings to overcome the perceived hyper-individualism of modernity by reclaiming a new communitarian ethos—a post-traditional form of collective solidarity based on the tenets of a new system of values. Tracing the history of postmodernism's ongoing struggle to transcend modernity will therefore contribute to our understanding of the social and cultural forces that are currently paralyzing America's democratic process.

According to the analysis of Deirdre McCloskey and other economic historians and political scientists, for a relatively brief period between 1789 and 1848, in Western Europe and America the newly ascendant worldview of modernity was celebrated by elites and commoners alike as a moral triumph. Liberty, equality, and fraternity became the watchword of the times, and the new freedoms afforded by liberal values—"the Rights of Man"—were widely acclaimed as the marvelous new order of the age.

During this honeymoon of modernism, many traditionalists continued to view it with suspicion. But even from its very beginnings modernity's secular-rational worldview attracted critics who were not traditionalists. Stirrings of discontent within modernist ranks began with the poets and writers of the Romanticism movement who reacted to a fading faith in God by attempting to rediscover some form of ultimate meaning in nature and in human emotion. Yet for the most part, artists and intellectuals in the first half of the nineteenth century welcomed the innovative and commercial spirit of modernity as a fresh wind of progress.

THE REVOLT OF MODERNITY'S ARTISTS AND INTELLECTUALS: 1848 TO 1968

While the cultural honeymoon of modernity would last at least until the disillusioning calamity of World War I, strong opposition to modernism's increasingly evident pathologies began to appear around the pivotal year of 1848. By the mid-nineteenth century many of modernity's elite thought leaders had become critical and even disdainful of what they saw as the vulgar pursuits of the bourgeoisie. Modernism's driving engine of free market capitalism accordingly became the focus of an "intellectual organization of political hatreds."[1] The most prominent figure in what is now recognized as the "revolt of the artists and intellectuals" was Karl Marx, whose *Communist Manifesto* was first published in 1848. But this loss of confidence in modernity cannot be conflated with the rise of Marxism. Other influential writers such as Charles Dickens and Thomas Carlyle expressed their own versions of dismay at the depredations of the industrial revolution.

In the period between 1848 and the similarly pivotal year of 1968, a significant portion of highbrow society in Europe and America, and nearly all of modernity's cultural elites, took a dim view of what they saw as "the evil of profit, the curse of materialism, the insincerity of advertising, the scandal of excessive consumption, the irreligiousness of commercial dealing, the corruptions of corporations, the ruination of the environment, [and] the inevitable poverty consequent on a system of market capitalism ..."[2] Even as millions achieved middleclass prosperity and technological innovation continued to advance at staggering speed, the flourishing scientific and commercial civilization brought about by the modernist worldview was viewed from within by many of its best and brightest citizens as morally bankrupt.

There were, of course, many good reasons to hold modernism in contempt. Beyond the perceived vulgarities of capitalism, the rapacious colonialism of the nineteenth century, followed by the devastating world wars of the twentieth century, provided seemingly ample justification for its rejection.

However, from the perspective of developmental politics, which focuses on the competing value systems that drive the evolution of culture, there was another, deeper reason why many sensitive thinkers for the last hundred and fifty years have found modernity to be intolerable. Although it was rarely clearly articulated or even fully realized by the contrarian artists and intellectuals themselves, the liberal values of modernity were deemed unacceptable because they lacked a strong vision of *the transcendent*—a form of ultimate meaning that is more important than the needs of the individual self.

Modernity's individualistic ethos was focused on liberating its citizens and protecting them from the oppressive dictates of the collective. But because classical liberal values were chiefly concerned with the sovereignty of the individual self, this made it seem as though self-interest was modernity's only guiding principle. And this helps explain why many of the thought leaders of Western civilization found the modernist worldview to be morally repugnant.

"The liberal values of modernity were deemed unacceptable because they lacked a strong vision of *the* transcendent."

Every version of the traditional worldview past and present employs a robust concept of the transcendent to serve as the focal point of its moral system. Notions of God's will or "the one true way" provide the heading for traditionalism's progress, and the very reason for its existence. Indeed, all socially viable moral systems identify some worthy object of ethical obligation that defines a greater good for which the sacrifice of self-interest can be justified. And in practically all traditional societies this ethical object is found in devotion to some kind of transcendent Deity. But as modernity escaped the bonds of Christianity's medieval political power during the Enlightenment, it also became simultaneously separated from the law-giving moral power of the transcendent itself. Even though most modernists continued to believe in God, and even though large portions of the population in both Europe and America remained loyal to traditional values, the unifying power of traditionalism's moral system was increasingly delegitimized as modernity became the dominant worldview of the West.

Although the unifying authority of traditionalism's moral system had been gradually decreasing since the Enlightenment, the publication of Darwin's

Origin of Species in 1859 dealt a death blow to traditional Christianity in the minds of many elites. Traditionalism's claims on political power had been largely repudiated during the eighteenth century, and then in the nineteenth century science overturned traditionalism's foundational creation story. Yet even though traditionalism's moral authority had been substantially discredited in the minds of many elites, Christianity continued to provide the default moral system that underpinned much of Western society through at least the first half of the twentieth century. However, as discussed in the next section, the year 1968 marked the beginning of the end for the mainstream cultural truce between traditionalism and modernism.

At a deep, and in many cases unconscious, cultural level, the gradual delegitimization of traditional morality throughout the nineteenth and twentieth centuries precipitated the search for a substitute ideal of transcendence. With the justifying authority of God's natural law increasingly absent, modernists needed a new way to ground their notions of justice and morality in something higher—something more worthy than self-interest alone. "Modern Westerners rejecting God found other gods, in will or despair or history or spiritualism or science or the environment."[3] But among all the candidates for a new moral object of ethical duty, "the people" became the primary stand-in for a religious concept of the transcendent. For many modernists, the secular love of others seemed to suffice as a worthy cause on which to ground their morality.

However, as modernity became untethered from its traditional moorings, this seemingly benign devotion to the collective morphed into two dangerous, and in hindsight predictable, social trends. Communism and ultra-nationalism, each in their own way, became focal points of this new devotion to the quasi-transcendent cause of the people. For the communists, this new object of ethical concern was defined as the proletariat masses who had been oppressed and exploited by the bourgeois ruling class. And for the fascist ultra-nationalists, the cause of the people was defined largely in ethnic or racial terms as the collective will of "the Volk." The religious fervor with which both communists and ultra-nationalists pursued their newly framed devotions to the people eventually led, of course, to the titanic clash of the Second World War.

The catastrophic failure of both communism and ultra-nationalism during the twentieth century provides strong evidence that the worldview of modernism is not capable of generating a functional moral system of its own.

Lacking the constraints and civilizing influence of traditional morality, both communism and ultra-nationalism, although originating within modernity, ultimately devolved into malignant forms of pseudo-modernity. And although communism and fascism have been defeated for the most part, pseudo-modernity, defined as a society that has mastered modernity's scientific technology but has failed to embrace modernity's liberal values, continues to plague humanity into the twenty-first century.

Even though communism would not collapse until 1989, by the 1960s modernism's failure to provide a free-standing, post-traditional moral system of its own had become evident to many in the West. While a new moral system founded on the vision of an exalted collective humanity still seemed like a hopeful possibility, it was becoming clear that this new moral agreement structure could not take root within the individualistic worldview of modernity itself. Attempts to substitute humanity for God while still remaining within a modernist value frame inevitably led to pseudo-modernity. Therefore, in order to safely establish "the people" as a new transcendent ground of moral obligation, it would be necessary to break out of modernist culture altogether.

Yet although the morality of modernity had been called into severe question by the events of the first half of the twentieth century, following World War II and before the upheavals of the Sixties, America's national unity and revitalized prosperity resulted in a kind of golden twilight for the cultural truce between modernism and traditionalism. The brief interlude between 1945 and 1968 was marked by strong social solidarity among Americans and a functional political consensus between Democrats and Republicans. This period of consensus was brought about by traditionalism's temporarily renewed influence. However, for reasons outlined in the last chapter, the postwar armistice between the individualistic liberal values of modernity and the communitarian religious values of traditionalism could not last. Their political partnership had become rationally incoherent.

Prior to the mid-Sixties, the intellectual and artistic opponents of modernity had remained a small, culturally elite group. But as the baby boom generation came of age, many found the message of Western civilization's critics appealing. In light of the horrific events of the twentieth century, this new generation was persuaded en masse that traditionalism had been delegitimized by science and philosophy, and that modernity had been discredited by war and the degradation of the environment. For this sensitive post-war generation, the prevailing establishment truce was no longer tenable, so the quest for an entirely new worldview seemed to be the only viable option.

POSTMODERNITY IS BORN AS A DISTINCT WORLDVIEW

Even though they had positioned themselves as modernity's cultural critics, the artists and intellectuals who rejected bourgeois liberal values prior to the Sixties nevertheless remained embedded within modernist culture. Marxists, for example, viewed social change primarily in economic terms and were committed to materialist metaphysics and atheism. But beginning in the 1960s, America's middleclass youth, who already enjoyed practically everything modernity had to offer, began to feel a sense of collective discontent with the society they had inherited. It was thus from the heart of modernity's most successful expression up to that time—the prosperous American society of the early Sixties wherein the cultural truce between modernism and traditionalism still prevailed—that postmodernism would first emerge as a historically significant worldview in its own right.

Just as the advent of modernity in the Enlightenment is now recounted with a standard narrative (described in the last chapter), the cultural changes that began in the 1960s also have a similar standard narrative. By this telling, the baby boom generation had been spoiled by privilege and had become restless. This led to an indulgent revolution of youthful idealism, fueled by drugs and a sense of liberation from oppressive traditional social norms. According to this standard narrative, the turbulent Sixties made society incrementally more tolerant and achieved some permanent social changes, but as the hippies matured, most were eventually assimilated back into bourgeois society. Indeed, this self-serving modernist account of a "failed revolution" and the subsequent demise of Sixties idealism seemed to be confirmed in the 1980s as Ronald Reagan and a re-emergent religious right temporarily restored the political authority of the modernist-traditionalist cultural alliance.

However, the standard narrative that paints the countercultural emergence of the Sixties as merely the folly of self-indulgent young baby boomers who have since grown up is merely wishful thinking on the part of modernists. The contemporary circumstances of the early twenty-first century reveal that the rejectionistic spirit that began in the Sixties has not been subsumed or assimilated within a continually growing modernity. Rather, the postmodern worldview has now become a politically significant cultural force that is supplying much of the existential discontent which continues to fuel America's ongoing culture war.

Although artists and intellectuals had been voicing their discontent for over a century, before the emergence of postmodern culture in the Sixties, their criticisms of modernity remained mostly within elite circles. And as noted, despite their suspicions, these critics were themselves culturally modernist in many important respects. But as the postmodern worldview began to emerge, anti-modernist opinions took on a new character and became widely democratized. As a result of powerful new forms of countercultural music and fashion, together with the worldview-shattering experience afforded by psychedelic drugs, the personal rejection of a modernist cultural identity was made attractive and exciting to large numbers of people. Moreover, the alternative forms of spiritual culture that blossomed in the Sixties seemed to offer the enticing promise of a fresh, emancipative lifestyle that could leave the rat race behind.

"The postmodern worldview has now become a politically significant cultural force supplying the existential discontent that is fueling America's cultural war."

These newly minted counterculturalists were politically progressive and decidedly leftist, but their politics constituted a new left. Whereas the old socialist left had been stoic and direly serious, this new postmodern left was more irreverent and playful (at least at the beginning). The new left inherited the moral righteousness of the civil rights movement, which it then combined with the youthful spirit of the anti-Vietnam war movement to create the political consciousness that would eventually develop into contemporary forms of postmodern resistance.

By 1968, the cord that bound anti-modernist intellectuals and their followers to the seemingly inescapable culture of modernity had finally snapped. Just as modernity itself had originally broken with traditionalism in 1789 through the rallying cry of "liberty, equality, and fraternity," postmodernity similarly declared its new-found freedom from modernity with the slogan: "turn on, tune in, drop out."

As noted, however, by the late-Seventies the promise of the hippie movement had been largely coopted by modernist culture. As the liberating music of the Sixties was superseded by disco and punk, hopes for the new "Age of Aquarius" faded, and many came to the conclusion that Sixties culture was merely a passing fad. But even as early postmodern culture became less visible within the mainstream, it continued to flourish in elite enclaves, most notably in academia and the entertainment industry.

Then after a period of relative quiescence in the 1980s during the Reagan years, postmodern culture witnessed a kind of rebirth in the 1990s. Although it was no longer merely a youth movement, the values of the postmodern worldview found fresh expression in a revitalized environmental movement and in a new push for diversity and multicultural inclusivity.

The ongoing vitality of postmodern culture was also nourished in the 1990s by the florescence of New Age spirituality. Youthful fascination with the mystique of Eastern religions and alternative forms of spirituality was a significant part of the counterculture from the start. But in the 1990s alternative spirituality experienced a boom as popular authors such as Deepak Chopra and Marianne Williamson rose to prominence, and this progressive form of spirituality became the publishing industry's largest category by far.

And now, as postmodern culture continues to develop into the twenty-first century, its momentum is being quickened by the coming of age of the millennial generation. Millennials evince a strong affinity for postmodern values, as shown by their enthusiastic support for Bernie Sanders' candidacy and by their staunch political correctness. While the postmodern culture of millennials is not identical to the original postmodernism of their baby boomer forebears, the worldview of progressive postmodernity nevertheless demonstrates tenacious intergenerational continuity.

Unlike traditionalism or modernism, contemporary postmodernism can be hard to pin down. Because of its inherent pluralism, and because it consists of many disparate cultural currents, it can sometimes be difficult to recognize as a coherent system of values. Yet like traditionalism and modernism, postmodernism engenders strong loyalty from those who make meaning using its perspectives. Moreover, the postmodern worldview defines who and what is valuable in ways that are clearly distinct from previous worldviews. As discussed in the last chapter, the influence of postmodern values can be seen in the increasing popularity of socialism, environmentalism, feminism, critical academia, and many other identifiable expressions of progressivism. Despite the diversity of views that are embraced by the postmodern worldview, what generally binds postmodernists together is their agreement regarding the abundant pathologies of modernism. Anti-modernism is thus the hallmark of practically all forms of postmodern culture.

Beyond the provision of political opinions and social norms, the distinctive culture of postmodernism gives its adherents a sense of cultural belonging. Postmodernists can usually recognize each other through their common styles of dress, by their scrupulous diets, and by their social associations. As will become increasingly apparent as our discussion continues, the postmodern counterculture that first emerged in the Sixties has now become a kind of counter-establishment—a politically influential structure of value agreements that can be compared and contrasted with modernism and traditionalism.

POSTMODERNISM IS FOUNDED ON A NEW COMMUNITARIAN ETHOS OF SENSITIVITY

In order to function smoothly and stave off social decay, all complex societies need systems of morality that can foster cooperation and ensure pro-social behavior among their citizens. And as we've seen, to be effective over the long term, moral systems depend on a communitarian ethos supplied by shared values nurtured within a common worldview. Recounting the history of postmodernism's nativity helps us see how this emerging worldview has been instinctively striving from its beginnings to create such a new communal ethic—a collective solidarity through which an entirely new moral system can be established.

As discussed in the last chapter, because the liberal values of modernity were founded on an individualistic ethos rather than a communitarian ethos, modernity's self-oriented "liberty values" could not sustain an effective moral system on their own. Throughout most of its history, modernity has accordingly relied on the moral system of traditionalism to help induce its citizens to forego some of their self-interest for the common good of the larger society. Patriotism, for example, is a value rooted in traditional morality that has been employed in the service of modernity's nationalistic interests.

Systems of morality depend on communitarian-oriented worldviews because it is through the mutual commitments brought about by collective solidarity that the requirements of moral systems are imposed on their members. Although some aspects of morality are inevitably enforced through actual laws, much if not most of any given moral system's social guidance and constraint is achieved by social norms that do not have the force of law. Moreover, a society's collective will—its political will—is largely dependent on the binding force of its moral commitments. As discussed in the previous section, in traditional societies this binding communitarian ethos is based primarily on a common belief in a transcendent God. But as traditionalism lost much of its moral authority in the West, those who sought to build a substitute moral system needed to find a non-religious yet greater-than-self focus of moral belonging.

"Postmodernism's uniquely emergent strength is an enhanced sensitivity to the feelings of others."

This quasi-transcendent binding element was eventually discovered through postmodernism's uniquely emergent strength: *an enhanced sensitivity to the feelings of others*. As a result of this enhanced sensitivity, postmodernists are afforded increased access to the subjective interiority of other people. And this enlarged sense of empathy for the feelings of others has now become the cornerstone of postmodernity's moral system. The rise of postmodernity thus marks the beginning of a new era of sensitivity—a new ethic of care that now defines the moral community of progressive culture.

Postmodernism's moral sensitivity finds its focus in a deep concern for the perceived victims of Western civilization. Postmodern morality is accordingly focused on righting the wrongs that the globally ascendant culture of modernism has inflicted on the world. From the perspective of postmodernism, those who have been wronged by modernity include: victims of racism and ethnic discrimination at home, victims of colonialism and imperialism abroad, female victims of sexism and an oppressive patriarchy, gay victims of homophobia, working class victims of capitalism, animal victims of an unethical food industry, as well as modernity's overall victimization of the world's natural environment.

Considering this list of postmodernism's recognized victim categories, we might conclude that many of these wrongs have resulted from the ethnocentric limitations of traditional values, and that modernity itself is not wholly to blame. But it is precisely because modernity has relied on and necessarily carried forward the traditional moral system of the West—for both good and bad—that postmodernists now view modernism as primarily culpable for the damage inflicted by the rise of Western civilization.

As we have seen, modernity's ascent was partially predicated on its cultural truce with traditionalism. And because modernity continued to rely on the underlying social solidarity provided by traditionalism, it could not effectively purge traditionalism's negative features from its politics and culture. Moreover, because modernity was far more powerful and expansionist than premodern Western traditionalism had been, as the senior member of its partnership with traditionalism, modernity has understandably been viewed as the establishment perpetrator of the perceived wrongs listed above. As the crimes and misdemeanors of Western civilization have become more evident, these wrongs have now galvanized postmodernists into a new critical worldview that largely defines itself in opposition to modernity.

In order to understand the postmodern worldview and its system of values, we need to appreciate the good that postmodernists are trying to do. Modernity's unprecedented success at creating economic and political progress has created a new set of problems that modernists themselves are ill-equipped to solve. The rise of the modern world has thus created a new opportunity to contribute to humanity's social progress by overcoming modernity's negative externalities. Postmodernists are accordingly working to stop the oppression of people and halt the degradation of the environment. By working to ameliorate these problems, postmodernists find a kind of personal self-actualization in protecting that which they hold sacred. By "fighting the system" and "speaking truth to power," progressives are serving the quasi-transcendent higher purpose that gives them a sense of identity and belonging within a new collective culture of moral solidarity.

This understanding of the identity-providing function of value systems helps explain why those who have suffered the greatest victimization are often those to whom postmodernists are most attracted. For example, "intersectionality," or overlapping disadvantaged identities, has become a particular focus of progressive concern (in its popular expressions) because honoring and empowering people who have suffered multiple kinds of injustice achieves the greatest possible good as defined by postmodernism's value priorities.

In summary, the focus of progressive culture's new collective solidarity—its binding communitarian ethos—is now defined as the group consisting of those who have suffered and those who empathize with that suffering. In other words, the new "we" that coheres as the worldview of postmodernism is comprised of the victims of modernity (including individual people, races and cultures, and the overall natural environment), together with those who are sensitive to the pain of that victimization, even though they may not have been directly victimized themselves.[4]

POSTMODERNISM IS BOTH A BLESSING AND A CURSE FOR WESTERN CIVILIZATION

The postmodern worldview is the most recent politically significant values system to emerge along the timeline of human history. And because it is relatively new it is understandably immature. Progressives are accordingly prone to zealotry and illiberal postmodern fundamentalism, as seen on militant college campuses and in the stridency of many environmentalists and social justice activists. For instance, "social justice warriors," as their opponents call them, are fierce and often tyrannical in their demands for immediate and uncompromising reform.

However, like every other significant worldview that has preceded it in history, the postmodern worldview includes both positive value aspirations that are necessary for our further progress, and debilitating pathologies that result from this value system's blind spots and shortcomings. For modernists and traditionalists, it is postmodernity's pathologies that are most evident because these aspects are the most threatening. Indeed, one of the characteristics of the culture war is that each worldview tends to see the others only for their downsides. Moreover, each worldview tends to confuse its historical successor for its historical predecessor. Modernists, for example, often characterize postmodernists as the adherents of a new religion. But while there are certainly similarities between the devotions of the postmodern moral system and the traditional moral system, these two worldviews are animated by different sets of problems and by different notions of the transcendent object of ethical obligation.

Mainstream modernist pundits who lament militant postmodern fundamentalism in academia are keenly aware of the threat that extreme versions of postmodernism pose to liberal values. But as they decry the privileged hypoc-risy of postmodernists, these commentators never ask the obvious question: Why has this novel set of progressive values gained so much traction among intellectuals (especially academics), artists (especially the film industry), and a significant portion of America's young people?

According to the World Values Survey, there is a clear and predictable trend toward postmodern values in the developed world. There is therefore little doubt that the postmodern worldview is in the process of becoming a relatively permanent feature of American culture that will continue to gain ground. So given that postmodernism is here to stay, the question becomes: What is the best response?

As we consider this question it is important to keep in mind that even if progressive postmodernism does threaten Western civilization's value foun-dations, it also seeks to address real problems that neither traditionalism nor modernism are capable of solving. In order to advance to the next level of civilization—in order to prevent modernity from running completely amuck—we do need to find a way to care more about the fragility of the environment and the needs of disadvantaged people worldwide. Postmodern values thus represent an indispensible new layer of moral concern that will be necessary for the ongoing progress and sustainability of human civilization.

It is therefore crucial that modernists and traditionalists recognize post-modern culture not only in the illiberal excesses of its zealous recent converts, but also in the important work of its venerated heroes and sages. As examples, the environmental activism of John Muir, the civil rights crusade of Martin Luther King, the second-wave feminism of Betty Friedan, the liberating music of John Lennon, the respectful pluralism of Joseph Campbell, the labor lead-ership of Cesar Chavez, and even the accepting optimism of Oprah Winfrey, all stand as important and enduring cultural contributions upon which the postmodern worldview has been founded.

But just as it is crucial for modernists and traditionalists to recognize the upsides of postmodernity, it is also crucial that postmodernists themselves acknowledge how the advance of their values ultimately depends on the ongo-ing viability of both modernist and traditionalist values. In the same way that modernism's system of liberal values relies on the values of traditionalism in order to function properly, postmodern values are similarly dependent on the moral (and physical) capital of previous worldviews. Postmodern morality is not free-standing. Without the liberal protections of individual freedoms provided by modernist values, and the foundational norms of fair play and honesty provided by traditional values, postmodern culture would soon regress to a "pretraditional" level of warring factions.

The key to receiving postmodernism's moral gifts, while avoiding its concomitant corrosion of our society's pre-existing value structures, therefore involves working to integrate postmodernism's emergent level of moral concern with the legitimate and still needed values of modernism and traditionalism. Put differently, because postmodern morality is both a blessing and a curse for our society—both a needed new level of ethical care and a reckless repudiation of the best of what has come before—we need to tease apart its dignities from its disasters, carrying forward the best while pruning away the worst of postmodernity's excesses and immaturities.

"Postmodernism is both a needed new level of ethical care and a reckless repudiation of the best of what has come before."

In response to this deep-seated cultural challenge, the goal of developmental politics is to help bridge and harmonize the divergent value systems that now compete for the moral soul of America. Toward this end, developmental politics offers a variety of promising new methods for achieving political integration and cultural maturation that can bring together postmodernism, modernism, and traditionalism into a more unified and cooperative level of development—a transcendent yet inclusive new whole. So in the next chapter we will begin our examination of these emerging methods for achieving agreement, which can help us move beyond our society's current political stalemate.

4

Reaching Political Agreement Through Values Integration

AMERICA'S CONTEMPORARY POLITICAL DYSFUNCTION is a complex problem with many contributing causes and no straightforward solution. Yet at the same time, the problem is simple: Americans have become unwilling to compromise politically or otherwise agree with each other. And from this perspective the solution is unambiguous: we need to find new ways to agree.

In response to this challenge, this chapter describes the method of *values integration*, which is developmental politics' primary strategy for building political agreement. First we consider why conventional methods for reaching consensus are not working. Then we focus on the actual locus of our national political discord: The conflict between bedrock values where the cultural battle is joined. Clarifying the bedrock values that are at the root of our political discord entails analyzing both the positive and negative features of America's major value systems, as well as charting the fault lines and dynamic tensions that exist between each of these political positions. As I hope to make clear, within the very value conflicts that divide us there can be found points of interdependence. And it is by working with these interdependencies that the values integration method gains traction on the potential for agreement. After covering the basic outlines of this method, we then consider examples of the method in action to see how this approach is already working in the case of some issues, and how it can be expanded and pursued more deliberately with other political issues. The chapter then concludes with a discussion of the integrative perspective that is ultimately needed to effectively build agreement by integrating values.

The values integration method outlined in this chapter is connected to a larger suite of related "agreement technologies." But these other methodological approaches to building agreement are more philosophical in nature, and will thus be considered in the context of Part II's discussion of political philosophy. The basic method of values integration discussed in this chapter, however, serves as a pragmatic foundation for developmental politics' overall approach to reaching agreement and building political will. Moreover, this foundational method ties together the discussion of worldviews in the first three chapters and accordingly provides a fitting culmination of Part I.

CONVENTIONAL PROPOSALS FOR REACHING POLITICAL AGREEMENT

Over the last ten years or so, a cottage industry of nonprofit institutions and think tanks has emerged seeking to promote respectful inter-party dialogue and political compromise. "Civil discourse" is the watchword of these groups.[1] The idea being that if both politicians and ordinary citizens could only listen to each other and be more open-minded about common goals and potential solutions, we could move forward without rancor and incrimination. According to this strategy, by building channels of respectful dialogue between opposing camps, we can eventually overcome the artificially imposed divisions that keep us apart.

This civil discourse strategy is hopeful and well-meaning, and bipartisan compromise is certainly good where you can get it. But after closely observing this method in real-life political contexts over the last few years, my sense is that it is only marginally effective at best. Overcoming our political impasse will not be accomplished by a better *process*; we must address the actual *content* of our disagreements, which are ultimately about values.

Another strategy being advanced to overcome political stagnation and persuade citizens to act prosocially in how they vote and consume comes from the fields of evolutionary psychology and behavioral economics. This approach includes the practice of "reframing conceptual metaphors" (advocated by George Lakoff), and "disentangling matters of fact from the cultural cognition of opposing group identities" (championed by Dan Kahan). The attempt to apply evolutionary psychology to politics also entails the crafting of subtle incentives and "gentle nudges to opt-in to the right choice," as described by proponents of "libertarian paternalism" (such as Sunstein and Thaler).[2] Like the civil discourse approach, this psychological-rhetorical persuasion strategy for building political agreement is also well-meaning. But in practice it can quickly become condescendingly manipulative and even disturbingly Orwellian in its implications. Because of its inherent deviousness, this approach is ultimately misguided. Increasing sympathy for a wider spectrum of values requires a persuasion strategy that is fundamentally transparent and sincere.

Yet another strategy for fostering political agreement focuses on campaign finance reform. Advocates of this strategy contend that the dominance of big money in politics is the primary cause of our gridlocked condition. These activists argue that the ideological purity demanded by large donors makes politicians unwilling to compromise or work with the other side. Passing legislation to curtail the outsized influence of oligarchs and corporations is thus seen as the best way to overcome hyper-partisan polarization.

While I will not deny that the outsized influence of money in politics is indeed problematic, I don't believe campaign finance reform is a panacea for our democracy's dysfunction. In fact, reforming our electoral system's financial structure is itself a project that depends on the existence of political will that is clearly lacking under present conditions. In order to reform the "politics industry" in general, and the influence of money in politics in particular, we must first overcome the cultural barriers to political agreement that currently stymie any attempts at structural reform.

Moreover, the notion that our political system is now completely bought and sold by plutocrats has been called into question by the results of 2016. One positive outcome of Donald Trump's election is how it has shown that our system is not completely controlled by money alone. Election results are not fixed or predetermined by an oligarchy; popular democracy is still powerful. And if voters have the power to sweep aside the political establishments of both parties and elect a reckless and unfit outsider, they also have the power to elect an extraordinarily innovative—even "developmental"—presidential candidate.

That being said, we cannot rely on the appearance of a magical candidate to solve our problems. As Plato understood more than two thousand years ago: "The states are as the men are; they grow out of human characters."[3] Therefore, in order to overcome the fractious and frozen condition of contemporary American politics, we need to improve and evolve the electorate itself.

The idea of overcoming our political dysfunction by changing American culture is, however, usually ruled out by advocates and pundits because they have no idea how to go about the process of fostering cultural evolution. Some commentators even argue that trying to change peoples' values is disrespectful. But developmental politics does not seek to change the values people hold dear. Rather than trying to convert or replace existing values, this new approach seeks to *expand the scope of what people are able to value*. Simply put, we don't want to erase or subtract peoples' values, we just want to add to them.

> "Rather than trying to convert or replace existing values, this approach seeks to expand the scope of what people are able to value."

Focusing on the Bedrock Values at the Heart of Our Political Disagreements

To grow out of our political dysfunction, we need to concentrate on the actual locus of the conflict: the bedrock level of values. This bedrock level of politics can be understood through an analogy with geological strata, as illustrated in figure 4.1. This graphic suggests that below the familiar levels of conventional political discourse and engagement, below the campaigns and party politics covered by the media, and even below the specific issues and interests that animate political factions, there lies a bedrock layer of foundational values.

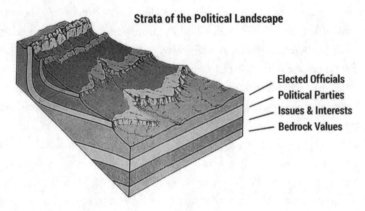

Strata of the Political Landscape

— Elected Officials
— Political Parties
— Issues & Interests
— Bedrock Values

Figure 4.1. Levels of politics can be compared to layers of geological strata

Even though this bedrock layer is apparently solid and seemingly difficult to influence or change—even though culturally foundational values inevitably become hardened by multigenerational investments of loyalty and identity—values are nevertheless subject to being modified and reconfigured by the larger "tectonic forces" of history. Despite their presumed solidity, bedrock values can shift and change, and sometimes they do so with the force of a dramatic earthquake, as seen in pivotal years such as 1776, 1848, and 1968.

Continuing this geological analogy, the tectonic pressure that causes bedrock values to shift or expand arises from the presence of existential problems that cannot be solved within the confines of existing value structures. Admittedly, sometimes the pressures of problematic life conditions result in cultural retrenchment and a narrowing of values that makes compromise impossible, and often leads to war. But as the historical record indicates, under certain pressurized conditions, the "rocks" can become plastic and metamorphic, resulting in a new cultural substratum with more flexible characteristics.

Prior to the national election of 2016, centrist Democrats seemed to be the only ones worried about the problem of hyper-partisan polarization. But after the election of Donald Trump, the pressure to fix our nation's dysfunctional politics is now being felt by the majority of Americans. The pain of our contemporary political stagnation has moved from being a chronic background condition to an acute and urgent affliction that we can no longer sublimate or ignore. Fortunately, the pressure of this acute political pain is forcing us to look for new ways to reach agreement—new methods for building political will and achieving social progress.

Recognizing the need for a fresh approach, the methods advocated by developmental politics do not seek to simply meet in the middle; nor are they focused on merely improved "civil discourse." The strategies for achieving agreement being advanced by this new political approach are far more ambitious. As we explore in this chapter and throughout the rest of this book, these new methods for reconciling and integrating bedrock values seek to ameliorate seemingly intractable problems such as our rapidly changing climate, our broken healthcare system, our insolvent social programs, our corrupt system of campaign finance, our misguided immigration policy, and even our questionable foreign policy.

We begin our consideration of these emerging strategies by examining the central method of values integration, which is arguably developmental politics' most promising and powerful form of agreement technology.

VALUES INTEGRATION: PRELIMINARY CONSIDERATIONS

The method of values integration is an approach to building political agreement that seeks to synthesize and harmonize the valid concerns of multiple conflicting worldviews. In order to understand and apply this method, practitioners must be able to sympathetically appreciate the full spectrum of foundational values that constitute the bedrock of American culture. Our discussion of worldviews in the previous three chapters accordingly provides the background perspective on cultural evolution through which this method was derived, and by which it can be successfully employed.

As a quick review, we saw how America's deadlocked political condition is primarily a cultural problem stemming from fundamental disagreements about core values. Because values generally cohere in sets, they can only be understood adequately in the context of the worldview structures through which they arise. As I argued, worldviews are the foundational structures of cultural evolution and are therefore the most basic units of cultural analysis.

In the previous chapters we also considered why American culture has become starkly divided among the three demographically significant worldviews known as modernism, postmodernism, and traditionalism. Our examination of these competing value frames showed how they are each focused on solving different sets of perceived problems. Modernism is focused on overcoming poverty and ignorance, and on liberating each individual to achieve their full potential. Postmodernism is concerned with righting the wrongs of modernity by building solidarity for the protection of the environment and the achievement of social justice. And traditionalism seeks to preserve our heritage and conserve the best of what has come before. Because each of these discrete problem sets continue to afflict our society, the problem-solving focus of each of these worldviews is still very much needed. Each form of culture thus has a necessary and ongoing job to do.

The complication, however, is that while each of these worldviews contains important values that we need to preserve and carry forward, each set of positive values remains closely tied together with accompanying pathologies that we need to leave behind. So the first step in framing a new politics of culture that can overcome the animosity that is stymying our governing process involves helping each worldview to see the others more clearly and more sympathetically. And to foster greater sympathy among worldviews, we need to start by carefully distinguishing between each worldview's enduring positives and its corresponding negatives. Indeed, it is the ongoing presence of each worldview's pathologies that is the real source of our nation's political rancor.

The foremost task of this new politics of culture is therefore to provide a method that can help us tease apart each worldview's upsides from its closely related downsides. Developmental politics' method of values integration therefore begins by tracing the value contours of these three major worldviews. The first move in this mapping process was originally shown in figure 2.2 in chapter 2, which is reproduced here as figure 4.2 for easy reference.

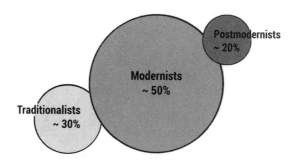

Figure 4.2. Approximate demographic sizes of America's three major worldviews, arranged along the timeline of their original emergence (figure 2.2, reproduced)

Framing America's three major worldviews as demographically proportioned circles arranged in the order of their original emergence helps us see both the current relative size of these foundational cultural structures, and their sequence in history. This framing, however, does not provide an accurate picture by itself. To supplement this picture we need to examine these structures from another perspective that shows how they fall along the conventional left-right political spectrum, as shown in figure 4.3.

Figure 4.3's highly simplified mapping of America's competing value frames places postmodernism on the far left and traditionalism on the far right, which may seem more familiar to most readers.[4] But notice how modernity, shown as a singular worldview structure in figure 4.2, has been divided into two distinct circles in figure 4.3. This division of modernity reflects the fact that while postmodernists are almost all leftists, and traditionalists almost always side with the right, modernists are fairly evenly divided between the left and right wing of American politics.[5]

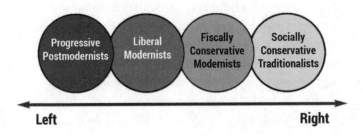

Figure 4.3. The political positions of America's major worldviews, arranged across the left-right spectrum

"The viability of modernity's individualism depends on a solidarity-building communal moral system that is not capable of supplying itself."

Modernism is politically divided because, unlike these other two major worldviews, it is organized around an individualistic ethos. As discussed in chapters 2 and 3, traditionalism and postmodernism are both oriented toward a communitarian ethos that emphasizes the sacrifice of self-interest for the sake of the larger group. By inculcating their respective forms of group solidarity and community obligation, both traditionalism and postmodernism have established strong moral systems of their own. Modernist values, by contrast, are focused on the rights of individual citizens. While this individualistic orientation is modernism's signature strength, the viability of modernity's individualism ultimately depends on the presence of a solidarity-building communal moral system that modernism is not capable of supplying by itself.

As a result of ongoing cultural evolution from traditionalism to modernism, and now increasingly toward postmodernism, contemporary American culture is being pulled apart by the competition between two seemingly incompatible communitarian moral systems—one premodern and traditional, and the other postmodern and progressive. These divergent moral systems are currently engaged in an intense political struggle for the allegiance of the modernist majority. The tug-of-war between these contending communitarian worldviews helps explain why modernists are consistently pulled toward one side or the other, and thus why centrism is not viable in our current political climate.

Building on the four political positions charted in figure 4.3 above, the next figure illustrates the major fault lines or multiple forms of political polarity that divide these positions. Figure 4.4 shows how the overarching polarity between the left and the right as a whole is mirrored within the modernist worldview, which again is evidently divided between fiscally conservative Republicans on one side and liberal Democrats on the other. Even though a large portion of the American electorate now identifies as Independent, most Independents nevertheless reliably vote for either Democrat or Republican candidates.[6] So regardless of official party affiliation, there is no effective middle in American politics.

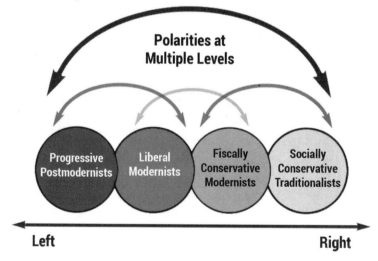

Figure 4.4. America's major political positions are divided by multiple polarities

The large arched arrow at the top of figure 4.4 reflects the familiar polar divide between Republicans and Democrats overall. However, as most political observers now affirm, the dynamic currents of contemporary American politics can no longer be accurately analyzed or explained within the simplistic framework of left and right. Figure 4.4 therefore illustrates the more nuanced complexity of current conditions by also charting the sub-polarities that exist *within* both the left and the right sides of American politics.

These intra-party schisms were clearly evident in the 2016 primaries. The polarity within the left was seen in the evident cultural differences between Hillary Clinton and Bernie Sanders. Even though these two candidates agreed on most issues, there was a difference in their values that voters, especially millennials, could detect.

Although the cultural conflict between modernists and traditionalists on the right is not as severe as the division between modernists and postmodernists on the left, polarization within the Republican Party itself has nevertheless hampered its legislative effectiveness. Gridlock and stagnation on the right helped fuel the perception of Republican indifference to the plight of the working class. This failure to help working people, coupled with the right's inability to contain the growing cultural power of postmodernism, resulted in the widespread dissatisfaction with Republican politics as usual that led to the election of Donald Trump.

"Traditionalists hired Trump as their bouncer."

Most traditionalists backed Trump, despite his flouting of traditional values, because of their felt need for protection against postmodernism's delegitimation of traditional culture. Although clearly not a traditionalist, Trump has positioned himself as an enemy of postmodernism. Traditionalists therefore hired Trump as their "bouncer" or cultural bodyguard. And when hiring a bouncer, one may be inclined to overlook his arrest record.

Beyond explaining electoral tensions, the multiple forms of political polarity shown in figure 4.4 begin to reveal the underlying features of American culture's bedrock values. Each of the four positions illustrated in figures 4.3 and 4.4 above represent strongly coherent sets of values that have arisen over the course of history. The authentic existence of these distinct value categories is therefore evinced by the strong polar tensions—the natural aversions—that prevail between them. The arched arrows in figure 4.4 suggest how these multiple polarities can be compared to magnetic forces, which attract agreement to each pole's positive values, while at the same time repelling agreement as a result of each pole's abiding negatives. Charting these multiple polarities thus starts to show how each value pole is composed of attractive values that almost everyone shares to some extent, as well as pathologies that the other poles find particularly repulsive. However, in order to see these competing value sets more clearly, we need to map out the specific positive values of each of the four poles, together with the negative shortcomings that plague each position. As described in the next section, this operation leads to the detailed values charts that are at the heart of developmental politics' integrative method.

DEVELOPMENTAL POLITICS' VALUES CHARTS—FOUNDATIONS OF ITS INTEGRATIVE METHOD

As shown on the next two pages, figures 4.5 and 4.6 build on figure 4.4's depiction of America's four major political positions by charting the positive values and accompanying pathologies of each political position. Please take a moment to read through these values charts, which have been derived through an analysis of the multiple polarities that currently divide our electorate. These charts are like the "circuit boards" of developmental politics' agreement technology. Or using another analogy, these charts provide the pallet of colors used by the method of values integration to paint the pictures of new political agreement that this method makes possible.

Considering the four value poles mapped by these charts, note that I have given each pole a nickname that summarizes the primary concerns of that political position. The traditionalist values category charted on the far right champions "heritage values." Fiscally conservative and libertarian modernists, while also on the right, are more concerned with what are best termed "liberty values." Moving to the left, we come to the values of liberal modernists, which can be typified as "fairness values." On the far left, progressive postmodernists bring a new layer of "caring values" to our cultural discourse. While the values shown in the top half of each position are respected to some extent by most Americans, the cultural center of gravity represented by each category has a dominant focus of moral concern, which these nicknames evoke.

Note also that each of the four positions charted in figures 4.5 and 4.6 includes a list of potential pathologies, which again, are closely tied together with that position's positive values. As explained above, the method of values integration begins by carefully distinguishing the positives from the negatives of each pole. Once the positive values of each pole are differentiated from its abiding negatives, it becomes easier to sympathize with the positive aspirations of that position. From inside the cultural purview of any one of these value categories, the negatives of the other categories appear most prominently. Yet when we take a larger perspective and stand outside our own position, we can begin to appreciate the larger substratum of bedrock values that underpin American culture as a whole, and this helps depolarize our thinking.

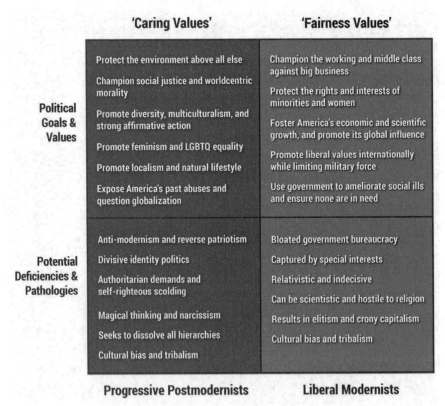

	'Caring Values'	'Fairness Values'
Political Goals & Values	Protect the environment above all else Champion social justice and worldcentric morality Promote diversity, multiculturalism, and strong affirmative action Promote feminism and LGBTQ equality Promote localism and natural lifestyle Expose America's past abuses and question globalization	Champion the working and middle class against big business Protect the rights and interests of minorities and women Foster America's economic and scientific growth, and promote its global influence Promote liberal values internationally while limiting military force Use government to ameliorate social ills and ensure none are in need
Potential Deficiencies & Pathologies	Anti-modernism and reverse patriotism Divisive identity politics Authoritarian demands and self-righteous scolding Magical thinking and narcissism Seeks to dissolve all hierarchies Cultural bias and tribalism	Bloated government bureaucracy Captured by special interests Relativistic and indecisive Can be scientistic and hostile to religion Results in elitism and crony capitalism Cultural bias and tribalism
	Progressive Postmodernists	**Liberal Modernists**

Figure 4.5. Value polarity chart of America's two major left-wing political positions

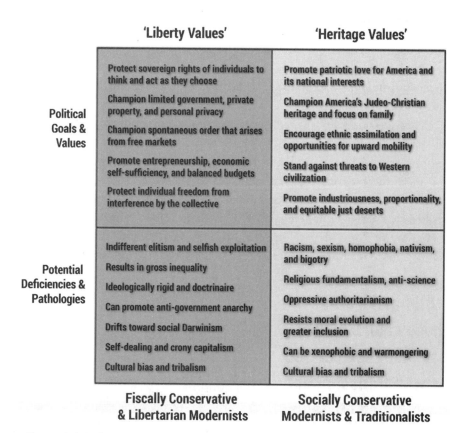

'Liberty Values'　　　　　　　**'Heritage Values'**

	'Liberty Values'	'Heritage Values'
Political Goals & Values	Protect sovereign rights of individuals to think and act as they choose Champion limited government, private property, and personal privacy Champion spontaneous order that arises from free markets Promote entrepreneurship, economic self-sufficiency, and balanced budgets Protect individual freedom from interference by the collective	Promote patriotic love for America and its national interests Champion America's Judeo-Christian heritage and focus on family Encourage ethnic assimilation and opportunities for upward mobility Stand against threats to Western civilization Promote industriousness, proportionality, and equitable just deserts
Potential Deficiencies & Pathologies	Indifferent elitism and selfish exploitation Results in gross inequality Ideologically rigid and doctrinaire Can promote anti-government anarchy Drifts toward social Darwinism Self-dealing and crony capitalism Cultural bias and tribalism	Racism, sexism, homophobia, nativism, and bigotry Religious fundamentalism, anti-science Oppressive authoritarianism Resists moral evolution and greater inclusion Can be xenophobic and warmongering Cultural bias and tribalism
	Fiscally Conservative & Libertarian Modernists	**Socially Conservative Modernists & Traditionalists**

Figure 4.6. Value polarity chart of America's two major right-wing political positions

In other words, by carefully distinguishing each pole's dignities from its corresponding disasters, the authentic good that each of these cultural categories is attempting to achieve becomes easier to appreciate. By increasing our sympathy for each set of values in this way, we can expand the scope of what we are able to personally value. And this increased sympathy allows us to effectively bring these diverse values together within our own positions and opinions.

But even after distinguishing between the positives and negatives of each pole, acknowledging, for example, that not all heritage values are racist, or that not all caring values are anti-establishment, questions remain, such as: Why should I revere heritage values? Or why should I care about the concerns of postmodernists? Beyond the instrumental goal of making American politics functional again, or otherwise solving social and economic problems through the restoration of a minimum degree of political consensus, there lies the deeper question of why these bedrock values really matter. Are they merely instrumental and politically expedient, or is there something intrinsically valuable about them?

This question goes to the heart of developmental politics' understanding of the evolution of human consciousness and culture. According to this perspective, which is grounded in research from developmental psychology and social theory, consciousness coevolves with culture.[7] Although there is certainly more to the growth of human consciousness than one's cultural worldview, the sequential emergence of wider frames of value does provide an important "line of development" through which individuals come to embrace more inclusive estimates of that which is good, true, and beautiful.

"Ultimately, all of these values matter because they connect us with transcendent meaning an guide us toward the overall improvement of the human condition."

For example, the gradual evolution of cultural worldviews has resulted in an expansion of the scope of those deemed worthy of moral consideration, from the family, to the tribe, to one's fellow believers, to one's countrymen, and now to increasingly worldcentric ideals of morality. Similarly, it is through the historical emergence of more sophisticated worldviews that humans have expanded their grasp of what is real and true—from magical, to mythical, to rational-scientific, and now to increasingly sensitive and holistic conceptions of truth. The emerging sequence of historically significant worldviews mapped out by the various charts in this chapter accordingly provide the rungs in the ladder of humanity's ongoing social progress.[8]

However, the sustainability of each worldview ultimately depends on the ongoing work of previous cultural structures. As discussed in chapters 2 and 3, the advance made by each successive worldview uses and relies on the continuous functioning of the earlier accomplishments of prior value frames. Although cultural evolution cannot be conflated with biological evolution, like all forms of evolution, cultural evolution advances through a sequence of development wherein later appearing structures build on the successes of previous structures. Following this evolutionary pattern, the sequence of viable cultural worldviews that have emerged in human history have not only *transcended* but also partially *included* the best of what has come before. This structure of emergence in consciousness and culture thus forms a kind of *interdependent cultural ecosystem* wherein the values of each cultural category provide an ongoing foundation for the sustainability of the overall structure.

To be specific, traditional heritage values are civilizing; they create the cultural container of decency and law-abiding fair play that makes our society possible. Similarly, modernist liberty values safeguard the basic freedoms we depend on as Americans. The positive liberty values shown in figure 4.6 serve to limit and restrain the overreaching tendencies of the other value categories.

While heritage values and liberty values are foundational, fairness values and caring values are also crucial in the way they make us kinder and point toward a more compassionate and inclusive society. Fairness values and caring values help make us better people, and it is through these values that we can ultimately create a better world.

The values represented in these charts are not just my values; these are the values that have been discovered over time and affirmed by millions of people in the process of trying to make their lives more fruitful and rewarding. These value categories and the worldviews they represent are therefore evident social facts and relatively permanent features of our cultural landscape. While the specific values and disvalues listed in the charts are not completely dispositive—while we could also illustrate these categories with a somewhat different list of positives and negatives—the reality of the categories themselves is established by the way they reflect our civilization's historical development.

Under current cultural conditions, nearly all of us identify most directly with one of these four value categories to the partial exclusion of the others. But according to the analysis of developmental politics, in order to mature into the next phase of our evolution and grow out of our gridlocked politics, we need to more fully embrace the positive values of every one of these cultural categories. As we explore further in Part II, expanding the breadth and depth of the values that Americans can hold is a worthwhile endeavor that is intrinsically valuable for its own sake, regardless of the laws it may pass or the candidates it may be able to elect. Ultimately, all of these values matter because they connect us with transcendent meaning and guide us toward the overall improvement of the human condition.

* * *

Building on our discussion in the first three chapters, figure 4.2 above portrayed the fundamental structures of American culture in terms of three politically significant worldviews arranged along the timeline of their original emergence, from oldest to newest. Figure 4.2 thereby suggested a developmental progression among these worldview categories. Figure 4.3 then reconfigured these three worldviews into the four basic political positions that were used to derive the values charts introduced in this section. The horizontal positioning of these charts, however, is not meant to imply that these discrete value categories are all relatively equal. As discussed further in chapters 7 and 9, developmental politics avoids both value relativism and value absolutism by carefully justifying an authentic dimension of vertical social development. Yet although this emerging perspective recognizes a definite trajectory of cultural progress, it nevertheless honors and includes every step in our historical journey.

The detailed charts shown in figures 4.5 and 4.6 provide a schematic picture of the bedrock values, and corresponding disvalues, that underlie our political culture. However, to adequately understand these value categories we need to see them in action. That is, these four categories are not static or stationary, they are dynamically engaged with one another in an ongoing cultural contest. In fact, it is the dynamic tensions between these categories—the multiple polarities within our body politic—that constitute the formative forces that shape and charge these competing positions in the first place. But as described in the next section, the very forces that are pulling us apart can also be harnessed to achieve new levels of synthetic agreement that can bring us together. So the next step in the explanation of the method of values integration involves gaining a working understanding of these formative polar forces.

POLARITY THEORY—AN INTRODUCTION

Over the past few decades a promising theoretical perspective has arisen that sheds new light on the forces that cause polarization. This way to think about conflict, known as polarity theory, posits that certain types of polar opposition are actually generators of value that, when effectively managed, can build agreement and produce meaningful progress.[9]

While polar dichotomies are ubiquitous in human experience, most of these forms of opposition can be recognized as straightforwardly positive and negative. Prosperity and poverty, for example, is a kind of polar relationship that exists between a value and a disvalue. In a positive-negative opposition such as this, the positive pole represents our goal and the negative pole describes what we're trying to avoid or overcome. Positive-negative polarities thus represent problems to be solved. Continuing with this example, even though poverty is a chronic human condition, it has been largely eradicated in some parts of the world. And I believe some day we may be able to eliminate it entirely.

Although most polar dichotomies are of this positive-negative type, there is another, rarer form of polar opposition wherein both poles are essentially positive. Unlike positive-negative forms of opposition, these positive-positive polarities are permanently recurring or indestructible, so they cannot be solved or laid to rest. An authentic positive-positive polarity is a kind of perpetual recursive system that can only be managed more or less well.

> "Polar opposition is a fundamental feature of the dynamic behavior of value."

Examples of positive-positive polarities include: individual-community, liberty-equality, real-ideal, competition-cooperation, mercy-justice, freedom-order, challenge-support, relative-absolute, defense-offense, grievance-gratitude, simplicity-complexity, immanent-transcendent, and even masculine-feminine.

These permanently recurring polarities continue to show up in the course of human affairs because polar opposition is a fundamental feature of the dynamic behavior of value. As explored further in Part II, values are energetic forces that naturally cohere in opposing pairs that are nevertheless interdependent. This interdependence can be seen in the way each pole uses the other to achieve its value-creating potential. In the pairs of polar values listed above, the strengths of each pole serve to mitigate and correct the downsides of its opposing pole in a recursive stepwise process that results in synergistic progress. Managing these relatively indestructible forms of opposition accordingly involves bringing out the best of both sides while avoiding the limits of each.

In the case of the competition-cooperation polarity, for example, unrestrained competition, in the absence of a larger agreement to play by the rules and cooperate, can quickly devolve into a dog-eat-dog condition wherein defensiveness saps productivity. Conversely, cooperation by itself, without the incentive or opportunity for individual excellence or creativity, can similarly devolve into groupthink or stifling bureaucratic mediocrity. But when competition and cooperation are brought together in a mutually correcting relationship that provides for both *challenge and support*, the value-creating potential of each side is maximized.

While polarity theory is fairly new, the mutual interdependence of positive opposites was realized as early as the sixth century B.C. And notably, this realization occurred independently yet relatively contemporaneously in both the East and the West, in the writing of the Chinese sage Lao Tzu and the Greek philosopher Heraclitus. The philosophical significance of this "coincidence of opposites" was also described by Nicholas of Cusa in the fifteenth century. The fact that many values cohere in complementary polar sets has even been recognized in the context of science by Nobel Prize-winning physicist Niels Bohr who wrote, "the opposite of a small truth is a falsehood, but the opposite of a great truth is another great truth."[10]

However, as we discuss further in chapter 6, while positive-positive value polarities exhibit opposing yet interdependent relationships, their poles are not necessarily equal or otherwise perfectly balanced. Some polarities, such as masculine and feminine, are of course equal in most important respects. But even the most equal forms of positive-positive polarity invariably reflect the *creative motif of part and whole*. Indeed, even within the otherwise balanced equality of the masculine-feminine polarity, the characteristics of part and whole are nevertheless evident. This pattern of part and whole can be seen in personality traits commonly associated with each pole, and even in the physical form and function of male and female reproductive anatomy. As we will see, this creative motif of part and whole is the key to the generative or *procreative* capacity of these value-creating polar relationships.

A common mistake in human affairs generally, and politics in particular, is to confuse a positive-negative dichotomy, representing a problem to be solved, with a positive-positive polar system that needs to be continuously managed. Partisans on both the left and right, for instance, approach most political issues from a win-lose perspective wherein their side is seen as straightforwardly good and the opposition's position is seen as simply bad or even evil. While some political issues are in fact unequivocal matters of right and wrong wherein one side needs to win and the other side needs to lose, most political conflicts are not of this kind. As the values charts introduced in the last section show, many political polarities arise from the competition between opposing values that are best recognized as different kinds of goods.

Recalling the geological strata analogy from the beginning of this chapter, we can acknowledge that in the context of politics, opposing *interests* are often irreconcilable—at the level of perceived interests we are often faced with a win-lose proposition. But when we approach political oppositions at the deeper level of bedrock *values*, the potential for compromise and reconciliation is greatly increased, especially when we appreciate the insights of polarity theory. The simple reason why values are easier to integrate than interests is that an authentic bedrock value is something that

> **"Values are easier to integrate than interests because an authentic bedrock value is something that almost everyone already shares."**

almost everyone already shares. Once we have clearly distinguished between the positives and negatives of each set of values, the positive values of each category become easier to affirm and integrate into our own positions.

By disclosing the presence of interdependent value polarities, polarity theory shows how the values we hold dear are almost always part of a complementary recursive system wherein the positive values of those we oppose are essential to the realization of our very own values. As an example, consider the interdependent polarity of modernism and postmodernism. Notwithstanding its rejection of modernity, postmodern culture depends on the free and prosperous social conditions created by modernism. And modernism in turn depends on the growth of postmodern values to help mitigate the environmental degradation that ultimately makes modernism unsustainable. Each pole therefore needs the other to help bring about the good that these opposing sets of values are ultimately trying to create. This approach to values integration can be stated as a general principle: When faced with a positive-positive value polarity, the best way to advance the values of our preferred pole is to actually affirm the foundational values of the pole we oppose.

When a positive-positive polarity is confused with a positive-negative dichotomy, the situation can become stuck or deadlocked. But when an authentic positive-positive polarity is managed according to this principle of complementary interdependence, a "stuck polarity" can become a "generative polarity"—a cooperative relationship of challenge and support that makes higher levels of agreement possible. Examples of how this principle works in the context of politics are discussed in the next section.

EXAMPLES OF VALUES INTEGRATION IN ACTION

The first and most powerful example of the kind of progress that can be created through the integration of interdependent value poles is found in our society's evolving mores around masculinity and femininity. Over the last fifty years, our collective idea of what it means to be a "real man" has grown to include being sensitive and even occasionally emotional. Likewise, our ideals of femininity have also evolved to include strong and independent women. This progress in gender norms has come about through the realization that mature masculinity and mature femininity both require a partial integration of the qualities that are most frequently associated with the other. And this evolution of our gender norms has had tremendous political and legal consequences.

This move toward integration, however, does not involve a fusion of the two poles, which in this case would mean a move toward androgyny. While there is nothing wrong with androgyny, it can represent a kind of "centrist compromise" that eliminates the procreative tension inherent in the masculine-feminine polarity. Stated otherwise, the evident progress made in our society's concepts of gender has not come about in an attempt to split the difference between the poles. Rather, both sides have been augmented and improved through the partial integration of their respective strengths in a way that also preserves their natural differences. This example thus begins to show how the method of values integration uses the creative tension inherent in an indestructible polarity to "true up" both sides.

A more politically specific example of values integration that has produced progress over a shorter time span is found in the issue of gay marriage. Advocacy for the right to marry has been instrumental in the larger success of the gay rights movement overall because the cause of gay marriage integrates important values from each of the four major value systems illustrated by the charts. Gay marriage advances caring values, fairness values, liberty values, and crucially, traditional family values (heritage values). Traditionalists who otherwise object to "decadent homosexual lifestyles" find it much harder to resist calls for the basic right to make a family commitment through the institution of marriage. While perceived traditionalist *interests* are not included in the new right for gays to marry, traditionalist *values* are included nonetheless. It was thus through values integration that this previously polarized issue has not only become law, it has also gained widespread social acceptance.

Another recent example of rapid political progress achieved by integrating values from across the spectrum, even in the context of our hyperpolarized political environment, is found in the issue of marijuana legalization. This once vilified botanical has now become partially or completely legal in thirty-three states, with more soon to follow. And like gay marriage, this issue has succeeded because it integrates the values of all four major categories. The cause of legal pot integrates caring values by decriminalizing the drug, it integrates fairness values by making a useful medicine available to those who need it, it integrates liberty values by ending morality-based prohibition, and again crucially, it also integrates the conservative values of federalism and subsidiarity, which seek to allow local populations to determine what's best for their community when it comes to political issues such as prohibition.

Conversely, in the same way that the successful integration of values explains the recent success of issues such as gay marriage and the legalization of marijuana, the lack of adequate values integration helps explain why other issues remain stuck.

The issue of climate change, for example, has yet to achieve political success because its advocates have failed to sufficiently integrate the values of the right side of the spectrum into their cause. As I discuss at length elsewhere,[11] the strident anti-modernism of the postmodern leaders of the climate change movement has produced strong resistance from those on the right, who would be less opposed to action on climate change if their values were better integrated into this issue's policy proposals.

In their otherwise admirable efforts to preserve the environment, climate change activists often repudiate both modernist prosperity values and the traditionalist values which seek to protect the status quo. Conservative opposition to action on climate change, however, could be reduced by better integrating modernist concerns regarding the fragile ecology of markets, and the need to carefully consider the health of the economy in environmental policy decisions. Modernist values could also be integrated into this progressive cause by showing more interest in engaging the creative power of business, and by acknowledging that the gradual transition to sustainable forms of energy can be accomplished more readily by the private sector than by the Federal government.

In addition to climate change, the stuck issue of immigration could likewise move forward if the left's values of fairness and caring were better combined with traditionalist heritage values (promoting immigrant assimilation) and the meritocracy values of fiscally conservative modernists (favoring immigrants with talent and resources).

In each of these examples, the process of integration requires more than simply combining values. Working with an interdependent polarity also involves using the upsides of each pole to mitigate the downsides of its opposing pole. This process is illustrated by considering the interdependent relationship between globalism and nationalism, which provides our next example.

Globalization as an economic trend, and globalism as an ideal, both depend on the ongoing viability of nation-states. Nations provide the underlying political structures that make increasing globalization possible. And every nation requires a degree of nationalistic patriotism to maintain its existence as a sustainable political entity. So at this time in history at least, the continuing integration of the peoples of the world relies on healthy civic nationalism as a support structure. But not only does globalism depend on nationalism, individual nation-states also depend in turn on global cooperation and the smooth functioning of the global economy. Even beyond economic considerations, national citizens worldwide, and especially the young, are encouraged by the promise that continuing global integration will lead to the overall betterment of people everywhere. Aspirations for increasing global solidarity and worldcentric morality thus provide hope for the ongoing progress of humanity. Although the perceived interests of nationalism and globalism may often seem to be at odds, the reciprocally intertwined nature of these levels of political development confirms their relationship as an interdependent polarity.

Figure 4.7 below illustrates the interdependent polarity of nationalism and globalism, taking the same form as the polarity charts of bedrock values shown in figures 4.5 and 4.6 above. Yet even more than the bedrock value charts, this nationalism-globalism polarity chart clearly shows how the positive values of each pole provide an effective remedy for the pathologies of its polar counterpart.

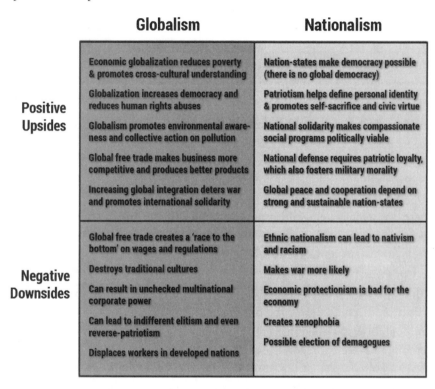

	Globalism	Nationalism
Positive Upsides	Economic globalization reduces poverty & promotes cross-cultural understanding	Nation-states make democracy possible (there is no global democracy)
	Globalization increases democracy and reduces human rights abuses	Patriotism helps define personal identity & promotes self-sacrifice and civic virtue
	Globalism promotes environmental awareness and collective action on pollution	National solidarity makes compassionate social programs politically viable
	Global free trade makes business more competitive and produces better products	National defense requires patriotic loyalty, which also fosters military morality
	Increasing global integration deters war and promotes international solidarity	Global peace and cooperation depend on strong and sustainable nation-states
Negative Downsides	Global free trade creates a 'race to the bottom' on wages and regulations	Ethnic nationalism can lead to nativism and racism
	Destroys traditional cultures	Makes war more likely
	Can result in unchecked multinational corporate power	Economic protectionism is bad for the economy
	Can lead to indifferent elitism and even reverse-patriotism	Creates xenophobia
	Displaces workers in developed nations	Possible election of demagogues

Figure 4.7. Value polarity chart for nationalism-globalism

Looking over figure 4.7's polarity chart, notice how nationalism's patriotic loyalty can help preserve the unique features of a nation's traditions in the face of globalism's cultural homogenization. Conversely, notice also how globalism's commitment to free trade and international cooperation can counter nationalism's predilection for a bellicose foreign policy. Other downward diagonal comparisons reveal additional ways that the positives of each pole provide remedies for the negatives of its opposite pole. As further examples, strong national governments can serve as a check on the power of multinational corporations, and a sense of global solidarity can counter nativism and xenophobia. All of the potential upsides and downsides of globalism and nationalism are obviously not included in this simple chart, but showing some of the positives and negatives side by side helps us better recognize the interdependent relationship between these poles, as well as the benefits that can be realized through their effective integration.

At the time of this writing during the Trump administration, many of us feel called to resist the isolationist downsides of nationalism. But according to developmental politics, our resistance will be more effective if we are able to conscientiously affirm the upsides of nationalism that need to be preserved. This kind of inclusive resistance, however, also requires us to acknowledge the downsides of globalism and admit that America may have indeed over-extended itself in this pole's direction over the last several decades.

These examples begin to show how the method of values integration can help us use the solutions found in each major values system like tools in our policy toolbox. If the problem is economic stagnation, then the application of liberty values may help, and if the problem is a shrinking middle class, then liberal fairness values may prove most useful. Unlike rigid partisans who are ideologically constrained from ever adopting the solutions of the other side, developmental politics can employ a wider spectrum of policies. For instance, rather than seeing familiar remedies such as smaller government (on one side) or increased spending (on the other) as universal solutions to be sought in almost all cases, a developmental approach is free to use both of these opposing solutions depending on the circumstances.

However, even if all the steps outlined above are carefully followed, this method will not succeed in overcoming gridlock and producing political progress until a critical mass of Americans come to adopt the *integrative perspective* that this method requires.

THE METHOD'S SECRET SAUCE: INTEGRAL CONSCIOUSNESS

By defining the values and providing a sense of identity for major segments of American society, each major worldview enacts its own distinct kind of cultural consciousness, namely, *modernist consciousness, traditional consciousness,* and *postmodern consciousness.* And as we've seen, each of these major worldviews is contributing to America's dysfunctional politics in its own way—each kind of consciousness is thus part of the problem. So in order to find a comprehensive solution to our broken political process, we need to approach the problem of hyperpolarization from a different *level of consciousness* than the ones that are creating the problem in the first place. This new level of awareness is known by a variety of names, but as used in the title of my 2007 book, I think the most generally descriptive label is "integral consciousness."[12]

Integral consciousness is a perspective that affirms the positive values of each of the cultural categories we are examining. Although it includes and builds on the accomplishments of progressive postmodernism, it also strives to be "post-postmodern." That is, integral consciousness represents a transcendence of postmodern consciousness because it does what postmodernism cannot: It fully recognizes the legitimacy and evolutionary necessity of all previous worldviews. Integral consciousness thus grows up by reaching down.

Some degree of integral awareness is necessary for the successful application of the values integration method because it is only from an integral perspective that we can appropriately *value* the values of each category, making them our own. From within any of these existing cultural structures, the other worldviews appear wrongheaded. But by adopting an evolutionary overview perspective, viewing these structures from "outside and above" so to speak, the legitimate concerns of each worldview become more evident. This wider cultural perspective

> **"Integral consciousness can champion each worldview's values at a more inclusive level, while simultaneously acknowledging each worldview's pathologies."**

accordingly begins to reveal how these competing value sets can ideally work together as an interdependent cultural ecosystem. Stated otherwise, integral consciousness can help heal the rifts created by the culture war because it can champion the essential core of each worldview's values at a more inclusive level, while simultaneously acknowledging the pathologies of each worldview. Moreover, by showing that it actually cares deeply about the enduring ideals and rightful concerns of all of these forms of culture, the integral perspective can effectively disempower each worldview's zealots and fundamentalists. By thus breaking out of these existing types of consciousness, which see their own worldview as mutually exclusive with the others, integral consciousness can cultivate the kind of higher-level agreements that can quell the current conflict.

As I'm arguing, in order to overcome hyperpolarization, we need people to expand their own values so they can better recognize the validity of their opponents' values. This kind of growth in values, however, requires the raising of people's consciousness. While raising consciousness is the long-term goal of developmental politics, as activists from across the political spectrum have discovered, raising consciousness takes time and can be exceedingly difficult. But by employing the method of values integration, we can begin to craft the new political positions that *would be possible* if values had already been expanded and the consciousness of the electorate had already been raised. In short, we don't have to wait for people to raise their consciousness, we can do it for them! Because the integral perspective deeply appreciates the values of each worldview, it already includes the valid concerns of each category in its positions without requiring potential opponents to argue for their side. The method of values integration thus allows us to approach political issues with the best interests of each value category already in mind. In fact, by adopting an integral perspective we might even be able to revere and defend the values of each category better than that category's own partisans.

However, it is important to emphasize that the polarized values represented by the charts cannot be easily combined in a friendly "both/and" consensus because these value categories are in a partially antithetical developmental relationship with each other—a dialectical relationship—wherein each category is formed and shaped through ongoing conflict with the other categories.[13]

As we have discussed, America's major worldviews have emerged by pushing off against each other in history, so they cannot be simply *included* all together in one static position because that would sap the charge that gives them life. Rather, they must be *integrated* in a way that continues to preserve their respective challenge to each other. This is why polarity theory is so important to the values integration process. When we use this approach to effectively manage the value polarities that exist in between America's major political positions, these polar oppositions become transformed into dynamic bridges or connecting links that result in relationships of both support and challenge. Therefore, even as we seek to bring about greater political cooperation, we must not try to eliminate the existential challenges that are an essential element of the dialectical process of cultural evolution overall.

This argument leads to a subtle but important point: The integral perspective is itself a kind of agreement technology—a new kind of "cultural intelligence" that can transform the way our democracy works. The method of values integration that this perspective makes possible can accordingly produce issue positions that many will naturally find more agreeable than the excessively polarized positions that currently dominate our political discourse.

The example of gay marriage cited in the previous section shows how a political cause that embodies values from across the spectrum can succeed by virtue of its own inherent rightness. The agreeable quality of the cause of gay marriage was not achieved through political horse trading or by attempts at coalition building, rather, its political power was baked into its very nature by dint of the diversity of values it embodied. While the early proponents of gay marriage might not have integrated these values consciously or strategically, we can nevertheless learn from the success of this issue, and others like it, by integrating values more deliberately and methodically in the positions we espouse. Through the application of this values integration technique, we can transform stuck issues, like climate change or immigration, into more potent political propositions that can garner agreement even within our hyperpolarized political climate.

VALUES INTEGRATION: SOME FINAL CONSIDERATIONS

Notwithstanding the promise of this values integration method, it is important to acknowledge that no matter how many values we may integrate, we will still encounter political opposition. Continuing with the gay marriage example, even though many former opponents of gay rights were won over by the basic morality of marriage equality, and even though most Americans now assent to gay marriage, many continue to oppose it. Yet even though disagreement will almost always remain—even around issues that well-integrate the full spectrum of values—developmental politics nevertheless aspires to discover win-win solutions wherever positive-positive value polarities can be found. Unlike the standard modernist approach of making tactical compromises to try to get most of what our side wants, developmental politics seeks to include the values of each camp into the mix from the beginning because it actually affirms these values and wants to see them forwarded. At the level of conventional political issues we're often faced with a win-lose proposition. But at the level of bedrock values it becomes possible to discover something closer to a win-win solution, even if such a solution does not completely satisfy all parties. Simply put, a developmental approach to politics seeks to accommodate the concerns of all sides, not just to get its way, but to make authentic progress for all sides by creating new value agreements.

Considering the operational details of the values integration method, remaining questions include: Where opposing values exhibit an irreducible conflict, how can priority be decided? And, when the positive features of a given category of values become politically empowered, how can we prevent the corresponding negative features of that category from also becoming empowered at the same time? These concerns are addressed by the central role of integral consciousness, which as I'm arguing, is necessary for the proper use of the method in the first place. Integral consciousness provides a new way of seeing—an expanded epistemology—that can recognize how two seemingly conflicting propositions can work together as a system of development. This way of seeing involves more than simply weighing the alternatives and assigning different degrees of worth to various components; it's a method of understanding that requires an intuitive sympathy achieved only by *entering into* the alternative perspectives that generate the opposing values. When we look at value conflicts without this ability, winning or losing seem to be the only options. But when we come to recognize how these cultural structures are working together within a larger overall trajectory of historical development, this allows us to engage these structures more creatively. Developmental psychologist Robert Kegan actually defines integral consciousness as "the capacity to see conflict as a signal of our overidentification with a single system."[14]

It must be emphasized that the process of values integration is not a formulaic procedure that can be reduced to a mechanical methodology; creativity is clearly required. So static examples can only provide an inkling of how this creative process works. Nevertheless, in answer to the first question above, priority among competing values is decided according to the nature of the problem being addressed. The idea is to apply the values of each distinct category to the specific types of problems that those particular values are focused on addressing. Simply stated, the preferred value in any given situation is the one that best corresponds to the problem at hand. Using a previous example, if the problem is economic stagnation, then the solutions of liberty values apply, and if the problem is a shrinking middle class, then liberal fairness values are probably most applicable. The nationalism-global-ism example above also demonstrates how this process works. In short, the priority of values is determined by the nature of the problem.

The power of this integral approach to politics accordingly stems from its ability to effectively *use* the values of each major worldview. In the case of traditional values for example, sometimes we need to invoke the defiant spirit of Winston Churchill to steel our backbones in the face of villainy. But in other situations, Mahatma Gandhi's postmodern spirit of nonviolent resistance will be most appropriate.

Regarding the second question about how to keep the negatives of each category in check, this concern is addressed by the essential functioning of the method itself. Continuously teasing apart the dignities from the disasters of each set of values—carrying forward the best while pruning away the worst—is part of the practice required to hold an integral perspective. So the process of distinguishing the good from the bad is ongoing. In the absence of this perspective, however, the eventual ascendency of each category's pathologies is almost inevitable. Yet when we manage interdependent value polarities through the continuous process of challenge and support, it becomes possible to consistently mitigate the downsides of each value pole.

In conclusion, I must emphasize that the most useful function of the charts and methodological steps outlined in this chapter is how these ideas demonstrate the integral perspective in action. Again, it is the perspective itself that is the real agreement technology. This integral form of awareness is based on an emerging "new truth" about the evolution of culture and consciousness. And this new truth is essentially philosophical. So next in Part II we turn to a deeper and more philosophical examination of developmental politics in order to get at the most essential, and thus most useful, aspects of this exciting new body of thought.

PART II

TOWARD A NEW POLITICAL PHILOSOPHY OF PURPOSE AND PROGRESS

5

Evolving Our Understanding of the Good

L ET'S BEGIN BY REAFFIRMING THE FOCUS of our concern: America needs to grow out of its current state of political dysfunction. Yet, as we've seen, our broken political system is actually a symptom of a larger "pre-political" cultural conflict whose resolution lies beyond the confines of Washington D.C. In chapters 1 through 3 we examined how this cultural conflict is being caused primarily by the rise of the postmodern worldview, which rejects many of the values of modernism and traditionalism. Then in chapter 4 we saw how the values of America's three major worldviews can be partially reconciled through an integrative method that affirms the legitimacy and necessity of each set of cultural values.

While the values integration method's pragmatic goal of building political agreement around specific issues provides part of the solution, this method is not sufficient by itself. In order to address the roots of America's debilitating culture war, we also need to focus on deeper philosophical questions about the essential nature of "the good." Each worldview has its own set of values and thus its own version of the good. And each of these value frames are concerned with overcoming a specific set of real and ongoing problematic life conditions. So in light of this evident divergence in values we are led to ask: Beyond this plurality of goods, is there an overall unity of the good? Is there a universal direction of progress that constitutes the good of humanity as a whole?

Finding a satisfying answer to this question is crucial for overcoming America's politically dysfunctional social condition because in order to grow out of our current state of hyperpolarization we need a new collective vision of authentic improvement. In short, we need an improved definition of improvement itself. Even though our democratic form of government is designed with political competition in mind, our democracy also relies on a minimum degree of cooperation and social solidarity—a solidarity that ultimately depends on a shared vision of the common good and a collective agreement about the direction of our collective progress. Such a renewed vision of a common good need not appeal to everyone, but the fresh ideal of progress we require does need to be attractive to politically significant numbers of people from each major worldview. Stated otherwise, we need a more inclusive vision of the American Dream that can inspire a broad spectrum of our citizens and help bring about a new cultural accord wherein the positive values of traditionalists, modernists, and postmodernists will all be welcome and respected.

The project of envisioning such a new and more inclusive American Dream itself requires a new and improved political philosophy. Philosophy is needed because supposedly value-neutral social science cannot establish a normative dimension of progress or otherwise clarify the direction of the good. Like the subject of ethics, the subject of progress in value is inescapably philosophical. While questions such as what is the good? or what is progress? may at first seem overly abstract or academic, these age-old philosophical inquiries are highly relevant for our current era. These theoretical questions about the nature and behavior of value are actually crucial for achieving the pragmatic political goals of reestablishing cultural solidarity and restoring hope for our collective political future.

"We need an improved definiton of improvement itself."

The goal of Part II is thus to describe the outlines of an emerging political philosophy of purpose and progress that can help establish a broad and inspiring vision of our collective way forward. What distinguishes this emerging political philosophy from previous philosophies is that it is based on a powerful *new truth* about evolution.

THE NEW TRUTH: CONSCIOUSNESS EVOLVES

Ever since the beginnings of Western philosophy in ancient Greece, philosophers have inquired about the essential nature of the good. In political philosophy, this inquiry is often narrowed to the question: What is justice? While the average citizen may be unconcerned with such questions, these philosophical inquires have nevertheless had a significant influence on the development of American democracy. Distinguished political thinkers from Plato, to Locke, to Kant, to Mill, to Rawls, to Habermas (to name a few) have each wrestled with the meaning of justice in their attempts to envision a more virtuous society. This thinking has guided the development of law and policy throughout our history.

But even though the meaning of justice and the nature of the good have been pondered for millennia, the recent appearance of the integral perspective's enlarged understanding of the development of human society gives us an opportunity to take a fresh look at these questions. This expanded integral perspective on human development provides new insight, new foresight, and even new hindsight about where we have come from and where we have the opportunity to go. As I will argue throughout Part II, this expanded understanding of human development is based on an important new truth. Yet although it will take the rest of the book to unpack, this "New Truth" (which I'll capitalize for emphasis) can be succinctly stated up front in just two words: *consciousness evolves.*

As I argued in Part I, this growth in human consciousness occurs though a process of coevolution wherein consciousness develops concomitantly with the development of human culture. Although every infant begins life with the same basic form of biological "human nature," the extent to which their consciousness develops is largely determined by the culture in which they are raised. It is thus in this way that human nature itself evolves through the evolution of human culture.[1]

And as we've seen, the most significant way that culture evolves is through the sequential emergence of values-based worldviews. In other words, consciousness evolves as values evolve, and conversely, as consciousness evolves it grows in its ability to perceive that which is truly valuable. Therefore, because the coevolution of consciousness and culture is directly tied to the evolution of values and our conception of the good, expanding the quantity and quality of what we can collectively value will create a more evolved society—a society that is freer, fairer, more inclusive, and more fulfilling for everyone.

(As a point of clarification, in this discussion the word "values" refers to the specific goals and aspirations that people esteem, desire, and strive for, whereas the word "value," when used as a noun, refers to the more general philosophical idea of quality or "the good.")

In light of this emerging evolutionary truth, we can begin to see almost everything as a process of development—a moving picture of change and growth. As philosopher Pierre Teilhard de Chardin famously wrote: "Evolution is a light illuminating all facts, a curve that all lines must follow."[2]

Even though the coevolution of consciousness and culture cannot be conflated with biological evolution, these distinct evolutionary domains are nevertheless united by a structural sequence of emergence wherein *something more keeps coming from something less*—a sequence that can be traced all the way back to the beginning of time and space in the primordial emergence of the big bang. Although evolution in the biosphere advances by different methods than evolution in the sphere of humanity's cultural and psychological development—the "thinking layer" or "noosphere" as Teilhard called it—comparisons between these domains can yield useful insights for politics.

In Search of an Understanding of Noosphere Energy

Of particular relevance in comparisons between evolution in the noosphere and evolution in the biosphere is the source of energy used in these respective macro-systems of development. We know that physical systems engage a continuous throughput of energy to maintain their ongoing organization in the context of a changing environment. In the case of biological organisms, this energy metabolism is powered by a variety of energy sources such as sunlight, oxygen, geochemical energy, and the energy stored in the plants and animals in the food chain. And we can see a similar throughput of energy in the case of manmade systems, which engage additional sources of energy beginning with the harnessing of fire and then expanding to include fossil fuels and nuclear energy.

Physical energy is the obvious source of power in biological organisms and human economies, but consciousness, and the agreements that constitute human culture, are not physical or material. While the domain of culture is closely connected to physical things and transactions in the exterior objective world, like consciousness itself, culture is largely an *interior* phenomenon which can only be fully known by participating in the subjective agreements that give it life. Culture cannot be fully fathomed by merely observing objective behaviors or physical surfaces. In the same way that learning a language requires a subjective understanding of the meaning of its words, the meanings and values that are the substance of every form of culture can only be fully appreciated from the *inside*.

Admittedly, the idea of the "inside" or "interior" of culture is a complex philosophical subject. In order to discern the dynamic behavior of cultural interiors we need to bring in the important idea of *intersubjectivity*. Intersubjectivity is a concept used in philosophy, psychology, sociology, and anthropology to describe the relational connections and structures of agreement that exist between conscious minds. That which is "intersubjective" is neither completely subjective nor straightforwardly objective. Intersubjective entities range from simple agreements about the meaning of words to the complex systems of agreement that cohere as the historically significant worldviews we explored in Part I. Even though these agreement structures "reside" inside the minds of those who participate in the agreements, these systemic structures are not merely subjective. These systems of agreement exist in an interior domain of development that is *in between* subjects, hence the term intersubjective. In other words, cultural systems such as worldviews are not physical or visibly objective, but neither are they entirely psychological or privately subjective. Even though these intersubjective entities connect with and depend on the physical world, and even though they interpenetrate the minds of individual subjects, they cannot be completely reduced to either objective things or subjective thoughts.

The recognition of the nature and behavior of intersubjective cultural systems is an important part of the new philosophy being advanced by developmental politics. But because this is an intellectually dense and somewhat difficult topic, I will address the finer points of intersubjectivity in appendix A at the end of the book. The point for now is that subjective systems of consciousness and intersubjective systems of culture coevolve and are deeply intertwined. Even though consciousness is individual and subjective, and culture is collective and intersubjective, these overlapping domains of interior development share the same source of energizing power. In the realm of consciousness this power is most often referred to as psychological energy or psychic energy, and in the realm of culture this power is known as *political will*.

The idea of psychic energy was originally introduced by Sigmund Freud, who used the phrase in a loose metaphorical way to compare the physical energy that acts upon objects with the source of desire that powers human intention. Freud's notion of psychic energy was developed further by Carl Jung and other psychologists in the first half of the twentieth century, but the idea continued to be used merely as a metaphor for the source of human motivation. Then in the 1960s behavioral psychologists challenged the idea of psychological energy, arguing that human motivation was merely a "mood" and not an actual force or form of power. Yet despite the lack of a clear definition of the nature of psychic energy, the field of psychology as a whole has been unwilling to give up on the concept because of its descriptive usefulness and evident reality. Although psychologists have continued to posit theories of motivation, the generation of both psychic energy and political will remain somewhat mysterious.

However, in light of the emerging New Truth about the evolution of consciousness and culture, the philosophy of developmental politics is able to see something new and say something more about the nature of psychic energy and political will. Many of these insights are found in the evident similarities that exist between evolution in the physical biosphere and evolution in the psychosocial (subjective and intersubjective) noosphere. Perhaps the most intriguing similarity is found in the way systems in both the exterior biosphere and the interior noosphere engage a throughput of energy to maintain their systemic vitality. That is, just as all living things maintain their organization through the ongoing metabolism of physical energy, the evolving systems of consciousness and culture engage a similar, albeit nonphysical, kind of energy to sustain their systemic continuity.

"In light of the New Truth, developmental politics is able to see something new and say something more about the nature of political will."

Although this interior equivalent of physical energy is only vaguely understood, the New Truth about evolution can help us gain further knowledge about the nature of human motivation. The promise of this inquiry into the source of energy used by the noosphere systems of consciousness and culture is that by coming to understand the behavior of this interior energy more fully, we can begin to effectively generate and harness this source of power to energize and enliven our political and civic life. By learning to work with this interior energy, we can discover new methods and strategies for improving the human condition by fostering the evolution of consciousness and culture on every front of its development.

Within academic social science, the line of inquiry that is most relevant to our search for a deeper understanding of psychic energy and political will is known as motivation theory. And in the pages ahead we will consider various theories of motivation. The word "motivation" by itself, however, cannot hold enough meaning to adequately convey the complex process through which humans are moved to make things better. Human motivations are largely determined by values, which are themselves circumscribed by the horizon of potential improvement that is defined by a culture's prevailing worldview. To fathom the complex process of human motivation we therefore need to employ a family of related words. These words, which surround and describe the phenomenon of human goal-directed behavior like iron filings around a magnetic field, include: "impulses," "desires," "intentions," "needs," "values," "ideals," "improvement," "progress," and perhaps most centrally, "purpose." Although all these words are relevant for our inquiry, I think "purpose" gets closest to the heart of the matter because the purpose to improve things is the primary impetus for cultural development. Unlike biological evolution, which unfolds inexorably through random mutations and environmental selection, cultural evolution usually only occurs when people *try* to improve their conditions. Except for occasional fortuitous accidents, almost all cultural evolution is "on purpose."

Notwithstanding our growing psychological knowledge, political scientists and social psychologists still do not really know how the political will that creates effective social movements is generated.[3] While pressing human problems are the most obvious motivators of political action, the question of why effective political will is generated under some circumstances but not in others remains undertheorized in political philosophy and social psychology. So in light of the evolutionary perspective we have explored thus far in the book, in our quest to better understand the source of motivation in politics we are led to ask: What can the properties of physical energy tell us about the psychic energy and political will that powers the noosphere? What is the basic nature of the *power* that attracts our purposes and causes us to recognize value? Is there a "physics of value energy" that can be discovered and used to improve our politics?

As Emerson understood, "every natural fact is a symbol of some spiritual fact." And if this is true then the ubiquitous natural fact of physical energy may provide a fruitful symbolic comparison that can help us better comprehend the "spiritual fact" of human values and their energizing influence on politics.

RECONCEIVING VALUE AS A FORM OF INTERIOR ENERGY

The idea of physical energy itself is a surprisingly recent concept. The word "energy" was not used in the modern sense until the beginning of the nineteenth century. And it was not until the 1850s that the laws of thermodynamics were discovered through the work of Lord Kelvin, Sadi Carnot and others. It was also around this time that Scottish scientist James Clerk Maxwell first showed that electricity, magnetism, and light were all manifestations of the same phenomenon. While Maxwell's equations constituted discoveries in the realm of mathematical physics, his theoretical breakthroughs laid the groundwork for the later development of electronic technologies.

Although physical energy has always been an evident feature of the natural world, observable in sunlight, heat, and even in the occasional lightning bolt, prior to the emergence of the modernist worldview humans could not conceive of these distinct phenomena as a unified field of power that we now understand as "energy." The phenomenon of physical energy as such could only be "seen" through the scientific perspective brought about by modernity. And in the same way that modernist consciousness enacted a new perspective that revealed previously unseen realities, the integral perspective introduced in the last chapter provides a similarly new vantage point from which additional discoveries can now be made. Just as Maxwell's discoveries in theoretical physics led to the development of the electronic technologies that have transformed our world, theoretical breakthroughs in philosophy can likewise lead to transformational political technologies—effective methods for reaching political agreement and revivifying our collective sense of common purpose.

In our search for a politically useful theory of the interior equivalent of energy, or what I term "value energy," the first step involves distinguishing between the internal sense of purpose (the drive from within) that arises in each person, and the external pull (the gravity of the potential for improvement) that draws people forward. In short, we are not only motivated from within, we are also attracted from without by the potential for an improved state of affairs. Distinguishing between the interior push and the exterior pull of human motivation allows us to see how the energy of value flows in a *circuit* from inside to out and from outside to in. Although our personal purposes and the goals we strive for are intricately intertwined, teasing apart the inner and outer sources of our impetus for improvement can show us how to generate psychic energy and political will more effectively.

As a result of my work in philosophy over the past twenty years, I've come to recognize how value or "the good" is really more of a verb than a noun. Even though we can identify countless things that possess the properties of goodness, the good in itself can be most accurately conceived of as *an upward current of perfecting energy*. Popular philosopher Robert Pirsig identified this flowing, energy-like nature of value through his concept of "dynamic quality," which he described as "the force of change in the universe."[4]

> **"The good in itself can be most accurately conceived of as an upward current of perfecting energy."**

As discussed at length in the next chapter, this rising current of the good moves in the direction of transcendence itself. And this idea helps explain why the higher purposes which we recognize as transcendent have a kind of magnetic power that draws us forward. As Oxford philosopher Iris Murdoch wrote, "we are spiritual creatures, attracted by excellence and made for the Good."[5] While the concept of transcendence does not necessarily imply the supernatural, it does require us to acknowledge that the desire to serve "something higher" is a fundamental feature of what it means to be human. As I will argue in the pages ahead, gaining a fuller understanding of how notions of the transcendent influence our society is crucial for reestablishing the social solidarity needed for a functional democracy.

The direct phenomenology of this deep-seated desire for transcendence—the sense of what it's like to be moved by the call of a higher purpose—confirms that we are being pulled by some kind of external force. Again, not only are we motivated from the inside to live up to our potential and strive to improve things, we are also palpably attracted from the outside by the enticing beauty that seduces us, the compelling truth that beckons us, and the excellent and righteous goodness that calls to us to be better.

Considering this idea of the exterior pull of value from another angle, we can see that beyond the negative pressure of the pressing problems that call for a solution—beyond the suffering whose tragedy and urgency compels us to try to make it stop—there is also a kind of positive pressure that arises from our persistent sense that a better world is possible.

The magnetism of value is a ubiquitous feature of life which we are only beginning to recognize and understand. Yet once we glimpse the potential benefits of developing a workable theory of value energy—a more robust philosophical understanding of the sources of human motivation and the generation of positive political will—we may begin to feel the exciting promise of the discoveries that lie ahead. The intriguing potential of this philosophical inquiry into the nature and behavior of value is that it can effectively ameliorate our political dysfunction, and in time, catalyze the emergence of a higher level of civilization.

6

Harnessing the Energy of Value

A S WE SAW IN PART I, the new politics of culture we need to overcome hyperpolarization works by integrating opposing values. And because the solution to our political dysfunction lies at the level of values, gaining a deeper understanding of the nature and behavior of value itself is essential for realizing the promise of developmental politics. Building on the discussion in the last chapter, this chapter explores in depth the idea that what we call value has a kind of gravity or magnetism. As I will argue, value is a basic and very real feature of our world that influences evolution in both the biosphere and the noosphere. This influence is seen in the way that value has an attractive, "to-be-pursuedness" quality that seems to be built into its essential nature.

In my 2012 book, *Evolution's Purpose,* I identified this attractive quality as "value gravity." And while I continue to find this analogy useful, I now think a somewhat more accurate comparison can be made with magnetism rather than gravity. Webster's dictionary defines the word "magnetic" as: "possessing an *extraordinary power* or ability to attract." Actual magnetism, of course, is a property of physical energy, and I'm not claiming that value is a physical thing. Nevertheless, in the same way that a magnetic field attracts metal objects, the magnetism of value attracts consciousness at every level of its manifestation. Although this "extraordinary power" has yet to be adequately analyzed or theorized, I believe a deeper understanding of the magnetism of value energy will prove to be highly relevant for the project of overcoming our political dysfunction and growing into a more mature stage of cultural development.

The remarkable attractiveness of value has been recognized since at least the fourth century B.C. In his dialogues, Plato described the ancient Greek idea of "eros," which begins as a sexual desire for another person's body, but which can be purified and refined through contemplation to become a desire for the ideal beauty found in the essence of that person. Although Plato grasped the connection between libidinous biological desire and the desire for higher levels of moral and aesthetic excellence, he did not make a clear distinction between the internal source of eros found in the heart of each person, and the external qualities that make the object of that desire attractive in the first place. For Plato, the beautiful, the true, and the good were seen as eternal forms that are objectively attractive in the same way that a beautiful person is attractive.

While I don't think Plato was completely wrong in his analysis of eros, from antiquity to this day philosophers have demonstrated significant problems with his theory of values as eternal forms. The main problem with Plato's theory of forms is that values are not "simply given." The good is not a substance or thing that can be located or observed in naked objectivity. Values always have a subjective or interpretive aspect of their discernment wherein the perceiver participates in constructing the value experience. Although this subjective component of evaluation is most evident in the value of beauty, even the value of truth contains an interpretive component.

Recognizing this subjective aspect of value, beginning in the Enlightenment philosophers began to assert that the good was merely a matter of personal preference rather than an objective entity in itself. Staunch empiricists such as David Hume argued that moral beliefs are essentially irrational, but are nevertheless "inevitable and convenient" for the functioning of society. The view that values are merely creations or projections of the human mind later became a central theme of existentialist philosophy, which took the concept even further. Inspired by the philosophy of Friedrich Nietzsche, existentialists maintained that because all values are created by humans, we are thus free to choose our values, and indeed have a responsibility to question every value rather than to passively receive our values from the society in which we live. According to existentialism, the universe is simply absurd and there is no meaning to be found in it beyond what meaning we give to it. The individual person is thus seen as tragically and heroically struggling against the abyss of cosmic meaninglessness.

However, just as Plato was partially mistaken in thinking of value or the good as simply objective, the reverse conception of values as merely subjective preferences is also problematically partial. As I argued at length in *Evolution's Purpose*, while values always have a subjective component, the most significant types of value also connect with external realities—real intrinsic qualities. Notwithstanding the necessary condition of an interested agent for the realization of value, the elusive phenomenon of the good is not entirely created or generated by the choosing subject alone. As Iris Murdoch understood, "The ordinary person does not, unless corrupted by philosophy, believe that he creates values by his choices. He thinks that some things really are better than others and that he is capable of getting it wrong."[1]

In short, something "out there" is valuable. But when we try to pin it down or grasp it in our thinking, the objective ontology of this "thing" slips through our fingers like water. Attempting to comprehend the dynamic properties of the inherent quality that is somehow *in* the world may at first seem like a rather esoteric philosophical exercise. Yet as I hope to make clear as we proceed, discerning the essence of value's not quite "objective" but nevertheless "exterior" attractiveness is an important key to our political evolution.

VALUE ENTERS THE UNIVERSE WITH THE EMERGENCE OF LIFE

Values are conventionally defined as the "important and lasting beliefs or ideals shared by the members of a culture about what is good or bad and desirable or undesirable." Value in itself, however, is more basic and natural than the culturally mediated agreements described by this standard definition. In fact, value enters the record of natural history at the very beginning of life.

The primary difference between life and nonlife is that living things strive to survive and reproduce. Physical dynamic systems such as tornadoes or ocean currents engage a throughput of energy that drives their motion and power, but nonliving systems such as these do not have a goal that they can fail to achieve. Living organisms, by contrast, actively try to stay alive; they strive and struggle tenaciously to achieve their goal of surviving and reproducing. In her description of the essential characteristic that makes life *alive*, eminent evolutionary biologist Lynn Margulis put it succinctly: "Life is matter that chooses."[2] Notwithstanding the preprogramming of genes or the automaticity of instinct, all living organisms exhibit agency or self-interest.

According to complexity scientist Stuart Kauffman, the capacity of agency—the power of choice—can be found even within life's earliest and most primitive forms, which he calls "minimal molecular autonomous agents." Writes Kauffman, "Without attributing consciousness to the bacterium, we can see in [its] capacity the evolutionary onset of choice and thus of meaning, value, doing, and purpose. The technical word for meaning is *semiosis*, where a sign means something. Here, the bacterium detects a local glucose gradient, which is a sign of more glucose in some direction. By altering its behavior and swimming up the gradient, the bacterium is *interpreting* the sign. The bacterium may, of course, be *mistaken*. Perhaps there is not much glucose to be found in that direction. Neither 'signs,' 'interpretation,' nor 'mistakes' are logically possible in physics ... getting food is the *purpose* of the activity and is the *doing* or *action* of the bacterium."[3]

The point here is that the presence of value is demonstrated by the choosing interest of every living agent. Indeed, life's striving to survive and reproduce is an indispensible feature of biological evolution as a whole. Darwin himself recognized the significance of striving in life forms. Describing what he called the "principle of fecundity," he wrote that all living things "strive to seize on every unoccupied or less well occupied space in the economy of nature."[4] Organismal striving can accordingly be recognized as a necessary precondition for the action of natural selection. If life did not strive to fill every niche it would produce no surplus of itself and there would thus be little competition between organisms. Without this competition, the selection pressure required for biological evolution through natural selection would be absent. The mechanism of natural selection therefore presupposes the presence of intentionality in living things. However, the momentous emergence of self-interested agency within life cannot be explained by purely physical evolutionary mechanisms. This is because the intentionality itself is not physical.

Realizing how intentional striving is a necessary and fundamental aspect of biological life begins to show how the magnetism of value is a foundational feature of evolution itself. Wherever we find an intentional interest we can recognize the presence of value. The value that the interest identifies and aims for is not solipsistically contained entirely within the intention or mind of the striving agent. The function of the interest—the purpose of life—is to either attain something the organism does not yet have (such as a meal or a mate), or to retain something the organism is at risk of losing (such as its life or the life of its offspring).

The evident purposefulness of life thus demonstrates how value acts as a kind of attractive or magnetic force that is indispensible for the ongoing existence of all living things. Stated otherwise, every organism "lives for" an intrinsic form of goodness—the good of itself for itself, and the good of its species as a whole. Describing the role of intrinsic goodness in the functioning of biological ecosystems, environmental philosopher Holmes Rolston writes, "No warbler eats insects in order to become food for a falcon; the warbler defends her own life as an end in itself and makes more warblers as she can. From the perspective of a warbler, being a warbler is a good thing. ... A life is defended intrinsically, without further contributory reference—unless to defend the species and that still is to defend a form of life as an end in itself."[5]

In the case of biology, even though the intrinsic goodness that every organism lives for is embodied within the organism itself or its larger species, this value can only be preserved and sustained by the active and ongoing pursuit of life by the organism in order to keep on living. That is, the value is not entirely self-contained or stationary. There is something about the value that is outside or beyond the agent itself, something that draws the agent forward and causes it to act intentionally and strategically to achieve its desired goal, which is the perpetuation of life itself. "Aliveness" thus evinces a purpose for its own progress.

Admittedly, the proposition that value is an attractive force that exerts a magnetic influence on the agency of living things might be disputed as an anthropocentric projection. Those who object to this idea may argue that the intentions of organisms are not magnetized by some metaphysical notion of the good, but rather merely directed by a set of genetic instructions that work like a deterministic algorithm. However, when we look beyond the biosphere and consider the active functioning of the human noosphere, the magnetic power of value becomes undeniable.

HUMAN CONSCIOUSNESS IS ATTRACTED BY AN EVER-EXPANDING DIMENSION OF VALUE

As I argued above, "the good" has a palpable gravity or magnetism on consciousness which is demonstrated by all living organisms through their tenacious will to live. As we saw, even creatures that lack neurons and may not possess actual consciousness nevertheless strive for the good of themselves and the perpetuation of their species. And as biological evolution unfolds, some forms of life, such as the higher mammals and even certain birds, come to exhibit something close to what we might call altruism.[6]

Then with the advent of humanity, the evolutionary significance of the attractive force of value becomes even more evident. One of the primary factors that distinguishes human consciousness from animal consciousness is that human needs can never be completely or permanently satisfied. Although our sense of self-interest remains rooted in our biology and we continue to feel the same natural urges as our animal cousins, unlike other animals we have the freedom to continually imagine how things can be better. As Plato understood, the sexual eros we feel in our bodies is connected to a larger spectrum of desire that points to something higher—something that goes beyond just surviving and reproducing. Human consciousness can feel the pull of values that transcend biological self-interest alone.

"Human consciousness can feel the pull of values that transcend biological self-interest alone."

The upper reaches of human self-interest were originally charted in the 1950s by developmental psychologist Abraham Maslow. Most readers are familiar with Maslow's famous hierarchy of needs, which posits levels of successive fulfillment that grow from the physiological need for food, shelter and safety, to the social needs of belongingness and self-esteem, and then to the quasi-spiritual need for self-actualization. Maslow's theory of needs, however, often leads to the false conclusion that the desire for self-actualization only arises once our lower and more physical needs have been satisfied. While this may be true in some circumstances, many of those who remain hungry and poor still yearn to give their gift to the world. But despite being speculative and overly simplistic, Maslow's theory of needs continues to be theoretically useful because it confirms in modern psychological terms what Plato realized over two thousand years ago: The satisfaction of human self-interest is ultimately bound up with forwarding the interest of something larger and more important than the self alone. And this felt need to serve something higher is not limited to only highly successful self-actualizers.

Throughout history humans have demonstrated a deep-seated need to connect with and serve something that is authentically transcendent. Yet notwithstanding the spiritual implications of this sense of moral duty to the good of a greater whole, evolutionary psychologists have sought to explain the presence of altruism and prosocial behavior in both animals and humans through the use of "multi-level selection theory." The idea is that not only does evolution favor individuals with a strong self-interest or survival instinct, the mechanism of natural selection also works at the level of groups. According to this theory, groups that can effectively cooperate outcompete groups that cannot, and thus reproduce themselves more abundantly than non-cooperating groups, propagating their genetic tendency to cooperate into future generations. Like our sense of self-interest, our sense of empathy or compassion is accordingly explained as a genetic mechanism that has arisen through selection pressure because it advances the ultimate goal of DNA, which is to survive and reproduce. Yet even as the proponents of evolutionary psychology attempt to reduce greater-than-self-interest to just another level of biological self-interest, they never ask why life has any kind of interest in the first place. Just as the original appearance of life has not been explained by science, neither has the intentionality of life.

In order to get at the root or ultimate cause of both self-interest and greater-than-self interest, we need to look beyond functionalist explanations that attempt to reduce all motivations to the underlying goal of biological adaptation alone. Neo-Darwinian materialists may assert that our minds are tricked into altruistic behavior by stone age programming whose "real" purpose is the propagation of our genes. But this proposition flies in the face of the actual lived experience of prosocial people. The motive to behave morally arises most often from authentic feelings of care and concern for others, and this intention is usually guided by a sense of decency and duty.

Beyond the heart-felt phenomenology of compassionate motives, functionalist explanations of human behavior are also shown to be inadequate by the fact that both self-interest and greater-than-self-interest *develop* in the direction of greater inclusivity. At the level of individual persons, our self-interest develops as we continually awaken to new horizons of potential improvement. And at the collective level of cultural worldviews, we can see how our semi-instinctual dedication to the welfare of our blood kin has also developed over the course of history to gradually encompass larger and larger estimates of those worthy of moral consideration.

Again, as culture evolves, the scope of moral concern grows beyond the family or tribe to include those of the same religion. Then with the emergence of the modernist worldview, the scope of moral concern is widened still further to include those of the same nationality, even if they subscribe to a different religion. And recently, over the last fifty years or so, the postmodern worldview has sought to transcend both traditionalism and modernism by advancing an even more inclusive moral system that extends the circle of care to encompass not only all of humanity, but animals and the environment as well. Even though the functionalist programming of our evolutionary ancestors still influences our motives and decisions, the fact that human interests continue to evolve in the direction of more inclusivity shows how we are not only driven from "below," we are also drawn from "above."

SELF-INTEREST AND GREATER-THAN-SELF-INTEREST COHERE AS AN INTERDEPENDENT POLARITY

Toward the end of his life, Maslow amended his theory of needs by adding a level above self-actualization, which he labeled "self-transcendence." According to Maslow, the ultimate human need "is to go beyond our ordinary human level of consciousness and experience oneness with the greater whole, the higher truth, whatever that may be." The idea that the pursuit of self-interest eventually leads to the desire to transcend the self altogether was also expressed by Viktor Frankl who wrote, "self-actualization is not a possible aim at all, for the simple reason that the more a man would strive for it, the more he would miss it. ... In other words, self-actualization cannot be attained if it is made an end in itself, but only as a side effect of self-transcendence."[7]

Echoing the psychological theories of Maslow and Frankl, numerous philosophers have also argued that self-interest is something we do well to transcend. According to John Rawls, for example, pursuing our own interests may be necessary, but only those acts that are motivated purely for the interests of others can be recognized as intrinsically moral. However, while I agree that the fulfillment of self-interest inevitably involves service to something greater than ourselves, I reject the idea that self-interest is inevitably selfish or otherwise amoral. As we'll discuss in greater detail in chapter 8, in addition to our moral duty to others, we also have a moral duty to ourselves. The pursuit of self-interest only becomes morally questionable when it is completely divorced from its connection with the interests of others. Conversely, a selfless concern for the needs of others, divorced from self-interest, can also become pathological when it exhausts the self's resources or otherwise becomes codependent.

Yet even though the good of the self and the good of the greater community may be closely related, and often overlap with each other, they also frequently conflict, pulling in seemingly opposite directions. The intersection of self-interest and greater-than-self interest is characterized by strong dialectical currents that tend to pull people exclusively to one side or the other. Thinkers who are strongly magnetized toward the common good of the whole tend to argue that to act morally we must transcend the interests of the self; while other influential philosophers, such as Nietzsche and Ayn Rand, have gone to the other extreme by championing self-interest and questioning the morality of selflessness.

But notwithstanding these one-sided arguments, after pondering this subject for quite some time, I've come to the conclusion that self-interest and greater-than-self-interest are inextricably related to each other, and actually form an interdependent polar system like the ones we examined in chapter 4. As a quick review, we saw how most positive values naturally cohere in complementary sets or polar pairs wherein each pole opposes, yet at the same time moderates and corrects, its polar counterpart. This unique reciprocal relationship is found in many familiar value polarities such as liberty-equality, real-ideal, and competition-cooperation. These interdependent polarities are permanently recurring conceptual and behavioral systems that are best approached as processes to be managed rather than as problems to be solved. And the best way to manage these positive-positive value systems is through an encompassing agreement or relational container that acknowledges the interdependence of the poles, thereby allowing each pole to true-up its counterpart in a ongoing recursive process that includes both challenge and support.

Because polarity theory is relatively simple and easy to apply, it can be very useful as a pragmatic methodology. But unless it is informed by, and indeed situated within, a larger understanding of dialectical development, it can tend to give the false impression that the two poles in a positive-positive polarity are a type of balanced system in search of equipoise. In other words, if we understand interdependent polarities primarily through the perspective of the masculine-feminine polarity, or otherwise take a kind of Taoist view of polar relations as yin and yang in search of harmony, we can lose sight of the generative capacity of these unique forms of oppositional relationship. In short, polarities have a tendency to produce growth. So rather than seeing the poles as *equals seeking compromise*, it is more accurate to recognize their interdependent relationship as *part and whole seeking integration*, as illustrated in figure 6.1.

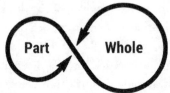

Figure 6.1. Part and whole seeking ongoing integration in an inter-dependent polar relationship

This dynamic part-whole relationship is an unstable system in constant search of higher levels of integration. These higher levels are achieved through the ongoing interaction of the part's impetus to seek individuation and differentiation, and the whole's countervailing impetus to integrate. This process thus unfolds as each new level of integration inevitably gives rise to a new impetus for further development by a differentiating part, which is in turn eventually followed by a still higher level of integration by an expanded whole. This sequential process of differentiation and integration helps explain how these polar relationships can, when managed appropriately, generate value and produce social progress. As further examples, the integration of the rights of individuals and the needs of the larger community results in greater social harmony, the integration of grievance and gratitude results in more persuasive rhetoric, and the integration of liberty and equality results in greater social justice.

Within part-whole polar relationships, the "whole pole" or "communal pole" is, of course, usually larger in scope and more important in significance. The common good of the community, for instance, is generally more important than the interests of any single individual. But despite being unequal in this way, the two poles of every authentic positive-positive value polarity are nevertheless interconnected in their respective value-creating capacity, such that the interests of the part and the interests of the whole are ultimately tied together.

Understanding how the two poles of every positive-positive polar relationship are thoroughly interdependent can help us avoid the traps and fallacies of "one-side-ism." In the case of the polarity of self-interest and greater-than-self interest we're considering here, recognizing the inherent complementarity of the poles shows how exalting greater-than-self interest over self-interest by claiming that the former is honorable and the latter is selfish is just as big a mistake as claiming that all interest is really only self-interest. The insights of polarity theory reveal how favoring one side of an interdependent polarity while rejecting the other side eventually leads to stagnation or pathology. Therefore, if we want to strengthen and expand greater-than-self-interest, widening the scope of groups and causes that people can identify with and care about, then we would do well to engage the opposing pole of self-interest to strengthen and empower its polar counterpart. Stated otherwise, by working to connect the circuit between self-interest and greater-than-self-interest, we can energize concern for the needs and interests of others.

The extent to which these two basic interests are interdependent and mutually cocreating is, however, not yet adequately understood within mainstream discourse. At a superficial level of understanding, the integration of these two poles might be approached by trying to show how each person's ultimate self-interest—their interest in self-actualization—can only be fulfilled by meaningful service to something greater than themselves. This proposition, however, is merely a banal truism that most people are well aware of as an abstract principle. Even though many of us already know that serving something greater than ourselves is the key to our personal fulfillment, this knowledge by itself is not producing the motivation needed to induce Americans to vote and spend and donate and organize in ways that more adequately consider the interests of the whole nation or the whole environment. So at this point in history, it is clear that simply asserting that caring about our society's collective wellbeing is good for us as individuals is not a winning strategy. Civic-minded prosocial behavior cannot be increased by mere exhortation to self-interest alone.

While we need to be able to "see beyond the opposition" and avoid thinking about value in strictly binary terms, we also need to recognize the indestructible nature of these polar relationships and work with them to realize their value-creating potential. Polarity theory accordingly provides a new approach that can help us grow out of the hyperpolarization that plagues our democracy. Yet to successfully employ this new approach to the problem of our political dysfunction, we need a deeper philosophical understanding of the motivational forces that drive the evolution of culture, which brings us back to the crucial subject of *transcendence*.

THE POLITICAL SIGNIFICANCE OF TRANSCENDENCE

By demonstrating the energetic dynamism of interdependent polar systems, polarity theory shows how the attractive power of value pulls in two directions simultaneously. Within every positive-positive polar relationship these opposing pulls form a kind of circuit of value energy. Within such polar circuits, the energetic potential of each pole is continually charged and renewed through its connection with its opposing polar counterpart. However, if these interdependent poles become isolated or disconnected from each other, they cannot hold their charge for long—their motivating energy becomes dissipated.

In the case of the interdependent polarity of self-interest and greater-than-self-interest, these value energy dynamics can be seen in the way that the pursuit of self-interest alone becomes unfulfilling if not connected to some higher purpose or larger cause. And conversely, selfless dedication to a good cause can likewise become tiresome if there is little or no personal reward received from the work. Unless there is "something in it for us" maintaining our commitment can become difficult over time. The individual pole of self-interest can, at a minimum, rely on the motivational resources of our biological urges and our perceived ego needs. But the communal pole of greater-than-self-interest depends on a more abstract and distant source of motivational energy, which is rooted in our cultural agreement structures. That is, the personal motivation to work or sacrifice for some higher common good finds its source in a vision of something more important than the self—something which lives on beyond us, and sometimes even something for which we would willingly lay down our lives.

For most people, this concern for a greater good is grounded in an intuitive sense that there is a point to life beyond life alone. This sense of obligation to a greater good is thus usually connected to the notion that there is, in fact, something that is truly "higher" than the normal concerns of our everyday lives. Recognizing this connection between greater-than-self-interest and ideals of transcendence therefore begins to show how the source of energy that magnetizes our commitment to the communal pole—our sense of duty to something greater than ourselves—comes from the magnetic pull of transcendence itself.

In light of this idea, as we explore in this section, clarifying and revivifying our collective vision of transcendence can lead to our political renewal. As I will argue, in order to generate the political will necessary to overcome our democracy's dysfunction we need to rediscover the transcendent meaning of our civilization at a post-secular level of understanding. In other words, the remedy to our cultural dilemma can be found in an enlarged ideal of a transcendent higher purpose (or a coherent set of higher purposes) that can speak to the hearts and minds of modernists, postmodernists, and traditionalists alike.

In addition to the intrinsic goal of moving closer to the philosophical truth about what is authentically transcendent, the instrumental goal of such a project is to better engage the power of individual self-interest in service to our collective common interests.

> **"Revivifying our collective vision of transcendance can lead to political renewal."**

As discussed above, this project is facilitated by the insights of polarity theory, which show how the pole of self-interest can be energized and motivated through the promise of some kind of *self-transcendence*. Indeed, according to Maslow, Frankl, and numerous other psychological theorists, self-transcendence is the ultimate destination of self-interest. Prominent virtue ethicist Candace Vogler describes what self-transcendence means to her:

> Self-transcendence shows itself when I understand my life as connected to a good beyond my own success, the security and comfort of my friends and immediate family, and the like. My life is lived through participation in a good that goes beyond my personal achievement, expression, security and comfort, beyond even the need to promote those goods for members of my intimate circle. I work on behalf of bettering the community in ways that will help strangers, say. I engage in spiritual practices that are not just designed to make me calmer and more effective in my daily life, but allow me to participate in a spiritual community organized by the need to be right with one another and to show due reverence for the sacred—community practice directed to

a good beyond the borders of the self-identified community. I devote myself to social justice. I devote myself to participation in the human search for truth, goodness, or beauty.[8]

Vogler's description suggests how authentic self-transcendence is explicitly or implicitly connected to some larger vision of collective transcendence. And this insight leads to an important point in our discussion: In order to serve as a consistent source of value energy and personal motivation, the goal of self-transcendence not only needs to transcend the needs and purposes of the self, it also needs to connect with a larger meaning for humanity as a whole—a higher purpose for the human race that goes beyond material flourishing alone. Simply stated, the drive toward self-transcendence is ultimately rooted in a more comprehensive notion of transcendence—a vision of collective higher purpose that can best be described as "cultural transcendence."

In most premodern societies, the idea of cultural transcendence was unproblematically associated with God. Working for the common good of the whole was therefore simply a matter of doing God's will, which redounded to self-interest through the promise of eternal salvation. But even though many Americans continue to feel the transcendent pull of the will of God and thus find their higher purpose in some notion of Deity, our nation can no longer be held together by traditional religious commitments alone.

As the traditional worldview has declined, the postmodern worldview has sought to advance its own ideal of a higher calling that entails liberating and compensating the oppressed victims of modernity, including animals and the natural environment. Postmodern culture's vision of a higher purpose might thus be summarized as "planetary healing." Yet while righting the wrongs of modernity may indeed be in our common interest, as discussed in Part I, postmodernism's reflexive vilification of modernity alienates too many mainstream Americans for its version of a transcendent ideal to ever become a unifying force for political solidarity. Moreover, postmodernity's vision of social progress lacks the moral resources to deal with the challenges of the pretraditional level of "warrior consciousness,"[9] as exemplified by gang and prison culture. Yet notwithstanding the postmodern worldview's inability to articulate a politically potent higher purpose for America overall, the biggest obstacle to reclaiming a collective vision of transcendence continues to be found in the staunchly secular values of modernity itself.

Modernism's proclivity for scientific naturalism and its corresponding allergy to transcendence has led to what eminent philosopher Charles Taylor calls "the challenge of our secular age." In his analysis of our contemporary cultural dilemma, Taylor invokes the polarity of immanence and transcendence, arguing that many of modernity's thought leaders advocate for a closed worldview that is cut off from the "horizon of the transcendent." According to Taylor, mainstream modernist culture is locked in an "immanent frame" wherein ideals of fulfillment are constrained within the material bounds of "human flourishing" alone. While human flourishing is certainly a commendable ideal, as long as this ideal remains exclusively within the immanent frame, it cannot access the moral sources of value energy that commitments to transcendence can supply. As he argues, transcendent commitments are ultimately necessary to realize the fullness of ordinary human lives. Writes Taylor, "Modes of fullness recognized by exclusive humanisms, and others that remain within the immanent frame, are responding to a transcendent reality, but misrecognizing it. They are shutting out crucial features of it."[10]

Although I'm inspired by Taylor's philosophical insights and agree with many of his cogent points, the definition of transcendence he articulates is not inclusive enough to provide the collective vision of higher purpose that we need at this time in history. Taylor identifies three types of authentic transcendence that go beyond the limited ideal of material human flourishing within a strictly immanent frame. These three meanings of transcendence include: 1) participating in a form of love or agape which goes way beyond any expectation of reciprocation or mutual exchange; 2) belief in some kind of afterlife; and 3) faith in a higher power whose source is beyond this world. While these ideas are authentically transcendent, and while I personally affirm all of them, these notions of transcendence are too closely associated with the traditional worldview to provide the unifying vision of transcendence we now require. Christianity may indeed play an important role in America's future cultural evolution, but the way forward does not lie in the revival of a liberal-friendly version of traditional religion, as implied by Taylor's arguments.

Nevertheless, Taylor is right that we need to reestablish a collective vision of human fulfillment that is energized and motivated by an authentic connection with the horizon of transcendence. And reestablishing this connection is the job of political philosophy. By employing the dialectical insights of polarity theory, the political philosophy I'm arguing for here brings together the polarity of self-interest and greater-than-self-interest with Taylor's polarity of immanence and transcendence. These two polarities are integrated through the following steps of logic: At the micro-level of individual motivation, the pursuit of self-interest, when relatively successful, moves toward forms of self-actualization that can only be found through self-transcendence. This relationship suggests how this polarity of basic personal interests can also be understood as "self-interest and self-transcendence." Continuing this line of reasoning, moving from the level of individual interests to the larger collective level of our overall social aspirations, we can see how the micro-level polarity of "self-interest and self-transcendence" translates into a similar polarity at the macro-level, which can be identified as "human flourishing and cultural transcendence." Put differently, in the same way that our personal fulfillment is ultimately connected to our own self-transcendence, our society's collective fulfillment similarly depends on its connection with an authentically transcendent purpose for humanity as a whole. Figure 6.2 illustrates how the overarching polarity of immanence and transcendence influences both the individual interests of the self and the collective interests of our culture as a whole.

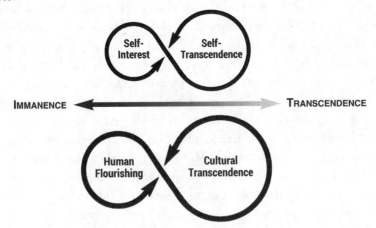

Figure 6.2. Showing how the polarity of immanence and transcendence influences both the personal polarity of individual interests and the collective polarity of social aspirations

Of course, at the individual level, many people do find a kind of fulfilling self-transcendence entirely within the immanent frame of human flourishing.

Working to improve the human condition certainly provides sufficient meaning for many. But at the collective level of mainstream American culture as a whole, a shared commitment to a higher purpose is now largely absent. The original American Dream of upward mobility and material success can no longer unify or inspire us as it once did. American society, and indeed modernity as a whole, needs to reinterpret its higher calling to respond to the challenges of the twenty-first century. While such a renewed higher purpose must include the fulfillment of human needs, the most important need of all is the spiritual need for self-transcendence. And as I'm arguing, self-transcendence is ultimately connected to some notion of cultural transcendence—something authentically "higher" for all of us collectively.

Many modernists and postmodernists reject the idea that anything "transcends" the physical universe. Yet many of those who deny the existence of any kind of transcendent reality nevertheless wholeheartedly devote themselves to various higher purposes which serve as substitutes for the transcendent ideals formerly supplied by religion. As noted in Part I, such stand-ins can include science, or art, or the needy, or the environment, or any ideal that seems worthy enough to devote one's life to. But no matter how meaningful or important such immanentized interpretations of transcendence may be, when interrogated philosophically, they all lead back to the same unanswered "why" questions. Why did this universe emerge? Why are we here? And why are we driven by an endless quest for betterment? How best to approach these unavoidably transcendent questions without falling back on traditional religious explanations is the subject of the next chapter.

Concluding this section, as I have argued, America needs a new vision of a higher purpose, one that can connect with authentic transcendence while still being acceptable to mainstream modernist sensibilities. And to be sufficiently unifying, this renewed higher purpose must also resonate with postmodern aspirations for social justice and environmental sustainability. Such an enlarged vision must accordingly serve as a bridge between the economic and political concerns of the immanent frame in which we are embedded, and our collective sense of hope that humanity has a deeper meaning and a higher destiny.

Notwithstanding denials by atheists and others hostile to the idea of authentic transcendence, our ongoing quest for something higher is an indelible feature of the human condition. As Taylor describes it:

Our world is ideologically fragmented, and the range of positions is growing as the nova effect is multiplied by expressive individualism. There are strong incentives to remain within the bounds of the human domain, or at least not bother exploring beyond it. The level of understanding of some of the great languages of transcendence is declining; in this respect, massive unlearning is taking place. The individual pursuit of happiness as defined by consumer culture still absorbs much of our time and energy, or else the threat of being shut out of this pursuit through poverty, unemployment, incapacity galvanizes all our efforts. ... All this is true, and yet the sense that there is something more presses in. Great numbers of people feel it: in moments of reflection about their life; in moments of reflection in nature; in moments of bereavement and loss; and quite wildly and unpredictably.[11]

This deep yearning for transcendence cannot be dismissed as wishful magical thinking; nor can it be explained away as merely a biological survival mechanism. Our attraction to a good that lies beyond ourselves—our ceaseless striving to create something better—is a fundamental part of what makes us human. And as I hope this discussion has conveyed, our transcendent ideals provide a crucial source of motivational value energy upon which the continued viability of our society depends. As argued by Taylor, and as confirmed by polarity theory, maintaining our collective connection to the energizing influence of authentic transcendence—allowing the immanent pole to be continuously supported and challenged by the influence of the transcendent pole—is the key to meeting the political challenges of our age.

Concluding this chapter, we've seen how the power of value exerts a strong energizing influence on the interests of humans, and indeed on all forms of life. We've also seen how, with humans at least, this source of psychic energy pulls in two essential directions: toward the immanent needs of the self, and toward the transcendent needs of something greater than the self. So, in order to overcome the debilitating lack of social solidarity that afflicts our democracy, we must reestablish our collective connection to authentically transcendent ideals. In the next chapter we will begin our exploration of an updated concept of transcendence that can supply an inclusive vision of higher purpose suitable for our twenty-first century civilization.

7

Cultivating Cultural Evolution Through a New American Dream

RECALLING OUR CENTRAL THEME, IN ORDER to overcome our nation's debilitating political dysfunction, we need to integrate and harmonize the conflicting values of America's three major worldviews. And as I am arguing, the key to integrating our diverse and discordant values will be found through the solidarity-building power of a new higher purpose. Yet to be sufficiently "higher"—to be inspiring and energizing—such a new proposition of collective cultural purpose must connect with aspirations that go beyond material security and prosperity alone. That is, in order to supply the motivational value energy needed to rouse us from our hyperpolarized political impasse, our new vision of higher purpose must connect with authentic transcendence.

As we explore in this chapter, the word "transcendence" can serve as an umbrella term that is potentially agreeable to a wide spectrum of metaphysical commitments. Again, connecting with the horizon of transcendence that lies beyond a closed immanent frame does not require us to either embrace the supernatural, or reject it out of hand. The ideal of transcendence advocated by developmental politics is accordingly broad enough to include religious ideas of God's will, as well as more secular notions of humanity's larger potential. While utopian idealism has been largely discredited, many secular people continue to believe that a more beautiful world is possible. So in order to harness the politically energizing power of an authentically transcendent ideal, our collective vision of a better future need only commit us to living up to the transformational possibilities that are already within our human potential.

Although both traditionalism and postmodernism are attempting to provide cultural leadership for modernity by asserting their own distinct versions of a transcendent higher purpose, as we have seen, neither of these visions is inspiring enough to serve as the higher purpose for America as a whole. At this time in history at least, God is too big and social justice is too small to serve as a solidarity-restoring ideal. To overcome our political grid-lock we need an updated and enlarged transcendent purpose that can *move modernity*, while also appealing to significant numbers of postmodernists and traditionalists.

But even though this new ideal of transcendence needs to appeal to modernists, it will not be found through focus group research or simply by devising clever political rhetoric. To be effectively inspiring and sufficiently unifying, this collective social goal must be founded on a higher truth—it must be saturated with the most concentrated form of truth we can know with relative certainty. In order to serve as an energizing vision, this aspirational ideal must be grounded in the kind of truth that can act as a bridge between the immanent and the transcendent. Which means that we must look for the ideational source of our new higher purpose in the intersection of science and spirituality.

To speak to the needs of our contemporary modernist society, our new vision of cultural transcendence must not only be consistent with science, it must be rooted in science. Science is modernity's authority on truth, so to move modernity we must look for the higher truth we need in the discoveries of science itself. Some modernists are of the opinion that science somehow disproves the transcendent or obviates the need for it. But as discussed in the last chapter, transcendent ideals are politically necessary for the long-term functionality of democracy. And as Charles Taylor argues, secular modernists are already "responding to a transcendent reality, but misrecognizing it."[1]

Science focuses primarily on that which is physical, so its methods and technologies cannot connect directly with transcendence or otherwise prove it. But the real truth delivered by science does reveal transcendence when properly interpreted. The amount of truth brought forth by science over the last three hundred years in general, and the last fifty years in particular, has given us a mother lode of truth that we have yet to fully digest or appreciate philosophically. And among all the truths revealed by science, the biggest and most profound truth by far is the discovery of evolution. It is thus within the new truths of evolution that we can find a vision of transcendence that can meet the political needs of our time.

TRANSCENDENCE AND THE STRUCTURE OF EVOLUTIONARY EMERGENCE

Although ancient Greek philosophers pondered "the becoming of things" over twenty-five hundred years ago, it was not until the beginning of the nineteenth century that modernist philosophers began to realize that everything on earth was in the process of becoming. Then later in that century, Darwin's discovery of biological evolution through natural selection would rock the Western intellectual world. By providing a naturalistic account of human origins, Darwin's theory helped overturn the West's religious creation story and led to the ascendency of science as modernity's ultimate authority on truth.

Then, in the middle of the twentieth century, a similarly momentous scientific breakthrough cast additional light on our origins. But this breakthrough—the discovery of the big bang and the dramatic beginning of time and space—would not be heralded by scientific materialists as an ideational triumph. The revelation that the universe as a whole was only three times older than the earth itself, and that everything could be traced back to the hydrogen and helium atoms that were the debris of the big bang, was deeply unsettling to those hostile to religion. Prior to the discovery of the big bang, most scientists presupposed that the universe was in an eternal steady-state. Albert Einstein even altered his physics equations to make them consistent with a steady-state cosmology. But as the evidence came in confirming that our universe first emerged only 13.8 billion years ago, scientists were faced with a profound mystery. And the "cause" of the big bang remains unexplained to this day.[2]

Although science has provided credible naturalistic explanations for the cosmological evolution of matter and the biological evolution of life, it has not been able to explain how or why these distinct evolutionary domains came into being in the first place. Not only is the cause of the big bang unexplained, but the origin of life remains unexplained as well. Moreover, the origin of humanity, which initiated the cultural domain of noosphere evolution, cannot be explained by natural selection alone. As the prolific polymath Arthur Koestler wrote, "The evolution of the human brain not only overshot the needs of prehistoric man, it is the only example of evolution *providing a species with an organ which it does not know how to use*; a luxury organ, which will take its owner thousands of years to learn how to put to proper use—if he ever does."[3] While our bodies may be only incrementally different from other primates, our minds are in another category altogether. As evolutionary biologist Marc Hauser observes, "cognitively, the difference between humans and chimps is greater than that between chimps and worms."[4]

The scientific story of our origins now reveals what philosopher Holmes Rolston calls *three big bangs*. These mysterious origin events mark the beginning of the three major domains of evolution: matter, life, and mind. Although evolution in each of these domains proceeds by different methods that cannot be conflated, what ties these different kinds of development together, confirming that they are all authentic forms of evolution, is the structure of evolutionary emergence itself. From the beginning, evolution has unfolded through a series of emergent steps, with each new step building on the accomplishments of what came before. In other words, within every domain of development, evolution grows from within itself as each level of emergent novelty transcends and includes the levels of development that preceded it: Molecules transcend and include atoms, cells transcend and include molecules, and complex organisms transcend and include cells.

"Something more keeps coming from something less."

This structural pattern of "development by envelopment" can be clearly seen in the human body. We embody the sequential steps of cosmological evolution from the hydrogen atoms in our water molecules through the periodic table of elements in our bones. Our bodies also contain practically all the stages of biological evolution. For example, we embody the evolutionary accomplishments of the eukaryotes in our cells, the vertebrates in our backbones, and the mammals in our neocortexes. These historical steps of emergence are not just events of the distant past; their achievements are being used here and now within us. Each one of these distinct forms of emergence is thus making an ongoing and vital contribution to the leading edge of evolution in the present.

Just as we embody and use the structures of cosmological and biological emergence in our bodies, we are likewise using practically all the stages of humanity's cultural development in our contemporary modes of awareness. The field of developmental psychology has shown how the accomplishments of previous stages of human history continue to contribute to the cultural consciousness of our current age. This can be seen in the development of children, who roughly recapitulate humanity's historical stages of evolution as they grow, moving from magical consciousness to mythical consciousness to more rational forms of consciousness as they mature, and potentially beyond that to more developed stages in adulthood.[5] These stages of humanity's psychosocial evolution thus form a kind of interior mental ecosystem wherein the accomplishments of each stage depend on the value achievements of previous stages. As explained in Part I, postmodern values rely on the previous cultural accomplishments of modernity, and modernist values likewise rest on the cultural accomplishments of traditional values.

This nested sequence of emergence is how evolution works at every level. Again, something more keeps coming from something less. Yet the "more" almost always takes up and uses the achievements of the earlier, less developed level from which it emerges. This evolutionary technique of transcendence through inclusion is what allows evolution to continually build on itself and make ongoing progress toward more complex forms of organization and greater degrees of awareness.

This discussion of the structure of emergence is meant to show that evolution has a definite direction. It's not a straightforwardly linear direction like the arrow of time, but evolution has been evidently moving toward "something more" throughout most of its history, despite occasional setbacks and regressions. Some scientists have defined this direction of advance as "greater complexity," but this rather thin description does not capture the radical nature of what is actually transpiring. Considered as a whole, the direction in which evolution is moving is best described as *the direction of transcendence itself*. Each step of sustainable emergence demonstrates what it means to "go beyond." And the most significant kinds of evolutionary emergence—the three big bangs—demonstrate this movement toward transcendence most dramatically. The primordial emergence of the original big bang transcended the "singularity" out of which it appeared by giving rise to space-time, energy-matter, and probably the laws of physics themselves. Similarly, the emergence of life, while made out of matter, transcended matter alone by bringing an entirely new kind of reality into the universe—the reality of intention. The emergence of humanity likewise gave rise to a transcendent new reality in the form of self-awareness and the ceaseless striving for higher levels of goodness.

Figure 7.1 illustrates the general direction of transcendence within the nested structure of evolution's three great domains of development. The way each domain encompasses its predecessor is empirically evident in the fact that the earth is now covered with life and increasingly enveloped by the physical structures of human civilization.

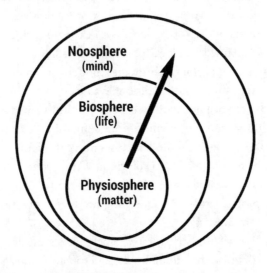

Figure 7.1. Each domain of evolution transcends and includes the realm out of which it emerges[6]

Neo-Darwinian materialists are fond of "debunking" the notion that humanity represents the leading edge of evolution. But when the noosphere is properly recognized as a distinct realm of authentic evolutionary development that transcends and includes the previous two domains of matter and life, we can see how the structure of emergence is now being extended primarily through the continuing evolution of human consciousness and culture.

So how does this analysis of the structure of evolutionary emergence relate to the new concept of cultural transcendence we need? How can these philosophical observations be used to reestablish common cause and reenergize our politics through a new agreement about our collective higher purpose? The short answer is that humanity's transcendent purpose can be discovered in the project of furthering the evolution of culture and consciousness on every front of its development. In other words, the modernist-friendly ideal of cultural transcendence that we need to restore our social solidarity can be found in an enlarged understanding of cultural evolution—an expanded conception of inclusive social progress that can advance the positive values of all three of America's major worldviews simultaneously, while also moving beyond their respective limitations.

Both the rational justifications for this proposed ideal of cultural transcendence, and the practical steps by which it can be implemented, are discussed in the pages ahead. But before I explain why and how the project of cultivating cultural evolution can ameliorate our pressing political problems, there is more to say about transcendence itself. As I am arguing, a common vision of cultural transcendence is ultimately necessary to sustain the social solidarity required for a functional democracy. In the same way that biological ecosystems can only flourish where there are abundant energy resources, in order to flourish culturally and politically, human societies similarly require sources of value energy—inspirational energy that can only be supplied by an authentically transcendent higher purpose.

"Humanity's transcendent purpose can be discovered in the project of furthering the evolution of culture and consciousness on every front of its development."

Yet, to be effective, the renewed sense of transcendent purpose we need must necessarily connect with the immanent political challenges of our time in history. The political philosophy of developmental politics can therefore help us meet this existential social need by acting as a bridge between the transcendent and the immanent. To serve in this way, this philosophical bridge must be firmly anchored to both the transcendent and immanent sides of the divide we need to span. And the key to establishing these connections and bridging this divide is found by returning to the central subject of human purposes and values.

Because the noosphere is the top layer or leading edge of evolution on this planet, and because humans are solely responsible for advancing evolution in the noospheric domain of cultural development, the values that motivate us point the way toward evolution's continuing advance in the direction of transcendence. Simply put, we make contact with the horizon of transcendence primarily through our most cherished values, which provide compass headings for "which way is up." Therefore, it is through a deeper appreciation of the nature and behavior of human values that we can begin to discover the vivid vision of cultural transcendence we need to establish a politically powerful higher purpose for twenty-first century America.

As a preview of the forthcoming discussion, the philosophical bridge we need to construct between the transcendent and the immanent will be described through the following connecting segments: Starting from the transcendent side, we examine the spiritual nature of values by focusing on the most intrinsic values humans can know—goodness, truth, and beauty. We then move toward the immanent side by exploring how each major worldview concretizes these abstract ideals by translating them into their own distinct versions of the American Dream. This leads to a consideration of how these competing visions of America's transcendent purpose can be harmonized and integrated through the new higher purpose of cultivating cultural evolution. As we will see, the goal of furthering the evolution of culture carries forward pervious versions of the American Dream while also opening new frontiers of compassionate and sustainable progress. The chapter concludes by examining the details of how cultural evolution can be approached as a political project. Then in the next chapter we ground these ideas on the immanent side of the divide by exploring the personal practice of virtues, which, as we will see, is a crucial component of developmental politics' project for political renewal.

GOODNESS, TRUTH, AND BEAUTY—TRACES OF THE TRANSCENDENT WITHIN THE IMMANENT

The farthest reaches of the ideal of transcendence are grounded in American culture's varying notions of ultimate reality. Yet according to my understanding, ultimate reality is not only transcendent, it is also fully immanent in the world.

Personally, I think the multitudinous spiritual experiences reported by both religious and nonreligious people alike provide considerable evidence for the transcendent presence of ultimate reality within our immanent frame. However, my intention is not to argue for a concept of transcendence that depends on a belief in God, Oneness, or similar ideas regarding an unseen spiritual realm. In order to be widely inclusive and politically compelling, the aspirational ideal of transcendence we require must be recognizable not only in peak experiences or mystical epiphanies, but also in the ordinary realities of our everyday lives. Simply put, the new national agreement we need to reestablish a collective higher purpose must be founded on experiences that are commonly accessible to everyone. And happily, ordinary experiences of transcendence are readily available in the intrinsic values that constitute our "matters of ultimate concern." As I argue in this section, goodness, truth, and beauty—the most intrinsic values—connect with authentic transcendence while still being widely accessible and metaphysically agreeable to the vast majority of Americans.

For the last twenty-four hundred years at least, numerous philosophers, theologians, artists, social scientists, and other sensitive thinkers have come to the conclusion that goodness, truth, and beauty represent the most significant kinds of value that humans can experience and create. Although this ancient triad is often associated with Plato, the veneration of these three values far exceeds the bounds of Platonic philosophy alone. Even though there is no general philosophical consensus regarding anything having to do with values, the special significance of goodness, truth, and beauty is nevertheless widely recognized by philosophers and spiritually inclined writers influenced by both Western and Eastern religions, and by some secular thinkers as well.[7]

While notions of love and freedom are also often thought of as belonging to the set of most intrinsic values, there is something very special about the triad of goodness, truth, and beauty. Taken together, these three values form a system wherein each value helps define and disclose the nature of the other two. Moreover, the special significance of these three values is seen in the way they each represent a "capstone quality" or guiding focus for the major domains of human experience and endeavor. To be specific, goodness is the essence of the moral dimension of human experience, truth defines the focus of the rational domain, and beauty can be broadly defined as the capstone quality of the aesthetic dimension of value.

The comprehensive nature of these most intrinsic values—the way they "cover the waterfront" so to speak—suggests an analogy with primary colors: In the same way that the entire visible spectrum of color can be depicted with just three basic colors, the entire field of human values can likewise be represented by these three "primary values." Figure 7.2 illustrates a "word cloud" of values that can be derived from, or otherwise related back to, goodness, truth, and beauty.

Figure 7.2. The primary values and some of their derivatives

While everyone experiences goodness, truth, and beauty in some form, the question of what these closely related entities actually are continues to be debated. The most simple and direct definition might be *aliveness*, or even *the flowering of the real*. These three interrelated terms, however, are not merely synonyms for "excellent" or "splendid." Although these concepts are highly abstract, considered together as a system, the good, the true, and the beautiful constitute a *conceptual cathedral* in which the polarized perspectives of science and spirit become harmonized. These primary values have been a major focus of my work in philosophy over the last twenty-five years, and during this time my appreciation of the special significance of these three fundamental qualities has continued to deepen.

In *Evolution's Purpose* I explored the philosophical implications of the primary values, arguing that these three qualities define the actual directions of evolution within consciousness and culture. This venerable triad of values functions as a "great attractor" that pulls evolution forward *from the inside* by influencing our hearts and minds. The way goodness, truth, and beauty lure us and draw us forward in an ongoing quest to improve our conditions was well understood by the eminent philosopher Alfred North Whitehead, who actually defined evolution as *an increase in the capacity to experience what is intrinsically valuable*. This consciousness-centric definition of evolution remains one of my favorite ideas in all philosophy.[8]

Then, in my 2015 book, *The Presence of the Infinite*, I considered the spiritual side of these qualities, arguing that these most intrinsic values literally represent the presence of the infinite within the finite realm of time and space. In my exploration of the spiritual dimensions of goodness, truth, and beauty, I argued that these qualities are comprehensible elements of divinity that provide "handles on spirit" that we can grasp in our experience and use in our work in the world. My account of "beauty, truth, and goodness spirituality" concluded with the claim that these value experiences communicate *personalized messages of love* that provide both instructions and assurances for our ongoing spiritual journey.[9]

Yet notwithstanding the authentic spiritual experiences that goodness, truth, and beauty provide, I am under no illusion that arguments alone, no matter how compelling, will change people's belief systems. Many modernists and postmodernists have a strong aversion to spiritual claims and will thus reject the contention that that which humans find beautiful, true, and good somehow justifies a spiritual reality that transcends the immanent frame of our mundane world. However, one of the best things about these most intrinsic values is that they don't demand a spiritual interpretation. The transcendent qualities of these primary values can be recognized and even venerated by atheists and agnostics within a completely secular frame of reality. As a recent example, staunchly secular Harvard professor Howard Gardner's book, *Truth, Beauty, and Goodness Reframed*, extols the special significance of these three values and argues that they should be the aims of education.

The great advantage of anchoring the transcendent meaning of our collective higher purpose in the ideals of goodness, truth, and beauty is that these values meet people where they are. That is, these ideals connect with authentic transcendence without requiring any supernatural commitments. So regardless of one's belief system, it is possible to wholeheartedly agree that transcending our culture's current conditions entails making things more beautiful, true, and good. Because they are widely inclusive and directly experiential, the ideals of goodness, truth, and beauty can therefore provide the necessary sense of authentic transcendence we need to support the higher purpose of "furthering the evolution of culture and consciousness." Simply put, these primary values well-define what "further" means at an existential level.

However, while these intrinsic values may connect with authentic transcendence from a philosophical and spiritual perspective, they are admittedly too abstract by themselves to be politically motivating for most people. In order to tap into the value energy that arises from a robust commitment to an inspiring higher purpose, we must move closer to the immanent side of the divide we are attempting to bridge. And as we move from these abstract ideals to the more concrete political values defined by America's conflicting worldviews, we are faced with the challenge of translating *different levels* of goodness, truth, and beauty into a common direction of advance that all Americans can potentially agree with.

DISCOVERING A NEW AMERICAN DREAM

In this chapter so far we have begun to explore both the need and the potential for an expanded vision of cultural transcendence—a new collective higher purpose for American society that finds its truth in the intersection of science and spirituality.

The new vision of transcendence that I advocate—transcendence through cultural evolution—connects with science because it is grounded in evolutionary development and focused on extending the structure of evolutionary emergence in the realms of culture and consciousness. As we've seen, evolution literally moves in the direction of transcendence—something more keeps coming from something less. So by tying our notion of transcendence to the evident process of universe development, this hopeful vision of America's future might find acceptance even among hardheaded skeptics.

"The universal values of goodness, truth, and beauty are grounded in culturally specific worldviews that give these values life and make them applicable to real world problems."

At the same time, this new proposition of America's higher purpose connects with spirituality by defining the trajectory of transcendence within cultural evolution as the quest for increasing realizations of goodness, truth, and beauty. These spiritual qualities represent the fundamental headings for cultural evolution in the noosphere. And the spiritual nature of these most intrinsic values is something that almost everyone can appreciate and affirm.

But again, while goodness, truth, and beauty may provide spiritual credibility and philosophical solidity, these primary values are too abstract to enact a new higher purpose by themselves alone. To be politically effective, the universal values of goodness, truth, and beauty must be grounded in the culturally specific worldviews that give these values life and make them applicable to real world problems. This need to ground the good, the true, and the beautiful in the political life of our nation brings us back to the distinct value sets described in Part I as "heritage values," "liberty values," "fairness values," and "caring values."

As originally mapped out in figures 4.5 and 4.6 on pages 54-55, each of these value sets can be understood as discrete bandwidths of value energy, or as distinct "octaves" in the ascending scale of our human aspirations for goodness, truth, and beauty. These four discrete sets of political values derive their magnetic power from the underlying intrinsic values which they help concretize and translate into accessible cultural identities. By rendering these intrinsic values into political agendas that are relevant to real-world problems and opportunities, each of these cultural categories defines its own version of the American Dream.

To be specific, for those who identify with traditional heritage values, their sense of being part of a nation that provides a moral example for the world—a "shining city on a hill" as Ronald Reagan put it—continues to serve as an inspirational form of patriotic higher purpose. Traditionalists take particular pride in American culture's enduring religiosity, as exemplified by the national motto: "In God We Trust."

By contrast, those who identify most closely with modernist liberty values define the American Dream primarily as the opportunity for upward mobility and financial prosperity, which is ensured through the protection of personal autonomy and economic freedom. Yet despite its focus on material prosperity, classical modernity's version of the American Dream also maintains its connection to transcendent ideals through the ongoing affirmation of Jefferson's vision of "liberty and justice for all."

Moving to the left, modernists who subscribe to a more liberal vision of the American Dream—those who identify most closely with the fairness values category—continue to affirm liberty and justice for all. But these liberal modernists also aspire to some version of Lyndon Johnson's "Great Society," wherein the American Dream is defined to include both personal prosperity and a government that takes an active role in ameliorating social problems and addressing unmet needs.

However, moving further left, we come to the caring values of postmodernists, whose notions of our society's most desirable future often include transcending the American nation altogether. Postmodernism's vision of a more evolved society accordingly entails overturning the original American Dream of individual success and national pride and replacing it with a transnational ideal of compassionate local communities dedicated to global social equality and environmental sustainability.

Given the disparity between these discordant notions of the larger meaning of American society and its best potential future, we might be tempted to conclude that finding common ground will be impossible, at least in the near term. The disruptive challenge of postmodernism, however, need not result in permanent political gridlock, or the gradual decline of Western civilization. Despite its threat to the established liberal order, and despite its immaturities and excesses, the emergence of the postmodern worldview can be interpreted more positively as the first tentative step beyond the culture of modernity. Because postmodernism's cultural power is largely fueled by discontent with modernity, the rise of the postmodern worldview can be recognized as a dialectical move of antithesis that is itself unstable. The antithesis of postmodernism is thus creating the need and presaging the potential for a subsequent step toward a cultural synthesis.[10] This anticipated synthesis will be found in an enlarged frame of values that can integrate and harmonize the enduring and necessary values of all four of the value categories we're considering.

> **"The synthesis will be found in an enlarged frame of values that can integrate and harmonize the enduring and necessary values of all four value categories."**

The challenge of framing a culturally synthetic and politically effective American Dream for the twenty-first century therefore requires us to employ evolution's own dialectical technique of *transcending and including*. This means that the expanded higher purpose we need must move beyond postmodernism's disruptive rejection of the old versions of the American Dream by affirming that both upward mobility and moral leadership can continue to be part of America's higher purpose going forward. Yet even as we reject progressive attempts to characterize America primarily as a shameful disgrace, it is also crucial that we validate and embrace postmodernism's important contributions. These contributions include postmodernism's sensitive new layer of moral concern, as well as its cogent critiques of America's past crimes and current shortcomings.

So how can we take postmodernism's existential challenge in our stride without giving up on the best of what has come before? How can we craft a new proposition of cultural transcendence—a new American Dream—that both includes and transcends the caring values and critical judgments of postmodernism? The answer proposed by developmental politics begins by recognizing how the postmodern worldview fits within the larger trajectory of cultural evolution as a whole. In fact, it is this expanded understanding of cultural evolution that allows us to see beyond postmodernism in the first place. This evolutionary perspective accordingly affirms that the new transcendent purpose we need can be found in the noble project of cultivating and supporting the evolution of culture and consciousness on every front of its development.

While this evolutionary project may at first seem politically unrealistic, as I will argue throughout the rest of this book, as the twenty-first century unfolds fostering cultural evolution can be, and most likely will be, an increasing priority for the world's most developed societies. As we've seen, the evolution of culture advances concurrently with the evolution of consciousness. So in order to address the major challenges of our age by evolving our culture, we must become better at raising consciousness. Indeed, the insights of developmental politics reveal how almost every human problem is partially a "problem of consciousness." It thus follows that working to develop and evolve consciousness can produce the cultural evolution we need to alleviate many of our national problems. To give a few brief examples: The problem of poverty can be mitigated through the development of modernist consciousness—modernist consciousness generates prosperity. The problem of global warming can be ameliorated by strengthening postmodern consciousness—postmodern consciousness cares deeply about the environment. And the debilitating problem of America's hyperpolarization can be similarly addressed through the cultivation of integral consciousness—integral consciousness sympathetically appreciates the full spectrum of American values.

This proposed revisioning of the American Dream in terms of cultural evolution carries forward the best aspects of previous versions of the American Dream. It continues to include the traditionalist dream of providing a moral example for the world by demonstrating a new kind of moral leadership through the harmonious integration of competing worldviews. As cultures throughout the world become stretched out through uneven development, the need to politically integrate diverse worldviews is a challenge that the rest of the world is increasingly facing. America can thus provide a new kind of moral example by effectively overcoming its own cultural polarization.

This new American Dream of cultural evolution likewise carries forward modernist aspirations for prosperity and upward mobility by revalorizing modernity, and by reaffirming the ongoing importance of its liberal freedoms. And crucially, this new American Dream also forwards progressive aspirations for social justice and environmental sustainability by recognizing the essential role of postmodernism's new layer of care in the unfolding development of American culture.

By integrating and consolidating the prevailing Dreams of every major worldview, the new American Dream of cultivating cultural evolution forwards each of these existing Dreams simultaneously by endorsing the myriad ways that people can contribute to the evolution of the noosphere. And by clarifying and advancing the transcendent aspirations of each set of values, the expanded higher purpose of universal cultural development effectively magnifies the inspirational power of each worldview's interpretation of the good.

Up until now, the evolution of culture has not been well understood. But as a result of the new insights and discoveries about the dynamic growth of values within America's cultural ecosystem being advanced by integral philosophy and developmental politics, fostering the growth of culture begins to seem like a realistic and promising endeavor. How such a project might be realistically undertaken is considered in this chapter's next and final section.

STRATEGIES FOR CULTIVATING CULTURAL EVOLUTION

As I contend, in order to grow out of our debilitating political impasse, we need to build agreement around a new vision of America's higher purpose—an expanded and inclusive American Dream that can accommodate the challenges of postmodernism while continuing to inspire modernists and traditionalists. And as I have argued, this new vision can and will be found in the project of evolving culture and consciousness. In our approach to this project, however, it is important to recognize that noosphere evolution does not unfold along a singular line of growth or a unilinear trajectory of advance. Culture evolves on multiple fronts of development.

Before considering the following strategies for fostering cultural evolution, it is also important to acknowledge that the world can be made a better place in countless ways that do not entail cultural evolution per se. Solving specific social problems, creating new innovations and technologies, and founding beneficial institutions, all provide familiar examples of good works that can improve our conditions without directly evolving our culture. But over the long-term, such improvements usually do eventually contribute to cultural evolution nonetheless.

As a preview of the forthcoming discussion, the first and perhaps most straightforward method for fostering cultural evolution in America involves working to improve and develop each existing worldview in accordance with its own goals and values. This project can be undertaken through the values integration method first introduced in chapter 4 and considered further below. The second approach to fostering cultural evolution involves encouraging the ongoing growth of consciousness into healthy versions of the existing worldviews that have emerged along the timeline of human history. This kind of cultural evolution presupposes a vertical dimension of development and is thus controversial. But despite its hierarchical implications, an integral interpretation of this normative dimension of growth recognizes the political equality and enduring necessity of each set of values, and thus honors and employs the values of all three major worldviews. And finally, the third approach through which we can help bring about America's further cultural evolution involves advancing a new and inclusive integral worldview that effectively transcends postmodernism. In the same way that modernism emerged from traditionalism, and postmodernism emerged in turn from modernity, it seems reasonable to expect that another new worldview will eventually emerge beyond postmodernism. These three distinct but related approaches to cultivating cultural evolution are examined in turn.

1. Evolving American culture by improving each existing worldview on its own terms

Here it bears repeating that mainly as a result of the cultural competition between the traditional and postmodern moral systems, the American electorate has now become polarized into the four value categories I'm labeling: caring values, fairness values, liberty values, and heritage values. As explored in chapter 4, each of these categories includes positive values that we need to honor and carry forward, and shortcomings and pathologies that we would do well to leave behind. (Again, the values charts on pages 54-55 provide a partial list of the strengths and weaknesses of each category.) Each of these value sets can accordingly develop by working to ameliorate and diminish its downsides while simultaneously strengthening and refining its upsides. In short, each value category can improve and evolve by teasing apart its dignities from its disasters.

The pathologies of each cultural category result from the struggles associated with that category's specific contribution to history. Yet while the downsides of each set of values can be clearly seen by the other competing categories, every one of these value sets tends to ignore or downplay its own unique negatives and shortcomings. Although some of these pathologies can be addressed politically and collectively through new laws, much of the work of overcoming these problems must be undertaken by the specific cultures that are responsible for creating them in the first place. For example, racism will only be fully eradicated when traditional culture will no longer tolerate it. And similarly, postmodernism's sweeping rejection of Western civilization will not be renounced until this form of culture recognizes how its ardent rejectionism is hindering the achievement of its own positive aspirations.

In response to this challenge, the insights of polarity theory provide a workable method for overcoming the unwillingness of each category to address its own shadow. As discussed in chapters 4 and 6, polarity theory shows how each category's own positive values can be effectively forwarded by establishing deliberative agreements with its polar counterparts wherein the moderating and correcting process of challenge and support can take place. By working with these principles of polar interdependence to form alliances across polarities, each major cultural block can become more aware of the burden of its own shortcomings, while also better recognizing the corresponding upsides of its cultural rivals. In other words, by engaging the value-creating power of the existential polarities that arise in the natural course of development, each distinct form of culture can increase the scope of its own values and thereby evolve into a more moral and effective version of itself. As America's disparate values become better reconciled and harmonized through this process of values integration, the particular kind of progress offered by each worldview will no longer be reflexively blocked or stymied by its political competitors. By thus reducing competitive resistance through the implementation of this method, each set of values can better advance its own positive agenda, albeit in moderated form.

2. Evolving American culture by fostering the ongoing growth of consciousness along the timeline of human history

Although the method of values integration provides the most direct and pragmatic approach to cultivating cultural evolution in the near term, developmental politics' greatest promise lies in its potential to help bring about a new synthetic worldview that transcends and includes all three existing worldviews. However, if this new post-postmodern or integral worldview is to be held out as being better or more evolved than postmodernism, then this necessarily implies that modernism is more evolved than traditionalism, and that somehow, postmodernism is similarly more evolved than modernism. While some readers may find this assessment of evolutionary development fairly evident, others will understandably resist or reject such a conclusion. Given the excesses and immaturities of postmodern culture, if it were to gain an electoral majority and come to provide the cultural center of gravity of American society, this could result in the precipitous decline of the American nation itself. For many modernists and traditionalists, postmodernism's rejectionistic cultural antithesis is accordingly seen more as a dire threat than as an attractive vision for America's future cultural evolution. Despite the fact that postmodernism is now close to constituting the majority worldview in countries such as Denmark and the Netherlands, for many Americans the potential political ascendency of postmodernism remains a chilling prospect.

Yet even though postmodernism may not be capable of providing comprehensive leadership for America, it is important to acknowledge how its emergence has nevertheless resulted in authentic cultural evolution. Moreover, the integrative worldview that we urgently need ultimately depends on the accomplishments of postmodernism for its own viability—in the dialectical logic of evolution, a synthesis requires a previous antithesis. Conversely, it is the inherent inadequacy of postmodernism that necessitates the need and thus paves the way for this subsequent integral worldview to emerge. In fact, every significant worldview that has emerged along the timeline of history has resulted in the evolution of values. The ability to recognize each worldview's enduring contribution to humanity's overall cultural ecosystem is thus a signature strength of integral consciousness. The growth in values that takes place as traditionalists embrace modernist values, and then as modernists come to adopt postmodern values is illustrated by the following examples.

The first and arguably most significant growth in values that results from the emergence of new worldviews can be seen in the case of inclusivity. The advent of each new worldview widens the scope of those deemed worthy of cultural inclusion and moral consideration. For instance, going beyond the ethnocentric limitations of traditionalism, modernism seeks to include multiple religions, races, and ethnic groups within its society, and postmodernism goes even further by working to include those who have been victimized, marginalized, or exploited.

In addition to this growth in inclusivity, we can also recognize the growth of liberty. Modernism liberates the individual from the religious constraints of traditional culture, and postmodernism in turn provides liberation from modernism's empty consumerism and materialism, and by encouraging cultural nonconformity and diversity. The evolutionary steps of liberation offered by both modernism and postmodernism can also be seen in the growth of the status of women. Undoubtedly, the relative equality of women is an objective marker of the degree of evolution achieved by any society.

The evolution of worldviews has also expanded our grasp on truth itself. Modernism has brought us the tremendous truths of science, and postmodernism has helped refine modernity's understanding of what's true by pointing out the limits of objectivity and by showing how many truth claims rest on subjective perspectives.

Despite these undeniable improvements, it is nevertheless important to reiterate once more how the emergence of each worldview also brings about new threats to humanity. With modernity comes the threat of nuclear annihilation and environmental destruction. And postmodernism in turn threatens to undermine Western civilization from within by repudiating its value foundations. The idea of "development" as conceived by developmental politics necessarily entails improvement and positive growth. But clearly, not all development is desirable, and some forms of development are decidedly unhealthy.

The fact that the evolution of culture is inevitably accompanied by a corresponding growth in the potential for destruction has led many to question whether real "progress" is even possible. However, the question of whether net progress has occurred since the advent of modernism, and whether positive progress is even possible in the long-term, will be addressed in chapter 9's consideration of the new vision of progress offered by developmental politics. There we will also consider whether the postmodern worldview constitutes the necessary next step for American culture as a whole.

Regardless of one's assessment of America's social progress, it must be acknowledged that each of these systems of value has been forged in the struggle to

> **"A fundamental tenet of developmental politics is that people have a right to be who they are."**

improve the human condition, and that each worldview represents the collective agreements of millions of people. The historical duration and global scale of these three major worldviews thus provides solid evidence that they are each making things better in their own way, despite their respective pathologies.

As we've seen, the process through which the consciousness of individuals evolves through the existing structures of history involves both a push and pull. The push comes from the accumulation of existential problems that cannot be solved at the prevailing level of development, and the pull comes from the magnetic attraction of the liberating values and empowering advantages offered by the next available level. These transitions from one worldview to the next are a familiar part of American life. For example, children raised in traditional homes frequently become modernists in adulthood because they are pushed by the limits of a mythic worldview and pulled by the lures of greater liberty and prosperity offered by modernist culture. Similarly, modernists become attracted to postmodern values when they begin to feel discontented with the vacuity of pursuing status and material gain alone, and are accordingly pushed to find more meaning in life. This push of discontent is usually accompanied by the appealing pull of postmodernism's creative freedom and communal belonging. These familiar cultural transitions are facilitated by many of the established institutions of our society, including education, the arts, political activism, and even by philosophy. However, the details of how this kind of evolution can be fostered are discussed extensively elsewhere in my work, so I won't repeat those methods here.[11]

But notwithstanding the benefits realized as consciousness moves into more developed worldviews, in order to be ethically inclusive, the project of fostering cultural evolution must show respect for every worldview and be transparent in both its methods and its goals. Indeed, a fundamental tenet of developmental politics is that "people have a right to be who they are," as long as they don't impede the rights of their fellow citizens. According to this principle, the development of values must remain a free and optional choice in our society. Modernists may insist that religious fundamentalists recognize the authority of science, and postmodernists may demand that mainstream society's focus on economic growth must yield to the needs of the environment. But developmental politics clearly recognizes how liberty values provide the foundation for all subsequent cultural advances, and this means that in most cases the evolution of consciousness can only be legitimately brought about by gentle persuasion rather than by legal coercion. This strategy of cultivating the evolution of conscious through gentle persuasion might be thought of as "gardening for emergence."

The bottom line of this subsection is that working to evolve consciousness up through the existing worldviews that constitute America's cultural ecosystem is an indispensible aspect of evolving culture overall. When undertaken noncoercively and with respect, the project of evolving consciousness along the timeline of human history can indeed achieve authentic cultural and moral growth. But again, this is a complex and controversial topic which we will revisit in our discussion of progress in the final chapter. Now we turn to the third and most exciting strategy for advancing the evolution of American culture: The project of building a new integrative worldview.

3. Evolving American culture by advancing an integral worldview that transcends postmodernism

The coming emergence of a culturally significant new worldview that will transcend postmodernism has been the main focus of my writing for the last twenty years. I must therefore reiterate that this emerging integral worldview can effectively do what postmodernism cannot—it can recognize the enduring legitimacy and embrace the positive values of modernism and traditionalism while continuing to honor the important accomplishments of postmodern culture. But even though this new integral worldview is generally friendly to progressive culture, it also rejects postmodernism's rejectionism. That is, the integral frame of values moves toward the synthetic inclusion of the best of what has come before by "negating the negation" of postmodernism's hypercritical political stance.

> **"The integral worldview rejects postmodernism's rejectionism."**

In both *Integral Consciousness* and *Evolution's Purpose*, I described this anticipated worldview in detail, and I continue to work for the advancement of this inclusive new cultural frame both in my writing and in my work with the Institute for Cultural Evolution think tank. While it is beyond the scope of this discussion to undertake a thorough description of this integral worldview, a large part of its perspective comes from knowledge of the dynamics of cultural evolution, which we have been exploring throughout this book. So readers who have come this far should already have a basic sense of what integral consciousness entails.

The exciting promise of the integral worldview first came to my attention in 1999. And until 2008, it seemed as though the political emergence of this stage of cultural development was actually taking place. During the first years of this century the audience for integral philosophy and integral culture was growing rapidly, and it appeared that the integral movement was starting to come of age. But beginning in 2009 the global recession diminished the vitality of underlying postmodern culture, and this had a significant impact on the fledging integral movement. In addition to the economic downturn, the movement's growth in the 2010s was also hindered by a lack of competent leadership and by professional rivalries between its factions.[12]

But given the history of the other historically significant worldviews we have examined, we should naturally expect that it will take some time for this integral worldview to emerge as a political force in American culture. As we saw in chapter 3, the postmodern worldview developed in relative obscurity for decades before it became culturally florescent and emerged as a politically significant worldview in the 1960s and 1970s. So it is hard to predict exactly when the integral worldview will gain cultural influence and recognition. The political emergence of this new worldview could be right around the corner in the 2020s, or it could still be decades away. Nevertheless, at the time of this writing the integral intellectual community continues to thrive in various places throughout the developed world. And my colleagues and I remain committed to both its promising potential and its eventual cultural and political emergence. Indeed, developmental politics is itself an attempt to help bring this new worldview into being.

However, we don't have to wait for the next cultural renaissance to begin working for the noosphere evolution we need. Even though the politically significant rise of the integral worldview has yet to take place, integral consciousness is available today through the new perspective enacted by integral philosophy and developmental politics. This emerging integral perspective helps us recognize the potential for a more politically functional era ahead wherein America's competing worldviews will come to cooperate more effectively.

It is thus through this new form of synthetic consciousness and its accompanying vision of cooperative cultural evolution that developmental politics discovers the potential of a new American Dream. By defining this Dream as the improvement of the human condition through cultural evolution, our collective sense of higher purpose becomes aligned with the larger purpose of the evolving universe as a whole. Whether we believe in God or not, we can see this universal purpose of evolution expressed in each person through their highest values and most idealistic aspirations. As we'll consider further in the final chapter, by pursuing the good, the true, and the beautiful according to our own lights, we each act as agents of evolution and thereby contribute incrementally to the realization of the universe's "final cause" or ultimate purpose. Once we recognize the larger cosmic significance of working for cultural evolution, we can begin to feel the inspiring power of this new vision of the American Dream.

* * *

In order for America to develop into a more integrated and cooperative version of itself, the methods for fostering cultural evolution outlined above will certainly be necessary. But while necessary, these methods are not sufficient in themselves. The work of building a better society ultimately involves improving the "civic virtue" of individual persons, and this cannot be accomplished by cultural evolution alone. To effectively cultivate character development and thereby foster the authentic betterment of our people, the project of evolving culture ultimately requires spiritual growth. How we can support and promote such spiritual growth within our contemporary secular society is accordingly addressed in the next chapter.

8

A Renaissance of Virtue

THROUGHOUT THIS BOOK I HAVE STRESSED the crucial idea that culture and consciousness coevolve. This means that the project of ameliorating America's political dysfunction through cultural evolution necessarily entails a corresponding degree of evolution in the consciousness of a politically significant number of our citizens. Even though the concept of human consciousness is easier to illustrate than define, it can be loosely defined as our sentient subjectivity or experiential awareness, which includes our feelings, thoughts, intentions, memories, and our personal sense of identity. Our waking consciousness is also impacted by our unconscious mind, and according to many, by a superconscious realm of mind that influences us as well.

Given the subtlety and complexity of human consciousness, an adequate account of how it evolves could fill a large book of its own. But for our purposes here we can recall Whitehead's concise definition of evolution itself as an increase in the capacity to experience what is intrinsically valuable. Under this definition, the evolution of consciousness can be straightforwardly recognized in all the ways we can come to appreciate and use a wider spectrum of intrinsic values. As described in the last chapter, this type of growth in consciousness can occur within each existing worldview through the broadening of perspectives brought about by values integration—the process by which competing worldviews come to recognize their mutual interdependence. Beyond this, consciousness can evolve by moving up through the existing worldviews of traditionalism, modernism, and postmodernism. And now, we can begin to recognize how consciousness can also evolve by participating in the emergence of a new integral or post-postmodern worldview that effectively transcends and includes all three of these previous worldviews.

But even though evolving consciousness by integrating values and building a new worldview will be absolutely necessary, this kind of growth in values alone will not be sufficient for overcoming the political problem at hand. In order to grow into a better version of ourselves, the evolution in consciousness we need must include both a growth in values and a growth in *character*.

"Values are the best of what we want, but virtues are the best of who we are."

While the concepts of consciousness and character overlap, character is best understood as a moral "line of development" within consciousness.[1] Fostering development along this moral line is the key to advancing the larger project of political growth and renewal. Again, as Plato understood early on, "states are as the men are; they grow out of human characters." Yet while improving the moral character of the majority of American citizens may not be a politically realistic undertaking, the goal of strengthening the character of a demographically significant minority is now becoming a real possibility. The good news is that we don't need everyone to become more moral, just a critical mass of people who are informed by the New Truth about evolution and energized by the enlarged sense of higher purpose that this New Truth entails.

The idea of character development, of course, begs the question: What is moral growth and how can it be measured? As noted, each worldview has its own version of morality and thus its own criteria for moral improvement. But as we explore in this chapter, developmental politics includes an effective approach to character growth that can appeal to every worldview and raise moral consciousness on every front of its development. This new approach is found in the rediscovery of ancient wisdom being brought about by the revival of virtue ethics.

Virtues are traits of moral excellence or strengths of character whose practice can lead to both ethical living and satisfying happiness. Although the concepts of virtues and values are interrelated, there is an important distinction. As we've seen, values are magnetic, they provide the aims and goals that attract us toward that which is more perfect, more real, and more right.

Values represent the improved future conditions we desire. Virtues, on the other hand, represent the good qualities we presently possess; the acquired attributes of excellence that become engrained into our basic nature through commitment and practice. Values are the best of what we want, but virtues are the best of who we are. Simply put, values are *headings* and virtues are *habits*—"habits of the heart," as they've been called.

In academic moral philosophy, positive psychology, and increasingly in popular culture, the time-honored practice of virtues is currently experiencing a revival. And now, as this renewed interest in virtues is being informed and empowered by integral philosophy, this ancient practice is coming alive at a new level. As we will see, the revival of virtue ethics promises to be highly relevant for addressing the political problems of our time. The practice of virtues provides a method for evolving consciousness that serves as a complementary supplement to developmental politics' primary method of values integration. Like the values integration method, the method of practicing virtues raises consciousness by channeling or harnessing value energy. Our exploration of this renewed practice of virtues accordingly begins by returning to the central subject of value energy.

THE ENERGETIC PROPERTIES OF GOODNESS, TRUTH, AND BEAUTY REVISITED

My intent in this chapter is to show how the practice of virtues provides direct access to the motivational energy of transcendence. But in order to ground this idea in what we have covered so far, I need to describe the relationship between the specific virtue concepts we are about to explore and the primary values of goodness, truth, and beauty discussed in the last chapter. In other words, I want to begin this discussion of virtue ethics by showing how the seven fundamental virtues we will consider can be derived from the system formed by the three primary values. This brief exploration of the relationship between

> "The practice of virtues provides direct access to the motivational energy of transcendence."

values and virtues is designed to show how integral philosophy can help take virtue ethics beyond the confines of its traditional religious origins and transform this ancient practice into a new form of personal political activism.

In the initial introduction to goodness, truth, and beauty in chapter 7 I explained how these most intrinsic values can be understood as forms of interior energy. So now I want to take this energy analogy further by showing how the intellectual light and motivational power of goodness, truth, and beauty enters into our minds and hearts through a natural circuit of receiving and giving. Stated otherwise, the power of intrinsic value flows through us as we take in and give out value energy in a process that can be compared to the metabolism of the nutritional energy that maintains the health of our bodies.

To be specific, the value of truth is realized through a circuit of *learning and teaching*, which is its natural practice. This circuit-like behavior of truth can be recognized in the way that we never fully learn something or "take it in" until it passes through us—until we teach it or share it with another person. Similarly, when we learn something that is deeply true, we are often filled with enthusiasm to "give it out," or teach this truth to someone else.

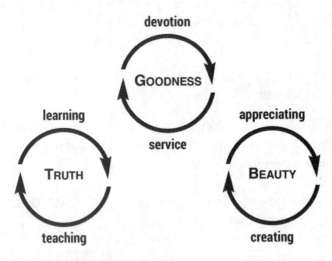

Figure 8.1. *Natural circuits of value energy metabolism*

As shown in figure 8.1, this same circuit of receiving and giving can also be seen in the practice of beauty, which is similarly realized through a circuit of *appreciating and creating*. For instance, if we want to paint a beautiful sunset, we must carefully observe the sunset's subtle details of color and form, as well as the overall majestic feeling produced by its colorful panorama. By working to express or give out the beauty of the sunset, we come to appreciate or take in that beauty with a depth of feeling only made possible by the attempt to recreate the sunset's beauty in paint. Through this process, the act of creating beauty opens the aperture of our hearts and helps us appreciate the beauty of the world more fully. Conversely, when we are moved by a powerful beauty experience, this often motivates us to express this feeling through music or images, or by simply beautifying our homes. It is thus by engaging the circuit of appreciating and creating that we can become spiritually charged with the value energy of beauty.

Of the three circuits of value metabolism shown in figure 8.1, truth's circuit of learning and teaching and beauty's circuit of appreciating and creating are the most evident and familiar. But the top circuit of *devotion and service*, which is the corresponding conduit for goodness energy, is not as obvious or well understood as the other two value circuits. That is, in the field of education we now have robust knowledge of the most effective methods and techniques for learning and teaching. And similarly in the arts, our culture has accumulated significant knowledge regarding the best techniques for appreciating and creating aesthetic experiences. In the realm of human relationships and the field of morality, however, contemporary American culture seems to have lost its collective knowledge of "how to be good."

While the idea of service as a method for giving out goodness may be familiar to many, the idea of devotion and its crucial connection with the impetus for service is not widely recognized. Devotion is the best word to describe how we "learn" or "appreciate" goodness—how its energy flows into us—because this term evokes a connection with transcendence. And it is the quality of transcendence within any thing or idea that gives it the power to kindle our enthusiasm, engender our loyalty, and strengthen our resolve. In fact, it requires devotion to adequately perceive and connect with transcendence. As philosopher Blaise Pascal understood: "Human things must be known to be loved, but divine things must be loved to be known."[2]

The central political significance of this emerging understanding of the circuitous flow of goodness energy—from devotion to service and from service to devotion—will become evident as our discussion proceeds. But in order to demonstrate why figure 8.1's simple schematic diagram is highly relevant for the renewal of our democracy, we must turn to a consideration of the virtues themselves.

As shown in figure 8.2, within the circuit of devotion and service we can find numerous methods and techniques for harnessing the power of the good. And the most accurate label for these "goodness technologies" is virtues. Figure 8.2's word cloud of virtue terms illustrates the wide array of traits and qualities that fall under the heading of virtues. How we might bring order to this chaotic cloud of words by narrowing down the list and systematizing these myriad notions of virtue is the focus of the next section.

Figure 8.2. *Some of the virtues associated with the practice of goodness*

DISCOVERING A NATURAL SYSTEM OF VIRTUES

Although virtues were venerated by many classical civilizations, our contemporary understanding of virtue ethics is rooted primarily in ancient Greek philosophy. For the Greeks, living a life of virtue was understood to be both a good in itself—the perfection of human nature—and the key to personal happiness. Plato summarized the list of "cardinal virtues" recognized by the society of his day as "temperance, prudence, courage (fortitude), and justice." Plato was then followed by Aristotle who, in his famous treatise on virtues, laid the foundations for this field of moral philosophy by describing how each virtue is a mean between extremes, and how the various virtues form a unity in which each virtue is necessary for the realization of the others.

The cardinal virtues of the Greeks were then carried forward by Christianity, which combined these cardinal four with Saint Paul's three "theological virtues" of faith, hope, and love.[3] This consolidated group of seven virtues—justice, temperance, prudence, courage, hope, faith, and love— was subsequently validated and solidified philosophically by the seminal work of Saint Thomas Aquinas. Through the influence of Aquinas and others, these seven classical virtues became part of the official Catechism of the Catholic Church and thus remain influential to this day.

But notwithstanding the Christian sanction of these classical seven, over the years hundreds of alternative ideals of virtue have been identified, and many different lists of preferred virtues have been proposed. There is, however, something very special or "fundamental" about these particular seven. Although many synonyms have been recommended as substitutes for these classical terms—for example, self-mastery for temperance, or practical wisdom for prudence—scholars working in the field of virtue ethics continue to be drawn to the specific ideas, if not the exact words, expressed by these ancient originals. For example, Alasdair MacIntyre, one of the leading academic proponents of virtue ethics, argues that: "The virtues that we need, if we are to develop from our initial animal condition into that of independent rational agents, and the virtues that we need, if we are to confront and respond to vulnerability and disability both in ourselves and in others, belong to one and the same set of [seven] virtues, the distinctive virtues of dependent rational animals."[4]

One of the strongest validations of the fundamental status of the seven classical virtues has come from the field of positive psychology. In their influential 2004 book, *Character Strengths and Virtues: A Handbook and Classification*, prominent academic psychologists Christopher Peterson and Martin Seligman summarized the findings of a significant body of empirical research which suggested a natural classification of six broad areas of virtue. Their research revealed "a surprising amount of similarity across cultures and strongly indicating a historical and cross-cultural convergence."[5] And the six basic kinds of character strength identified by Peterson and Seligman turned out to be remarkably similar to the seven classical virtues. The only reason they came up with six rather than seven "broad areas" is that they lumped hope and faith together into a single virtue they fittingly called "transcendence" (more on this below).

Commenting on positive psychology's empirical validation of ancient moral philosophy, Deirdre McCloskey observes that it is "striking that a group of modern clinical and social psychologists, using largely Western evidence, have on the whole confirmed what ur-Westerners such as Aristotle and especially Aquinas discerned by other means: that the virtues among us Westerners (at least) are these particular seven, and that they work as a system in the best of our lives and the best of our communities."[6]

These seven specific virtues have been tested and refined over a long historical period, and have thus been worked out within a living anthropological context. Moreover, the duration of their veneration has led to the accumulation of a significant body of philosophy and literature dedicated to their analysis and contemplation.

In the last chapter, figure 7.2 portrayed a word cloud of values organized around the three primary values of goodness, truth, and beauty. So based on the analysis above, we can now depict a similar word cloud of virtues organized around these seven fundamental virtues, as shown in figure 8.3.

Figure 8.3. The seven fundamental virtues emerging from a word cloud of positive character traits

Narrowing down the field of hundreds of potential virtue concepts to these seven broad yet explicit areas is the first step in naturalizing and systematizing the virtues. There is, however, more to say about the natural status of these fundamental virtues. Beyond the insights of contemporary moral philosophy, beyond the research of positive psychology, and beyond the weight of religious tradition, the validity and power of virtues in general, and these seven classical virtues in particular, is being confirmed by the new "physics" of value energy that we are just beginning to understand. And as we will see, by naturalizing the virtues and showing how they can be used to evolve people's character and consciousness, the practice of virtues can become an important part of the solution to America's contemporary political challenges.

THE OBLIGATIONS OF VIRTUE

Years ago, when I first encountered the philosophy of virtue ethics, I was unimpressed. It seemed overly idealistic and excessively moralistic, and its admonishments to be good felt like ungrounded religious commandments. But my opinion changed dramatically when I began to see the connection between the practice of the virtues and the harnessing of value energy. This connection can be recognized through an analysis of the ethical objects of duty revealed by the nature of the virtues themselves.

Most people think of ethics primarily as the obligations we owe to other people. The idea that we each have a basic duty of care for others—a minimum degree of required altruism—has been the central focus of the two ethical theories that have dominated moral philosophy since the Enlightenment. Unlike virtue ethics, these alternative systems of Kantian deontological ethics (based on the idea of natural moral rules), and utilitarian ethics (concerned with the greatest good for the greatest number), are primarily interested in the consequences of actions and the logic of proper conduct. But unlike these competing *action-centered* ethical theories, virtue ethics is *agent-centered*; its ethics are more about who we are than what we do.

In fact, the revival of virtue ethics in the mid-twentieth century came about precisely because this philosophy of ethics was more concerned with good character than with good actions alone. This modern revival was initiated by the distinguished philosopher Elizabeth Anscombe who argued that despite their secular framing, the prevailing ethical systems of both deontological ethics and utilitarian ethics were both grounded on theological assumptions that could no longer be justified. Anscombe accordingly contended that the concept of obligation should be jettisoned from morality because talk of moral duty no longer made sense.

According to virtue ethics, the first reason to be ethical is because it's in our own self-interest. This was Aristotle's original argument. He saw virtues as necessities for human flourishing rather than as the requirements of a theological moral law. For Aristotle, being excellent was both an end in itself, and the best strategy for achieving authentic happiness or *eudaimonia*.

Yet as virtue ethics became reestablished as a major branch of academic moral philosophy in the second half of the twentieth century, and as scholars in the field began to unpack the implications of the practice of virtues, they started to rediscover the full range of underlying obligations to which virtues are inextricably connected. Although Aristotle in antiquity, and Anscombe in modernity, had both grounded virtue ethics in the obligation we owe to ourselves, over the last few decades it has become increasingly apparent that the duty we owe to ourselves cannot be consistently fulfilled without also fulfilling a duty of care for others, and crucially, without also caring for something truly greater than ourselves—something that is authentically transcendent. As I argued in chapter 6, and as we discuss further below, the fulfillment of self-interest ultimately depends on a commitment to some kind of self-transcendence.

> **"The duty we owe to ourselves cannot be fulfilled without also caring for something truly greater than ourselves—something that is authentically transcendent."**

The connection between the practice of virtues and these three basic obligations of ethical concern—self, others, and transcendence—becomes especially evident once we put a stake in the ground around something close to the classical seven virtues. As shown in figure 8.4, these time-tested virtues clearly reveal three primary objects that are the natural focus of their moral attention. Stated otherwise, when the seven fundamental virtues are considered together as a unified system, the distinct focuses of duty or sources obligation that correspond to each of the fundamental virtues become apparent.

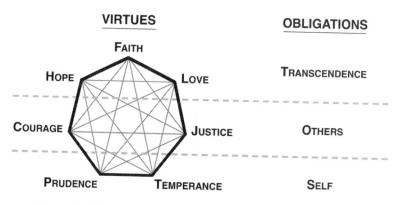

Figure 8.4. The seven fundamental virtues and their corresponding obligations (after McCloskey)

Temperance, prudence, and self-regarding courage help define the ethical obligation we owe to ourselves—the duty to control ourselves and act strategically and bravely to achieve our laudable self-interests. Justice and other-regarding courage describe the traits through which we fulfill our obligations to others, including our obligation to other people, animals, the environment, and even to the best of humanity's cultural creations. Independent of any external duty, we are called to be fearless and just in our dealings with others, not just for their sake, but also for the sake of our own character. Finally, faith, hope, and love, which are also held by virtue ethics to be indispensible to human flourishing, find their object of concern in that which is transcendent.

These three obligations of virtue are not founded on notions of deontological moral rules, they arise from the practice of the virtues themselves. According to McCloskey, for those who follow the virtue ethics of Aristotle and Aquinas, morality is "about the good life for a human, which requires a character of prudence and temperance toward oneself, and faith, hope and higher love toward the transcendent. And it requires justice and courage and lower love on behalf of other people."[7] This natural connection between these fundamental qualities of human excellence and the corresponding focus of their moral concern was recognized over seven hundred years ago by Aquinas himself, who wrote: "The principle ends of human acts are God, self, and others, since we do whatever we do for the sake of one of these."[8]

The idea of transcendence, however, needn't be equated with God or the supernatural. Transcendence can be readily discerned and appreciated within a secular reality frame. Scientists, for example, have faith that the universe is intelligible and that the truth about nature can be reliably discovered. Similarly, hope's trust and love's agape are each forms of virtue that connect with transcendence but are certainly not limited to believers alone. All three of these "theological virtues" can be practiced by secularists by putting their trust in non-religious ideals of transcendence. Yet regardless of one's metaphysical beliefs, positive psychology has now confirmed that some concept of transcendence is ultimately necessary for a fulfilling life. Again quoting McCloskey: "We humans, even we bourgeois humans, cannot get along without transcendence—faith in a past, hope for a future, justified by Larger Considerations, namely, the love of a transcendent. If we don't have religious hope and faith we'll substitute hope and faith and love in Art or Science or National Learning. If we don't have Art or Science or National Learning ... we'll substitute our family or the rebuilt antique car. It's a consequence of the human ability to symbolize, a fixture of our philosophical psychology."[9]

Recognizing the three essential ethical obligations that correspond to the seven fundamental virtues, as shown in figure 8.4 above, helps validate the claim that these virtues constitute a kind of natural system. In fact, the systemic quality of this model of virtues is grounded more in the three obligations than in the seven specific virtues themselves. As shown in figure 8.5, we can use alternative and somewhat more secular terms for the virtues, as long as these words adequately connect with the basic obligations we have to ourselves, to others, and to that which is transcendent.

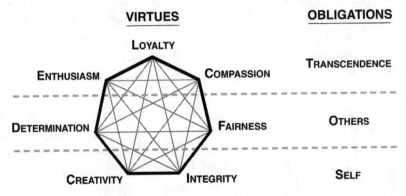

Figure 8.5. Alternative descriptions of the fundamental virtues that nevertheless correspond to the three basic obligations of virtue ethics

These three corresponding obligations of virtue, however, are not merely ethical burdens, they are also sources of motivational energy. These ethical duties are jobs that pay! As we saw in chapter 6, self-interest is a powerful motivator. This biologically-rooted interest in our own wellbeing drives us to protect what we have and draws us to pursue what we want. And for many, the deep-seated need for self-transcendence can also be a powerfully motivating interest. When we commit to a particular vision of transcendence—when we hear the call of a higher purpose or sacred cause that we can make our own— the pull of transcendence energizes and empowers us to serve that cause and even sacrifice our own self-interest on its behalf.

Each one of these virtues taps into the power of value energy in its own unique way. To give just a few of many potential examples: Courage acts as a shield against fear and gives us the strength to hold our ground. Hope works similarly by giving us the strength to persevere and carry on, and hope empowers us by providing confidence in our future success. Prudence gives us the power to plan and execute effectively, and temperance provides the power to resist being pulled off track. Love gives us the energy to care deeply about what really matters, and the capacity to recognize the spiritual bond we share with our fellows. Justice gives us the power to identify with the interests of the whole. And finally, faith connects us with value energy by continuously reassuring us of the good's ultimate righteousness and reliability.

These virtues function as conduits for value energy by molding our characters and thereby creating "receptor sites" in our consciousness into which this energy can flow. Stated differently, the virtues work by imprinting our psyches with "channels" through which the power of the good can circulate. These channels then work as a kind of "muscle memory" in our wills, habituating us to right-thinking and right-acting. And as we receive value energy through these virtue channels, it propagates down into our bodies. That is, the motivation we receive from both our natural interest in our selves, and our cultural interest in things that transcend ourselves, translates into the mental energy of attention and concentration, the emotional energy of excitement and passion, and ultimately the physical energy to stand up and act.

VIRTUES AND TRANSCENDENCE

Recognizing how the three basic obligations implicated by the virtues are not only duties, but also sources of value energy, brings us back to the relationship of self-interest and self-transcendence first discussed in chapter 6. There we saw how these opposing sources of motivation—our interest in our selves and our interest in something greater than ourselves—are bound together in an interdependent polarity. Within this natural polarity of interests, the energetic charge of each pole is maintained through a connection with its polar counterpart. In other words, while each pole of interest can be motivating by itself for a time, either pole will eventually lose its motivating power in isolation. But when brought together in a mutually reinforcing relationship of challenge and support, the two poles of this polarity function as a powerful generator of sustainable motivational energy.

The interdependent relationship between self-interest and greater-than-interest is well understood by the United States Peace Corps. In their application to join the organization, the Peace Corps requires their idealistic volunteers to clearly state what's in it for them, or how joining the Peace Corps will serve not only their greater-than-self-interest in promoting world peace, but their personal self-interest as well. Such a clear identification of self-interest is necessary because this organization has found that the volunteers whose motivations are entirely selfless often end up quitting before their term is complete.

As shown in figure 8.6, the energy-generating polarity of self-interest and self-transcendence serves as the "engine room" of the practice of goodness. Figure 8.6 combines the polarity diagram originally shown in figure 6.1 (now turned upright) with figure 8.2's circuit of goodness practice. By bringing these two energy circuit diagrams together, figure 8.6 thus illustrates how the encompassing circle of devotion and service is itself powered by the underlying interaction of the interests of self and the interests of transcendence.

In other words, that which we recognize as transcendent naturally attracts our devotion. But in order to translate the inspiration that comes from our devotions into sustainable action, our admiration of the transcendent must eventually connect with our sense of self-interest. Our ability to respond to the transcendent and receive its motivating energy is thus directly linked to the recognition of how our true self-interest will be served by this process.

And in the same way that engaging the power of self-interest helps connect us to the upward currents of transcendent goodness, the energy of transcendence likewise ennobles and empowers our self-interest. Effectively furthering the interests of some transcendent ideal helps to validate the necessary role of our distinct identities. In short, our pursuit of self-transcendence consecrates our self-interest.

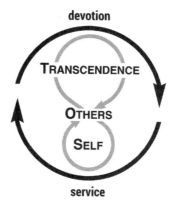

Figure 8.6. The circuit of goodness practice is powered by the energy-generating polarity of self-interest and self-transcendence

In addition to depicting this polarity of interests, figure 8.6 also includes the virtue obligation we have to others (as originally shown in figures 8.4 and 8.5), placing the "interests of others" in the middle of the circuit between the interests of the self and the interests of the transcendent. As the converging arrows of this polarity indicate, we serve the transcendent primarily through our service to others, and we likewise receive the inspiration of transcendence mainly through the exemplary fruits of others. Continuing with the Peace Corps example, this organization pursues its transcendent goal of "promoting world peace and friendship" by helping developing countries meet their needs for trained manpower. The Peace Corps thus makes its contribution to transcendence primarily by serving needy people.

It is also worth mentioning in this context that the interactive power of self-interest and self-transcendence is not only harnessed by the seven virtues working together as a system, this underlying value polarity is also the energy source for each virtue by itself. Each virtue connects with transcendence when, through the moderating influence of the other virtues, it causes us to act virtuously and morally. Each virtue also connects with self-interest at the same time by helping us live up to our potential and by making us happy. When properly practiced, each virtue thus becomes infused with the twin sources of motivational energy generated by the polarity of self-transcendence and self-interest. This philosophical understanding of the practice of virtues therefore reveals how it is ultimately in our self interest to be loving and just, and conversely, how being prudent and temperate can be of service to something greater than our selves alone.

Admittedly, this exploration of the connection between virtues and transcendence is conceptually dense and may take a while to digest. But before we turn to the political application of this model of virtues in the final section, allow me to make one more subtle but important point about the significance of the virtues and their corresponding obligations.

When we come to appreciate how the virtues provide a powerful spiritual practice that can connect us with transcendence and facilitate our self-actualization, we may also begin to sense how this practice can help answer the "why" questions underlying all intrinsic values, and especially the values of beauty, truth, and goodness. That is, why be good? Why be just, loving, hopeful, sincere, and the rest? I think the best answer is that, as humans, this is what we are uniquely empowered to do. As free agents of evolution we have both the privilege and the duty to participate in the gradual and incremental perfection of the universe of self, culture, and nature.[10] And when we come to see how the practice of the virtues allows us to fulfill this perfecting role by harnessing the upward currents of goodness, this helps confirm our true higher purpose within the cosmic economy. Again, as Iris Murdoch understood, "we are spiritual creatures attracted by excellence and made for the Good."

So how can we really know that working to "perfect the universe" incrementally in our own small way is our true purpose? Well, in the same way that a profound truth can often be recognized by its conceptual beauty, the truth of our higher purpose is indicated in the way that its fulfillment makes us happy. Our own eudaimonia can therefore provide personal validation of the idea that making a unique contribution to transcendence is why we are here.

HOW THE PRACTICE OF THE VIRTUES CAN AMELIORATE AMERICA'S POLITICAL PROBLEMS

The seven fundamental virtues (or similar synonyms) offer a powerful personal practice for being and doing that everyone can embrace. But the practice of the virtues is far more than just another self-help technique. This practice has the exciting potential to become a unifying political force in American society.

Values may differ widely, and even be dialectically opposed, but *virtues* are something that just about everyone can affirm. The political promise of this practice is accordingly found in its potential to provide a common moral language and a national standard of "civic virtue" which we can hold ourselves to collectively.

While this claim for the virtues may at first sound like idealistic wishful thinking, as I argue in this concluding section, the practice of the virtues contains all the ingredients necessary for it to spread virally and become widely popular. The potential popularity of this practice can be seen in the way that the virtues appeal simultaneously to the self-interests of each individual person and to the distinct collective interests of every major worldview. The fundamental virtues thus offer a neutral and universal picture of the good with which almost all Americans can identify. My contention that the practice of the virtues can become a politically unifying force in American culture is based on the following three lines of reasoning.

> "The practice of virtue can become a politically unifying force in American culture."

First, the potential for the virtues to become nationally popular can be seen in this practice's proven usefulness for both individual improvement and personal satisfaction. By offering these personal benefits, the practice of virtues lends itself to a comparison with the distinct but similar practice of mindfulness. Mindfulness is a secularized form of meditation that fosters calm introspection, a focus on the present moment of awareness, and an open acceptance of what is. Many readers will be familiar with the recent mainstreaming of mindfulness practice, which has "gone viral" and which now enjoys widespread popularity. Mindfulness is promoted as a technique for becoming more focused and productive in one's daily life, and its cultural success stems from the fact that it is a simple but effective spiritual practice that everyone can engage in regardless of their beliefs. Like mindfulness, the practice of the virtues also provides a method for becoming more focused and effective, and these two practices are even being promoted as natural complements to each other within the positive psychology community.[11] But although mindfulness and the virtues are both contemporary spiritual practices rooted in ancient philosophy and religion, the practice of the virtues surpasses mindfulness by fostering both an ethical commitment to others and an active pursuit of the transcendent.

The virtues have yet to become as popular as mindfulness because their practice demands more of a person, and because the idea of virtues is still perceived as being bound up with religious tradition. However, as the fundamental virtues become naturalized and systematized, and as it becomes evident that their practice provides a powerful technique for harnessing the interest-based sources of motivational energy we have explored, the potential for the virtues to become a nationally unifying common moral language may be realized.

Second, the potential for the virtues to become a popular, affinity-generating force in our culture can be seen in the way that their practice appeals uniquely to the values of each major worldview on its own terms, while remaining neutral and universal. Put differently, the virtues provide an approach to citizenship that is consistent with the goals and sensibilities of each distinct form of culture, while at the same time offering a basic practice that all Americans can participate in.

For traditionalists, the revival of the virtues promises to validate and carry forward the religious wisdom of Western civilization. The project of reintegrating the fundamental virtues back into our national consciousness therefore forwards the interests of heritage values and helps meet the perceived needs of social conservatives.

For modernists, the virtues offer an attractive, empirically validated technology for happiness that fits within a secular context and thus comports with mainstream sensibilities. This appeal is demonstrated by the ongoing success of positive psychology, which has built a cottage industry around the virtues by showing how their practice is as necessary for personal health and wellbeing as physical exercise. Social science's validation of the virtues also shows how they can be approached mainly as an opportunity for self-improvement rather than as a solemn ethical obligation. And because it advances the modernist values of personal progress and individual achievement, this practice has the potential to become, like mindfulness, a popular pursuit within mainstream modernist culture.

And crucially for postmodernists, the practice of the virtues can advance the causes of social and environmental justice, and ultimately lead to a more loving society—goals that are near and dear to the hearts of most postmodernists. The primary challenge facing the postmodern worldview is its relative lack of political influence. Even while its cultural influence continues to gain ground, its political goals remain largely unfulfilled. As noted, this lack of influence stems largely from postmodernism's repudiation of modernism and traditionalism. But by adopting and championing the practice of the virtues, postmodern activists can find a greater degree of moral affinity with their opponents, and thereby become more successful at integrating their caring values into America's collective vision of a better future.

An example of how adopting the practice of the virtues can forward the specific aims of postmodernism can be seen in the case of justice. Part of the reason why postmodernists can't get the rest of America to care adequately about social or environmental justice is that the postmodern concept of justice itself is not virtuous enough—postmodern demands for justice are often militant and authoritarian and thus threaten the very people they need to persuade. But when the notion of justice is situated within the system of seven virtues, postmodern demands become refined and moderated, and this helps infuse these calls for justice with the energy of goodness necessary to make them more magnetically attractive, and thus more politically agreeable. That is, to be truly virtuous, justice must be balanced with mercy born of love. It must be restrained by temperance, and made swift and efficient through prudence. Justice needs hope to maintain its focus on redemption and rehabilitation. And to be sustained over the long term, the project of working for justice must remain committed to the ultimate rightness of this endeavor through the power of faith.

"The postmodern concept of justice is not virtuous enough."

When the postmodern worldview first emerged fifty years ago, its proponents viewed the idea of virtues as outdated, moralistic, and even priggish. But now, as the virtues are being naturalized and systematized, the practice of the virtues is becoming something that even postmodernists can embrace. In fact, this practice has the potential to become widely admired and even expected within postmodern culture, like eating natural foods and pursuing a healthy lifestyle.

Third and finally, perhaps the most significant reason why the virtues have the potential to become a politically unifying force in American culture is found in the way this practice can help fulfill our acute need for a common higher purpose. As I've argued, America needs a new collective vision—a more inclusive and enlightened American Dream—and the practice of the virtues can help us find this purpose and thus meet this need by better connecting us with authentic transcendence. As discussed in the section on the "Obligations of Virtue" above, the practice of faith, hope, and love actually provides *a technique of perception* for the transcendent. As Pascal understood, "divine things must be loved to be known." So by helping us to better intuit the direction of authentic transcendence, the practice of the virtues can illuminate the fresh ideal of cultural transcendence that is at the heart of the larger national project of furthering cultural evolution. Indeed, building agreement around the universal wisdom of the virtues will generate cultural evolution in its own right.

Again, this practice has all the ingredients necessary for it to become nationally popular, it only needs to be adequately publicized and promoted, as has been done with mindfulness. Through the popularization of the virtues, American culture can become more virtuous overall, and thereby gain the strength to resist the impulse to regress to tribalism in response to the challenges of hyperpolarization. And perhaps most importantly, the advent of a national movement for the virtues can help foster our evolution by revitalizing our politics with the energy of transcendence.

Yet notwithstanding the benefits of finding common ground in the practice of the fundamental virtues, it must be said that building a cross-cultural agreement around this practice is not a political panacea; conflicts and competing interests will clearly remain. But by reviving the practice of the virtues within traditional and modernist culture, and by persuading a significant number of postmodernists to also undertake this practice, a modicum of cultural harmony can be restored. By helping to create greater cultural affinity in this way, the virtues can thus make a significant contribution to the larger project of overcoming hyper-partisan gridlock and restoring the functionality of American democracy.

There is much more to say about the virtues and their practice, but I hope this chapter has provided some sense of their powerful potential, and why they are crucial for the success of developmental politics' program for cultural evolution. For readers interested in developing a personal virtue practice, appendix B provides an exercise that can help you get started. For now, however, we will leave the virtues and turn to the final chapter on progress, which weaves together the various philosophical threads we have explored here in Part II.

9

A Transcendent Vision of Progress

AS I HAVE ARGUED, AMERICA'S HYPERPOLARIZED political condition is primarily a cultural problem that requires a cultural solution. And the cultural solution I have proposed is to cultivate evolution on every front of our culture's development. As we saw in chapter 7, this project can be approached by framing a new American Dream—a transcendent yet inclusive vision of a more mature and cooperative version of our society. A crucial part of this new American Dream is an agreement regarding the overall heading of our social improvement. So now in this final chapter we return to the central subject of cultural evolution to consider it in light of the controversial concept of *progress*.

As we've discussed, in order to recover our lost solidarity we need a fresh ideal of "cultural transcendence." And a key component of this needed new ideal is a shared notion of progress. In fact, the idea of transcendence itself is closely connected with the concept of progress. Therefore, in order to *go beyond* our current conditions, we cannot do without a collective sense of the way forward. The quintessentially modernist notion of the overall progress of human civilization has, however, been largely rejected within progressive culture. The restoration of our democracy's functionality accordingly requires not only a new American Dream, but also an accompanying vision of progress—an enlarged ideal of inclusive social betterment that can inspire a significant number of progressives while continuing to appeal to most modernists and traditionalists.

In response to this challenge, this chapter explores an expanded conception of progress that transcends and includes modernist concepts of social development, such as growth in GDP or the advance of science and technology. In this discussion I will define "progress" broadly as "growth in value over time," and this universal definition applies to both human societies and to evolution as a whole.

Developmental politics seeks to rehabilitate the idea of overall civilizational progress by showing how American culture's conflicting aspirations for improvement can be integrated and aligned. As we come to see how America's three major worldviews form an interdependent cultural ecosystem, this reveals the necessary and ongoing contributions that each type of culture is making to our society's functionality and sustainability. These contributions are necessary, not only to maintain what we have already achieved, they are also crucial for our further development. By thus recognizing the underlying interdependence of America's competing forms of culture, it becomes possible to harmonize each worldview's distinct notions of social betterment within an overarching ideal of universal social progress.

The chapter concludes by considering the idea that our near-term social and political progress is ultimately connected to the long-term cosmic progress of evolution. As I will argue, recognizing how the progress of humanity is actually forwarding the evolution of the universe can help us rediscover the transcendent meaning of our civilization at a post-secular level of understanding. By affirming our role as authentic agents of evolution, we can revitalize our collective hope for progress by recharging this ideal of ongoing development with the value energy of transcendence.

THE PROBLEM WITH PROGRESS

A defining feature of what it means to be human is the impulse to make things better. Our ability to imagine how things can almost always be improved is indeed one of our greatest strengths. Beginning with the advent of modernity around three hundred years ago, this impulse for improvement was expanded and exalted into a world-historical conception of the grand march of civilizational progress. And in the wake of the astonishing scientific, economic, and political breakthroughs achieved by the Enlightenment and subsequent industrial revolution, the ideal of progress became a driving force of the Western world.

Now, however, the very idea of civilizational progress is seen by many of our brightest intellectuals as a discredited myth. In the realm of politics, modernist culture's enthusiasm for unceasing growth and development is denounced by pundits on both the left and the right. Even though all political advocates continue to identify issues that need to be worked on and improved, and even though the expectation of a modicum of progress remains a prerequisite assumption for all meaningful political action, notions of overarching civilizational progress are either avoided or explicitly dismissed as naïve or hubristic. Within academia, this allergy to the concept of progress is even more pronounced, where writers must now bracket the word in scare quotes to maintain their credibility.

This current aversion to the idea of progress, of course, reflects the widespread dissatisfaction with modernity we have discussed. Progress is arguably modernity's most powerful idea, so it was perhaps inevitable that the accumulating pathologies of the modern world would lead to the downfall of civilizational progress as an aspirational ideal. While the disavowal of progress is a defining feature of the postmodern worldview, pessimism about "The Enlightenment Project," as it is sometimes called, is also growing among intellectuals influenced by the traditional worldview. Prominent writers such as David Brooks and Patrick Deneen decry the loss of social trust and the destruction of the moral bonds that once held American society together.

Despite the impressive rear-guard action being mounted in defense of modernity by intellectuals such as Jonah Goldberg and Steven Pinker (discussed below), the progress offered by the modernist worldview has lost its luster within much of American and European culture. Although the allures of modernity remain attractive to billions of people in the developing world, as we saw in Part I, it is the problems created by the rise of modernity that now occupy the attention of most American thought leaders. And according to numerous academics and environmentalists, modernity is caught in a "progress trap" in which its environmentally unsustainable growth will eventually lead to its demise.

Yet while modernity may indeed be environmentally and culturally unsustainable, this does not mean that its collapse is inevitable. As I've argued, in order to solve the existential problems that plague our country and our world, we need to improve and build on this indispensible stage of material and cultural evolution. The unprecedented accomplishments of the modernist worldview in science and technology, in prosperity and upward mobility, in our political freedoms, and in bringing about democracy itself, must be preserved if we are to avoid significant regression. With close to eight billion people now alive on the planet, and with billions more on the way before any expected stabilization of world population growth, we need to maintain the globalized systems of modernity in order to avoid a catastrophe of dire proportions. While many feel that climate change will eventually produce such a global catastrophe and that this justifies rolling back the globalizing tide of modernism, this thinking is misguided and ultimately part of the problem. We cannot safely rid the world of modernity, so we must work to overcome its threats and pathologies while simultaneously carrying forward its tremendous achievements.

"We cannot safely rid the world of modernity, so we must overcome its threats and pathologies while simultaneously carrying forward its tremendous achievements."

Like all forms of evolution, cultural evolution advances by building on past accomplishments. In order to foster the further cultural evolution we require, we must prevent modernity from being undermined or discarded. To ensure that its achievements are preserved, we need to revalorize modernism and restore its legitimacy in the eyes of both the intelligentsia and the common people. However, restoring our collective gratitude for the gifts of modernity involves recognizing that modernism is an important step in the development of human civilization, but not an end state. To adequately appreciate modernity we must come to see it within the larger timeline of human history. We must look beyond our contemporary culture war to envision a future cultural synthesis that can satisfy our longings for restored social cohesion. While such a cultural synthesis will itself be only temporary, eventually requiring further evolution to overcome the new pathologies it will inevitably bring about, our growing knowledge of the New Truth about evolution can help restore our faith in progress and ensure that it is sustainable and ongoing.

Although realizing the ideal of overall progress in human civilization is among modernity's greatest achievements, our concept of progress need not be constrained by the limitations of modernism's value horizons. In order to update and expand the American Dream and grow into a better version of ourselves, we need to revision our collective ideal of progress by improving our definition of improvement itself.

PROGRESS AND TRANSCENDENCE

As a boy growing up in the Sixties I remember being taken to the "Carousel of Progress" at Disneyland, an attraction that celebrated the technological advances of the twentieth century and glorified the charms of consumerism. This revolving theater ride, which moved across the decades to highlight the inventions and appliances that transformed American domestic life, concluded with its rousing theme song: *There's a Great Big Beautiful Tomorrow.* As I exited the ride I recall being filled with hope and confidence in the bright promise of an amazing future to come. Although the Carousel of Progress closed in 1973, and although it seems hopelessly corny in light of our current sensibilities, this attraction epitomized the sense of transcendence which once imbued America's expectations of ongoing progress.

Watching the Carousel of Progress's stage show on YouTube today, it seems more like a bad *Saturday Night Live* skit—an ironic satire of progress that no one could take seriously. And the fact that Walt Disney's earnest vision of modernity's progress has now become severely dated and even ridiculous, testifies to the degree to which postmodern consciousness has come to infuse American culture. In their attempts to discredit modernity, postmodernists have instinctively attacked modernism's sacred creed—the ideal of progress. Faith in ongoing scientific and economic progress provides modernists with their strongest sense of cultural transcendence, so it naturally became the target of modernity's opponents. But even though postmodernists are now largely in charge of American popular culture, as of this writing they have failed to offer a substitute vision of cultural transcendence with the power to inspire and energize an electoral majority.

Moreover, some modernists are still not willing to give up on the ideal of progress without a fight. Most notably, psychology professor and popular author Steven Pinker has marshaled an impressive body of evidence which convincingly demonstrates the ongoing material and social progress that modernity continues to deliver. In his 2018 book, *Enlightenment Now,* Pinker documents the clear improvements that have been made over the last few decades in personal health and longevity, in education, and in human rights.

He also cites the decreasing costs of basic human needs such as food, clothing, energy, and transportation. But despite his demonstration of the irrefutable trend lines of material improvement, Pinker has largely failed to convince postmodernists and traditionalists that the progress offered by modernity is something they can endorse and be proud of.

For example, on the traditional side of our three-way political divide, *New York Times* columnist David Brooks (seemingly a conservative modernist with traditional sympathies) rejects Pinker's optimistic thesis of unappreciated progress, writing: "Pinker doesn't spend much time on the decline of social trust, the breakdown of family life, the polarization of national life, the spread of tribal mentalities, the rise of narcissism, the decline of social capital, the rising alienation from institutions or the decline of citizenship and neighborliness. It's simply impossible to tell any good-news story when looking at the data from these moral, social and emotional spheres."[1] The fact that Brooks remains pessimistic, even in the face of Pinker's overwhelming evidence of ongoing social improvement, reveals the alternative vision of cultural transcendence held by most traditionalists. For social conservatives, authentic progress is not measured by growth in GDP, or even in improving physical health. Traditionalism's ideal of cultural transcendence is defined by the maintenance and development of virtues such as family loyalty, personal responsibility, piety, and patriotism, all of which are generally in decline.

And predictably, on the postmodern side of the divide Pinker's statistical defense of modernity has been even more vehemently rejected. Salon magazine, for example, characterized *Enlightenment Now* as an incoherent "grand apology for capitalism." As we've discussed, cultural transcendence for postmodernists is primarily defined in terms of protecting the environment and achieving social justice for the marginalized and exploited. These progressive ideals have been shaped and charged by the perceived pathologies of modernity, so the evidence of modernism's progress cited by Pinker is inevitably seen as only exacerbating the ongoing damage being wrought by globalizing "neoliberalism."

This widespread refusal to acknowledge positive progress, at least as defined by modernists like Pinker, points to the fact that American society's conflicting definitions of cultural transcendence are at the root of what's pulling us apart. It therefore bears repeating that ideals of transcendence are magnetic, and the value energy they supply exhibits behaviors that are roughly comparable to the behaviors of physical energy. This energy-like behavior can be seen in the way that the motivational pull of transcendence oscillates dialectically between poles. As previously illustrated by figure 2.3 on page 25, over the course of historical development the drawing power of cultural transcendence alternates between concern for the rights of individuals on one side, and concern for the needs of the larger community on the other. By seeing this dialectical evolutionary process at work, we can begin to recognize how these apparently conflicting ideals of cultural transcendence can actually work together by providing the two legs of our collective development, which carry us forward by dialectical steps.

Again, each worldview's concept of betterment has been formed in response to the specific set of problematic life conditions that prevailed at the time of its original emergence in history. Traditionalism's values are shaped by pretraditional culture's perpetration of never-ending war and chaos; modernism's values seek liberation from traditionalism's oppression and stagnation; and postmodern values

"Each worldview is responding to the pull of the upward current of good in its own way."

arise in response to the destruction wrought by modernity. Yet even though these discrete problem sets point toward different notions of transcendence, once we understand how ideals of transcendence exhibit energy-like behavior, we can appreciate how each worldview is responding to the pull of the upward current of the good in its own way. Stated otherwise, the expanded understanding of value energy being advanced by developmental politics shows how these dialectically alternating currents of transcendence, which are now largely working against each other, can be brought into overall alignment within the larger frame of ongoing cultural evolution.

It is crucial to recognize the role played by the magnetic pull of transcendence in the political life of our democracy because this form of value energy ultimately provides the foundation of our political will. While not all problems require a transcendent vision for their solution, humanity's most difficult and troubling problems usually cannot be solved without some kind of passionate concern. And hyperpolarization is clearly such a large and difficult problem, and thus one that requires a high degree of political will for its amelioration. Therefore, to prevent America's three major worldviews from effectively thwarting each other, and to generate the requisite political will to overcome the problem of hyperpolarization, we need a deeper understanding of how our varying ideals of transcendence and their accompanying concepts of progress drive our politics.

DANGERS OF TRANSCENDENCE

Admittedly, the magnetic pull of cultural transcendence can be dangerous. Because most people naturally long for a collective sense of higher purpose they can believe in, when their ideals of transcendence become frustrated or stymied, the pull of the upward current of the good can become reversed, leading to what might be called *false-transcendence*, or the pull of regressive evil. For example, the allure of the ill-fated Islamic State offered a twisted form of cultural transcendence that pulled many young Muslims to their doom, wreaking havoc in the Middle East and creating a disaster of global proportions.

Yet even though human history is littered with similar examples of destruction wrought by social movements fueled by the pull of false-transcendence, this should not be used as an excuse to deny or erase the existential human need to participate in some form of collective higher purpose. Even though transcendence provides a powerful form of motivational energy that can be harnessed for both good and bad, every human society needs some kind of transcendent vision. Indeed, when the energy supplied by a sense cultural transcendence drains away and progress seems impossible, social decay inevitably follows. As the author of the biblical *Book of Proverbs* understood over twenty-five hundred years ago, "Where there is no vision, the people perish."[2]

Nevertheless, in light of the horrendous consequences of the regressive pull of false-transcendence, we might be tempted to conclude that because misguided notions of transcendent progress can be dangerous, we should de-emphasize collective visions of overall social betterment and focus on the discrete needs of individuals rather than on the advance of entire cultures. But again, because investing loyalty in something greater than oneself is a basic human need, people will seek the fulfillment of this need in one way or another. So in order to prevent the human suffering that can result from either a commitment to false-transcendence, or the lack of any connection to cultural transcendence whatsoever, we must continually refine and renew our collective engagement with an authentically moral vision of progress. And this is precisely what developmental politics is attempting to do—to remedy America's political dysfunction by framing an enlarged conception of progress, one that is charged with a fresh vision of transcendence that can meet the unique needs of our time.

TOWARD A UNIVERSAL DEFINITION OF PROGRESS

Prior to the emergence of postmodernism, America's primary vision of progress was defined straightforwardly and unapologetically as economic growth for the nation and upward mobility for the individual. Yet while prosperity remains an important value for most, the promise of material gains alone cannot provide the unifying vision we need at this crucial juncture in history.

Recognizing that growth in GDP or the advance of technology no longer suffice as adequate metrics for overall positive development, a number of distinguished thinkers have attempted to redefine progress in more holistic terms. Social philosopher Jürgen Habermas, for example, proposes that progress be assessed according to three broad criteria, which he identifies as material wellbeing and security, freedom and dignity, and happiness and fulfillment. In a similar attempt to define social progress in terms of human wellbeing, economist Amartya Sen argues that positive development should be equated with the expansion of freedom, which he defines as "increasing citizens access and opportunities to the things they have reason to value."[3] But even though such enlarged conceptions of progress are welcome, they only beg the question of what constitutes wellbeing, and what is really valuable.

Building on the work of Sen and others, a consortium of philanthropists and academics has recently created the "Social Progress Index," which seeks to provide a holistic yet rigorously empirical standard of measurement for the overall progress of human wellbeing. Using fifty-four indicators of positive development, the Social Progress Index defines progress as an increase in "the capacity of a society to meet the basic human needs of its citizens, establish the building blocks that allow citizens and communities to enhance and sustain the quality of their lives, and create the conditions for all individuals to reach their full potential."[4]

Like the more comprehensive definition of progress proposed by Habermas, this attempt to broaden the assessment of progress beyond GDP alone is certainly worthwhile. However, the Social Progress Index's fifty-four indicators of progress are ultimately not that different from those cited by Pinker, which as we've seen, do not convince or inspire most postmodernists or traditionalists. Even though the Social Progress Index includes metrics such as "tolerance and inclusion," and "environmental sustainability," it is ultimately a technocratic expression of the modernist mindset, so it cannot provide the transcendent ideal of progress our society now requires.

Again, in order to inspire a politically significant majority of Americans and restore at least some of our lost social solidarity, we need a vision of progress that can speak to each major worldview's distinct yearnings for transcendence. Yet because the dialectical magnetism of transcendence is pulling each of these worldviews in different directions, getting them all to agree on a common direction of advance may seem like an impossible task. This dilemma, however, illuminates the unique advantages of revisioning progress in terms of overall cultural evolution. Unlike the well-meaning attempts to define progress holistically cited above, which ultimately remain within the value frame of modernity, developmental politics' conception of progress through cultural evolution can satisfy each worldview's yearning for transcendence on its own terms.

"Developmental politics' conception of progress through cultural evolution satisfies each worldview's yearning for transcendence on its own terms."

Although it may at first seem unlikely that the goal of cultivating cultural evolution could provide a unifying vision of progress for America, as we come to better understand the development of values through the insights of integral philosophy, we may begin to see the exciting potential of this project. As I've argued from the beginning, America's political dysfunction is ultimately a cultural problem whose solution lies at the level of values. So as we come to discover new methods for promoting the growth of values, the collective goal of cultivating cultural evolution on every front of its development will begin to seem increasingly desirable and achievable.

MAKING PROGRESS BEYOND HYPERPOLARIZATION

A fundamental tenet of developmental politics is that each worldview's distinct ideals of improvement—each worldview's bedrock values—are indispensible for our ongoing progress. By taking a perspective that is outside and above all three worldviews, this expanded view of progress can foster sympathy for the distinct notions of authentic transcendence that each set of values brings to our larger cultural ecosystem.

This point, however, brings us back to the questions first raised in chapter 4: If the differences that are bitterly dividing American politics are ultimately about bedrock values and core identities, what could possibly induce these opposing camps to compromise with each other? Why, for example, would postmodernists want to compromise with fiscally conservative modernists who are seen as destroying the environment and oppressing workers? Or why would traditionalists want to compromise with liberal modernists who are seen as suppressing religious freedom and murdering innocent fetuses? Indeed, why would socialistic postmodernists and theocratic traditionalists ever deem to compromise with each other when their respective moral systems seem to be diametrically opposed?

Although each worldview currently has a biased view of its cultural competitors, these respective forms of bias can be softened and reduced by using the New Truth about evolution to demonstrate how the existential polarities that divide these worldviews also make them interdependent. As discussed throughout this book, the polar oppositions that define the conflicting differences between traditionalism, modernism, and postmodernism result from the dialectical development of values over time. These polarities are indestructible features of American culture's developmental structure, and as such they work in an ongoing way to help define and enact each worldview's most cherished values.

When these political and cultural polarities are approached as problems to be solved rather than systems to be managed, this results in the gridlock we are presently experiencing. But when these polarities are recognized as value-creating systems and worked with accordingly, this perspective provides a practice that can effectively mediate the conflicts and facilitate progress. Under this method, the legitimate differences of opinion reflected in these polar oppositions are not ignored or explained away, they are rather preserved in moderated form so they can perform their proper function of both challenging and supporting their polar counterparts.

As described in chapter 4, this method of bridging or integrating value polarities involves creating a container of agreement—a deliberative truce—within which the positive upsides and negative downsides of each cultural category can be effectively distinguished and teased apart. Once the positives have been clearly separated from the negatives, this makes the necessary and enduring values of each pole easier to appreciate and integrate. By practicing this method, Americans from across the political spectrum can come to "metabolize" a wider spectrum of values, and thereby actively participate in creating the cultural evolution we need to overcome our nation's political dysfunction.

While this practice of managing polarities is well-established in the business world, it has yet to be tried in politics, so it lacks a track record. But the promise of resolving polarized political issues by creating deliberative agreements in which the integrative process of challenge and support can take place is foreshadowed in the success of issues such as gay marriage, as we've seen. Now that the negative impacts of a gridlocked democracy have become evident to the majority of Americans, the incentive to try new methods for reaching political consensus is being strengthened. And this new incentive for Americans to work with worldviews they otherwise oppose is justified by both instrumental reasons and intrinsic reasons.

On the instrumental side, each worldview has an incentive to work with the others because it is through this process that each set of values can most effectively forward its own positive agenda. Here we can recall the general principle stated at the end of chapter 4: When faced with an interdependent value polarity, the best way to advance the values of our preferred pole is to actually affirm the foundational values of the pole we oppose. Although it may seem counterintuitive, under our currently gridlocked conditions this principle actually provides the best strategy for each worldview to achieve its own laudable goals.

To be specific, by participating in developmental politics' program of values integration, traditionalists can help restore respect for their religious traditions and ensure that America's historical heritage is not eroded or discarded. Modernists can likewise forward their positive agenda through this process by restoring the cultural legitimacy of modernity and by reducing resistance to the progress that results from liberal freedoms in general, and from economic freedom in particular. And perhaps most importantly, postmodernists can also be induced to integrate the values of their cultural opponents because it is only through this process that they can overcome their relative political impotency.

Notwithstanding its caring values, because postmodernism generally rejects modernity and has contempt for traditionalism, it has not been able to persuade the majority of Americans to endorse its programs at the ballot box. But by becoming more sympathetic to the values of modernism and traditionalism, and by better integrating these values into its own worldview, postmodernism itself can evolve from its current position of staunch antithesis to America's established culture toward a more synthetic stance that will make it more politically effective.

Beyond these instrumental reasons, there are also deeper intrinsic reasons that can induce Americans to expand the scope of what they are able to value and better integrate the values of their political opponents into their own positions. These intrinsic reasons are found by seeing how each category of values represents an established channel for the upward current of the good. By demonstrating how each set of values connects with authentic transcendence in its own way—by showing how all of these categories serve as receptor sites for real value energy—the integral perspective sharpens the allure of each set of values and helps make each worldview more attractive to the others. And by making each category of values more attractive in this way, this enlarged cultural perspective can persuade the majority of Americans to tap into a wider bandwidth of cultural transcendence and thereby better fulfill their own existential need for self-transcendence. Examples that convey the universal appeal of each worldview's specific connection with authentic transcendence are discussed in the next section.

APPRECIATING EACH FORM OF CULTURE'S UNIQUE CONNECTION WITH TRANSCENDENCE

Here we briefly consider the intrinsic good that each worldview is attempting to achieve. This section's account of each worldview's specific ideals of betterment therefore builds on chapter 7's discussion of the distinct versions of the American Dream held by these different forms of culture. Even though postmodernists and traditionalists rarely use the word "progress," both of these worldviews clearly have their own agenda for improvement. In this iteration of our analysis, however, we will focus on each worldview's unique connection to transcendence itself, starting with modernity.

We don't have to become apologists for the establishment to recognize the many ways that modernist consciousness has helped humanity to go *beyond* the suffering of our past. Reflect, for example, on the wonder of scientific medicine—the millions of lives it has saved and the untold anguish it has prevented. Postmodernists may deny progress, but science as a whole continues to make indisputable advances that clearly demonstrate progress in truth.

The transcendent progress brought about by modernity can also be appreciated by comparing life in the developed world's democracies to the degraded conditions of the third world. Those of us who are privileged to live in modernist societies are no longer mired in debilitating corruption or trapped in extreme poverty, and we are free to be or say almost anything we want.

Modernity's authentic connection to its own bandwidth of transcendence is also exemplified in the heroic lives of its founders and champions. Consider, for example, the visionary genius of Thomas Jefferson, or the compassionate wisdom of Franklin Roosevelt. We could obviously make a long list of the heroes of modernity who have each improved the human condition immensely. The point is that we shouldn't allow the ongoing work of overcoming modernism's pathologies to alienate us from the real transcendence that modernist values continue to offer. The modern world that has arisen from the rational values of the Enlightenment is truly "the Great Fact." And the connection to intrinsic truth and goodness that these values continue to provide is an important part of every American's heritage. We can literally hear modernity's unique connection with transcendence—its sense of optimism and unbounded creativity—expressed in classic modernist compositions such as George Gershwin's *Rhapsody in Blue*, or Ludwig van Beethoven's *Ninth Symphony*. Listening to this music evokes the palpable feeling of freedom.

Turning now to traditionalism's ideals of betterment. Although many Americans remain ambivalent about the values of our Judeo-Christian cultural foundations, these ancient values represent aspirations for transcendence that remain highly relevant for our contemporary problems. For example, America's generous support for charity and our collective sense of responsibility to provide for the poor originate with Christianity. Even though many social conservatives resist the expansion of our social safety net, the transcendent value of caring for every member of the congregation remains a foundational American value that is rooted in traditionalism. As Charles Taylor writes, "In view of the importance of Christian universalism and agape in the constitution of the modern ideal of moral order, ought we really to hope for the utter uprooting of all the beliefs which Christianity has inculcated in our civilization? ... we cannot simply condemn it root and branch, as though it could be undiscriminatingly destroyed and rooted out; we have in fact to overcome it while preserving what is valuable in its roots."[5]

By adopting an integral perspective, even nonreligious Americans who are currently polarized against social conservatism can nevertheless connect with the authentic transcendence that can be found within the values of the traditional worldview. This traditional connection with transcendence, for instance, empowered the movement to abolish slavery in the nineteenth century, and this same sense of transcendence was carried forward by Martin Luther King, whose moral crusade for civil rights synthesized traditional values with postmodern values. And if these examples don't evoke a sense of transcendence, just listen to John Newton's *Amazing Grace* or Katharine Lee Bates' *America the Beautiful* to feel the pull of the upward current of the good that traditional values tap into.

Finally, consider the specific current of value energy that is the focus of postmodern values. The feelings of joy and freedom that arise from participating in the movement for a more peaceful and loving world

> **"The feelings of joy and freedom that arise from participating in the movement for a more peaceful and loving world need not be the exclusive possession of counterculturalists."**

need not be the exclusive possession of counterculturalists. Postmodern values represent authentic American values that point to a form of liberating transcendence that everyone can embrace. The upward current of transcendence that postmodern values tap into is expressed in myriad forms of art, and can be readily felt by listening, for example, to Joni Mitchell's song *Woodstock* or to Bob Marley's *One Love*.

Nevertheless, for the modernists and traditionalists who are appalled by the pathologies of postmodern culture, the idea that this countercultural worldview somehow represents progress is admittedly difficult to accept. But here too the practice of values integration allows us to affirm that we can protect the environment and elevate the disadvantaged, even while we simultaneously push back against a cultural movement that seeks to undermine much of what America has achieved. Notwithstanding the potential dangers of unchecked postmodernism, and despite the popular yearning for a mythical "Great America" of the past, there are few who would actually be willing to return to the American society of the 1950s. As with the achievements of modernity, the majority of Americans take the accomplishments of postmodernism (described in chapter 3) for granted. However, the undeniable cultural progress achieved by the rise of postmodernism shows that this worldview has indeed discovered and embraced an emergent new form of authentic transcendence—one that all Americans can endorse once they've teased apart postmodernism's disasters from its dignities.

It is important to acknowledge in this context that much of the resistance to postmodernism is predicated on the fear that if this worldview were to become the majority outlook in American culture, this could eventually result in the demise of our republic. According to academic developmental psychology, we can't skip stages in the evolution of our consciousness. And this suggests that American culture must inevitably "pass through" the postmodern stage on its way to a more integral future. But despite the evident connection between the evolution of consciousness and the evolution of culture, I do not believe that the postmodern worldview will eventually come to represent America's cultural center of gravity. While postmodern values must play an important role in our further development, we don't need to become a majority postmodern nation before we can become a more integral one.

Postmodernism has helped awaken us to the cruelties of traditionalism's bigotry and ethnocentrism, and it has disenthralled us from the empty lures of modernism's materialism. But just as we now see Walt Disney's naïve view of progress as woefully outdated, we must similarly become disenthralled from postmodernism's pessimistic irony, and its ceaseless promotion of grievance without gratitude. As we've seen, each of America's major worldviews have pathologies that we must overcome, yet each offers a unique and enduring connection to transcendence that we cannot do without if we are to grow into a better version of ourselves. The job of this new integrative political philosophy is therefore to show how we can tap into the motivational energy of all three of these distinct visions of transcendence and thereby go beyond our current cultural impasse.

The integral philosophy of developmental politics accordingly makes its own contribution to transcendence by elevating and harmonizing each worldview's existing visions of transcendence. And by doing this, developmental politics reveals a new layer of transcendent meaning that can help guide the further development of our civilization. Beyond the amelioration of our contemporary political problems, this cultural approach to politics can also inspire us at a higher level by connecting our nation's social progress with the cosmic progress of evolution as a whole. As integral philosophy makes clear, authentic cultural evolution moves toward the direction of transcendence itself.

CONNECTING OUR POLITICAL PROGRESS TO THE COSMIC PROGRESS OF EVOLUTION

At the beginning of chapter 7 I briefly outlined the overall structural sequence of evolutionary emergence, which began with the big bang 13.8 billion years ago, and which has continued to build on itself ever since. In the first phase of universe development, matter evolved up through the periodic table of elements, eventually producing solar systems with planets like ours. Then on this planet, and likely elsewhere throughout the universe, a distinct second phase of evolution appeared with the emergence of life. This second phase of development continued to extend the structure of emergence, building on the accomplishments of the first phase of evolution, but also transcending the evolution of matter alone through the advent of increasingly complex organisms. Evolution in the biological tree of life eventually led to the emergence of a uniquely aware species endowed with the power to transcend biological evolution itself. The momentous emergence of humanity accordingly inaugurated a third phase of universe development, which we are only now beginning to fully appreciate as an authentic kind of evolution—noosphere evolution.

The evolution of human civilization builds on and includes matter and life, but it also transcends these structures of development in the way that its advance is largely predicated on the intention and creativity of the human mind. Unlike cosmological and biological evolution, which proceed inexorably and apparently without intentional direction, noosphere evolution is "on purpose." And it is in the purposive quality of this most recent phase of universe development that we can anchor our assessment of universal progress.

Despite the many attempts to refute or deny the notion of progress in evolution, when progress is straightforwardly defined as "growth in value over time," and when value is identified in the intrinsic qualities of goodness, truth, and beauty, then the only way to deny progress is to deny value itself. That is, can there be any doubt about the real value that has resulted from the series of evolutionary emergences that transformed hydrogen gas into the myriad wonders of life and the glorious achievements of human culture? As we discussed in chapter 6, humans live for value—we are "attracted by excellence and made for the Good." Our uniquely human ability to appreciate and create value itself therefore provides clear evidence of evolution's value-creating behavior, and thus its irrefutable progress.

> "Can there be any doubt about the real value that has resulted from the series of evolutionary emergences that transformed hydrogen gas into the myriad wonders of life and the glorious achievements of human culture?"

Yet notwithstanding its progress, there is also an evident countercurrent in the universe's process of value creation. In cosmological evolution it is recognized as entropy—the force of decay that ensures that all forms of material organization are only temporary and fleeting. In the realm of noosphere evolution, this countercurrent can be recognized as the opposite of beauty, truth, and goodness, which manifests as the ugliness, ignorance, and evil that continue to plague our troubled world. As human culture has evolved, many of these horrors have seemingly increased, which has led many people of good sense and good faith to conclude that human progress is a pernicious myth that realism requires us to abandon.

However, despite the decay of entropy in the physical cosmos, despite the suffering of life in the biosphere, and even despite the persistent shadow of violence and oppression in the noosphere, something more keeps coming from something less. And the "something more" that is human freedom and intention has brought us to the point where we are now largely responsible for the further evolution of value in our corner of the universe. In the words of distinguished polymath Michael Polanyi, "the theory of evolution finally bursts through the bounds of natural science and becomes entirely an affirmation of man's ultimate aims."[6]

Once we acknowledge that the noosphere is in fact a new and significant layer of authentic evolution, then we must face the fact that humanity represents evolution's leading edge. Even though civilization may have developed much further on other planets, here on our planet we are creating the unique and intriguing story that is human history. And now more than ever before, we have the power to intentionally advance the evolution of the noosphere and contribute to the further progress of human history. Even though this new power also gives us the ability to destroy ourselves, it's not too late.

As a result of the advent of modernity we have a tiger by the tail; if we let it go it will devour us. We can, however, master the power that modernity has given us and use it to create a more beautiful world that transcends modernism itself. Simply put, by using the light and power that comes from the New Truth about evolution, we can actively foster the further development of human consciousness and culture.

Given America's contemporary political dilemma, this framing of human progress in cosmic terms may seem disconnected from the apparent regression we have experienced during the Trump administration. But taking an evolutionary perspective on our political problems helps reframe our hyperpolarized political condition as a golden opportunity to bring about the next emergent level of our own evolutionary development. As we've considered throughout this book, our gridlocked politics constitute a wicked problem that requires a new level of thinking for its amelioration. And the emerging integral worldview and its accompanying new politics of culture provides just the kind of new thinking we need.

In fact, the very problems that cause many to deny the possibility of progress actually provide the urgent push that is the indispensible counterpart to the pull of value—the magnetism of the good that draws us forward. In other words, the partial and imperfect conditions of the finite universe are what make evolution toward greater perfection possible in the first place. So even though these problems are daunting and often overwhelming, the opportunity to overcome them step by evolutionary step can be recognized as a sacred gift. We are the agents of evolution in the noosphere, and its further progress depends on us. As we awaken to our role as agents of evolution's progress, this reveals humanity's transcendent higher purpose: We are the bearers of the universe's teleology—our purposes are its purposes.

It is thus within this New Truth about evolution that we can discover a fresh vision of transcendence that can meet the political needs of our time. Stated otherwise, the inclusive higher purpose required to restore our social solidarity can be found in the expanded conception of social progress provided by developmental politics' program for cultural evolution. As we have discussed, this project of cultivating cultural evolution reveres and integrates the values of traditionalism, modernism, and postmodernism, and seeks to facilitate the unique kind of progress offered by each of these worldviews. Moreover, this evolutionary program also seeks to bring about a new and inclusive integral worldview that can effectively include the best and transcend the worst of America's three existing cultures.

"Our hyperpolarized political condition provides a golden opportunity to bring about the next emergent level of our evolutionary development."

By widening our collective vision of progress in this way, and by connecting our near-term cultural and political progress with the cosmic progress of the universe as a whole, integral philosophy can help bring about a post-secular appreciation of transcendence, and perhaps even a post-traditional conception of the will of God. It is thus by restoring our common sense of higher purpose and collective destiny that we can grow into a more advanced stage of cultural maturity and thereby save our democracy in the process.

* * *

By way of conclusion, allow me to end with a call to action. In order to adequately appreciate integral philosophy and grow into the expanded perspective it makes possible, this emerging body of thought needs to be both studied and applied. In short, the integral perspective takes practice. Practicing this perspective—metabolizing this New Truth—involves working with the three "practice circuits" discussed in chapter 8, namely, the practice of learning and teaching, the practice of appreciating and creating, and the practice of devotion and service. Taking action to develop integral consciousness can accordingly include reading some of the books in the selected bibliography, investigating some of the integral interviews and podcasts available online, and investing the time required to learn this new philosophy and share it with others.

Finally, and perhaps most importantly, taking action to help bring about noosphere evolution also involves practicing the virtues by taking them to heart. The virtues of faith, hope, and love can empower our personal motivation by establishing a stronger connection to the energy of transcendence. And the virtues of prudence, courage, justice, and temperance can empower the effectiveness of our individual political activism. When practiced together as a whole, these seven habits of the heart can evolve our character and our consciousness, and thereby facilitate our own personal contribution to the evolution of the universe.

On the Ontological Status of Worldviews

What are worldviews really? In chapter 1, I provided a formal definition, and in chapter 2 I loosely described these value systems as "types of consciousness within people." There is, however, much more to say about the reality, or ontological status, of these influential cultural entities. Developmental politics places a lot of theoretical weight on the concept of worldviews, so it is important to understand what they are and where they exist. In chapter 5, I briefly introduced the concept of intersubjectivity, which was defined as "the relational connections and structures of agreement that exist between conscious minds." However, I deferred the discussion of this complex philosophical subject to this appendix. Even though the existence of human relations and agreements is plainly obvious, the fact that these relational connections have a kind of systemic vitality—a partially independent life of their own—is only vaguely understood. Gaining greater knowledge of the systemic behavior of cultural relations in general, and worldviews in particular, can therefore help us work with these value systems more effectively in our efforts to establish a pragmatic politics of culture.

As I have argued, America's contemporary political dysfunction is primarily a cultural problem, and worldviews are the basic units of culture. In various places in this book, I referred to worldviews as having intentions and taking actions. But as I trust the context made clear, these were shorthand references to the collective intentions that worldviews embody, and were not meant to imply that worldviews have a mind of their own. Worldviews are not conscious entities, but they are more than merely summative numerical sets of shared individual values. These cultural entities are large-scale *systems* with their own momentum in human history. According to social philosopher Margaret Gilbert, "social groups, as opposed to mere collections of individuals, are formed by the members making joint commitments."[1] And the collective intentions that arise from these joint commitments evince a metabolism of value energy, which helps explain how they cohere into the larger intergenerational systems of agreement we identify as worldviews.

As we've seen, worldviews persist through time, and the collective intentionality they embody clearly has an influential impact on people's perspectives and values. Even though worldviews originate "from below" in the minds of individual people, they also exert influence "from above." The collective values and intentions they represent *supervene* on people's thinking. Recognizing the force of this collective intentionality does not require us to reify worldviews as individual actors, but it does require us to recognize how these intersubjective structures profoundly shape our social world.

OUR EMERGING UNDERSTANDING OF SOCIAL ONTOLOGY

The academic discipline known as "social ontology" has recently become a fashionable field within professional philosophy. In 2018, the *Stanford Encyclopedia of Philosophy* published its first substantial article on the subject.[2] This scholarly article, written by Stanford professor Brian Epstein, defines the field of social ontology as: "the study of the nature and properties of the social world. It is concerned with analyzing the various entities in the world that arise from social interaction." While this new field shows promise, as the encyclopedia article makes clear, researchers are far from a consensus regarding the ontological status of human groups. The article also reveals a general lack of awareness of how the intersubjective realm of relations functions as a domain of cultural evolution. While the article acknowledges the idea of intersubjectivity in general, it does not explain the metaphysics of this category, or how intersubjective entities can be compared and contrasted with both the objective realm of things and the subjective realm of thoughts.

Integral philosopher Ken Wilber has done some interesting work in this area with his four-quadrant model of evolutionary emergence. His model depicts four metaphysical categories of evolution: the interior and exterior development of individuals, and the interior and exterior development of collective groups.[3] While a thorough description of this model is beyond the scope of this appendix, it must be acknowledged that Wilber's quadrant map provides a useful way to think about the correlation between interior and exterior development. Wilber's model is among the first attempts to describe intersubjectivity as an actual ontological domain of development. As such, I commend it for providing a solid start to integral philosophy's ongoing quest to chart evolution's interior dimensions of development.

However, although Wilber's map provides a fairly accurate description of the structure of emergence in the biosphere, his model becomes distorted and leads to confusion at the level of noosphere evolution.[4] The limitations of this model are shown by the fact that it has not been taken seriously by mainstream intellectuals. While the model remains popular with many of Wilber's readers, since its original introduction twenty-five years ago it has failed to garner recognition in professional philosophy or in academia in general. For example, even though the recent *Stanford Encyclopedia* article on social ontology includes close to six hundred references, Wilber's work is not cited. I have discussed my objections to Wilber's model in detail elsewhere,[5] so I won't repeat those critiques here.

The limited goal of this brief appendix is to help us appreciate the subtle but important distinctions between the evolution of consciousness and the evolution of culture. Even though the structures of psychological development and the structures of cultural development are deeply intertwined, we must avoid the mistake of understanding worldviews primarily in psychological terms. As the rising field of social ontology is beginning to dimly see, cultural entities such as worldviews cannot be entirely reduced to shared subjective frames of mind. Worldviews are indeed made up of shared psychological perspectives, but their systemic existence extends beyond the psychological domain of subjective mind.

THE RELEVANCE OF DEVELOPMENTAL PSYCHOLOGY

Developmental psychology is the subfield within academic psychology that studies the developmental structures of the human mind. Although this branch of psychology is not well liked or integrated within the more prominent and well-funded quarters of the larger field of academic psychology in general, the findings of developmental psychology cannot be dismissed. This branch of psychology began over a hundred years ago and has amassed a significant body of research. Major figures in developmental psychology include James Mark Baldwin, Jean Piaget, Lawrence Kohlberg, Lev Vygotsky, Carol Gilligan, Jane Loevinger, Michael Commons, Abraham Maslow, Clare Graves, Howard Gardner, and Robert Kegan.

Researchers in this field have developed a variety of competing theories regarding the specific stages through which adult cognitive developmental takes place. There is, however, a fair degree of overlap between these various stage theories, with the stages originally identified by Piaget having garnered the most agreement. But notwithstanding the influence of Piaget, no clear consensus has emerged regarding the exact number or specific character of the structure-stages through which humans grow in adulthood.

Many of these competing stage theories now include their own psychological assessment instruments which purport to accurately locate people's overall stage of development. Yet because developmental psychologists do not agree about the stages themselves, this lack of consensus raises questions such as: Are developmental psychologists inadvertently measuring slightly different lines of psychological growth while claiming to measure cognitive development overall? Are their tests detecting the influence of cultural worldview stages that interpenetrate people's minds but which are actually grounded more in the intersubjective realm than in the subjective domain? Within developmental psychology, worldviews are usually conceived of as exclusively psychological structures. But while there is clearly overlap between cultural stages and psychological stages, is it wise to conflate stages of cultural development with stages of psychological development, and then attempt to assess the development of these stages by psychological testing alone?

As I argued in chapter 2, for most Americans worldviews "sound more in chords than in single notes." So while psychological assessment instruments may be able to detect a person's cultural center of gravity, conceiving of people as being "at" a given worldview stage in their personal psychological development can lead to confusion. People's cultural loyalties do tend to "locate" them within the larger cultural ecosystem comprised by America's major worldviews. But in order to understand the ontology of worldview structures, we must recognize how these systems of intersubjective development are not completely identical with stages of psychological growth.[6]

So how are collective worldviews partially independent from the psychology of individual minds? Well, worldviews are made up of agreements about values, and all active agreements reflect joint commitments that extend beyond the subjective intentions of single individuals. A legal contract, for example, represents a joint commitment that, once affirmed, comes to have independent economic value in itself. The independent value of enforceable contracts is what allows such agreements to function as the building blocks of modern economies. This example of legal contracts accordingly illustrates how agreements can extend the subjective intentions of individuals into intersubjective commitments that transcend the subjective psychological realm.

Beyond economic agreements, when intersubjective commitments form around values, they provide a connection with transcendence that reinforces people's sense of personal identity. And by establishing this connection with transcendence, these intersubjective agreements become active circuits of value energy. Recognizing how agreements about values come to metabolize value energy helps explain why intersubjective agreements exhibit their own systemic vitality and evolutionary dynamism. Indeed, it is this systemic dynamism that allows value agreements to cohere into large-scale worldviews with their own evolutionary momentum. Which helps explain how worldviews themselves cohere into the larger cultural ecosystem we have explored.

With the notable exception of Graves, developmental psychologists have not attempted to tie-in the psychological stages they recognize with the socio-cultural stages of human history. Although philosopher Jürgen Habermas has noted the "homologies" that can be found between historical and psychological worldviews,[7] the intriguing parallels between personal and cultural development have not been carefully explored outside the confines of integral philosophy. And as noted, integral philosophy itself is still in its infancy and has yet to receive mainstream recognition.

Like psychology in general, the current state of developmental psychology remains reminiscent of medieval medicine before the advent of the scientific method—there's a lot misplaced confidence and groping in the dark.[8] It is therefore important to acknowledge that the depth and breadth of the human mind is vast, and we are far from a comprehensive understanding of it. Moreover, the psychological structures of individual consciousness are partially governed by intentionality and subject to degrees of free will, which means that they are among the most complex entities that humans can attempt to fathom. Cultural structures, on the other hand, are not self-aware or self-acting, so in theory, they should be easier to discern than the far more complex structures of consciousness, with which they are correlated but not entirely identical.

Further, unlike human consciousness, which can step outside of history and make contact with untold depths of insight and creativity, and which may even live on beyond this world, human culture is bound up with history and limited by humanity's social development. So these respective domains of evolution cannot be accurately conceived of has being symmetrical in depth and breadth. The evolution of culture depends on the evolution of consciousness and vice versa, but evolutionary development in these distinct domains does not always unfold in a lockstep one-to-one correspondence. Therefore, in our quest to better understand the political and social significance of worldviews, we do well to recognize the ways in which these intersubjective systems of development are partially independent from the psychological structures through which individual consciousness evolves.

Mapping the Ontology of the Noosphere

Structures of consciousness exist in our heads. But where do the systemic structures of culture reside? While cultural structures interpenetrate our minds, as I argued above, they cannot be completely reduced to subjective psychological entities—they exist *in between* individual subjects. These intersubjective structures do have objective physical correlates, which for the most part take the form of human artifacts. These physical artifacts, however, are mostly surface features of deeper interior phenomena. Language, for example, extends into the physical world through vocal sounds and written symbols. But the primary corpus of language consists in the meaning it transmits; and this shared meaning is essentially intersubjective in nature. Without the shared meaning that gives it life, a language becomes dead. While the word symbols of a dead language may persist in the archeological record, once the shared meanings of the words are lost, the cultural system they once represented ceases to exist.

Therefore, even though cultural structures interpenetrate both the objective realm of things and the subjective realm of thoughts, these structures cannot be reduced to either of these other two domains. Which is why we need a clear conception of a third category of development beyond the objective and subjective—we need to recognize that the intersubjective domain is where most of cultural evolution actually takes place. So as a starting place for our thinking about the ontological status of worldviews, figure A.1 provides a conceptual diagram of the interior and exterior domains of noosphere evolution. This simplified two-dimensional figure only shows one conceptual slice of the complex phenomena constituted by the development of culture and consciousness. But figure A.1 does help illustrate how the objective, subjective, and intersubjective dimensions of the noosphere relate to each other.

In figure A.1 human consciousness (depicted in white) is located inside the physical bodies (depicted in black) of both the main subject shown in the figure and the "other people" that together make up the exterior social world. These individual subjects interact with the objective social world (depicted in dark gray) through their perceptions, communications, actions, and in other ways, as indicated by the two-way arrows. And as noted, most of these social interactions are facilitated by manmade artifacts such as languages, media,

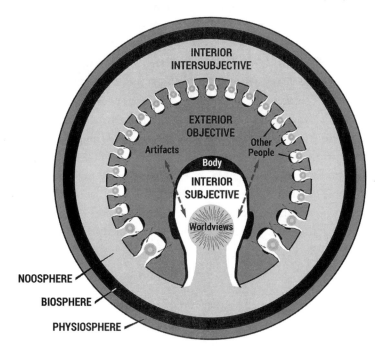

Figure A.1. A chart of the ontology of the noosphere[10]

institutions, political structures, and numerous other objective physical systems. Yet in addition to these psychological and physical realities, figure A.1 also shows a distinct intersubjective realm (depicted in light gray). This intersubjective aspect of reality extends partially into the consciousness of each subject, which is how worldviews, together with other aspects of intersubjective culture, influence our thoughts, feelings, and intentions.[9]

Figure A.1 also shows the encompassing domains of the biosphere and the physiosphere, as indicated by the two outside circles. Like the human body, the biosphere is depicted in black. And like the objective social world, the physiosphere is depicted in dark gray. By showing the noosphere as *arising within* the biosphere and the physiosphere, figure A.1 reflects the thinking described in note 3 to chapter 7. This extensive endnote and its accompanying chart explains how life can be conceived of as arising within the larger physical cosmos, and how subjective consciousness and intersubjective culture can be likewise conceived of as emerging within a biological context.

The New Truth about evolution reveals the interiors of culture and consciousness like never before. And in order to chart this newly revealed territory we need to make new maps. Yet because no single two-dimensional diagram can adequately depict all the nuances of the noosphere, we need a wide variety of maps. Indeed, accurately charting the interior contours of culture and consciousness requires us to view these domains from a variety of different conceptual angles. Figure A.1 therefore provides one such angle.

Just as the flowering of European civilization in the Renaissance was marked by the Age of Discovery and the mapping of the globe, now in our time we are witnessing the beginning of the next age of discovery. But in our age the mapping project is focused on charting the internal universe. While all early maps, including mine and Wilber's, will likely be overturned in the future by more accurate ones, this "inner cartography" is a necessary and exciting part of the next renaissance—the birth of the integral worldview.

An Exercise for Practicing Virtues: Creating a Personal Portrait of the Good

This final appendix builds on our previous consideration of virtues by providing an exercise designed to help you develop an effective virtue practice. As discussed at length in chapter 8, virtues are personal commitments to moral excellence that are best understood as "states of intention," "dispositions of the will," or even "habits of the heart." The practice of virtues accordingly requires conviction and personal dedication. This dedication can be strengthened by consciously choosing your preferred virtues, and by creating simple rituals through which you can regularly evaluate the growth of your character. This appendix's exercise is therefore designed to help "habituate" the practice of virtues by personalizing and routinizing the process through which these ideal traits can become ingrained into your basic nature.

What follows is a three-step exercise that can serve as a starting place for your virtue practice by providing some structure and a finished product to contemplate. This finished product is a personal *portrait of the good* which symbolizes and concretizes the specific virtues you choose to live by. Thinking deeply about your core virtues is an important part of a virtue practice, and this exercise is designed to help you do just that.

The exercise requires a pencil and paper and should take about fifteen minutes to complete. The exercise is also online at the Institute for Cultural Evolution's website: www.culturalevolution.org.

STEP 1: CONTEMPLATE YOUR ESSENTIAL INTERESTS (THREE QUESTIONS)

To start this exercise, take a blank piece of white paper and place it in front of you in a horizontal or "landscape" orientation. (You can see an example of a finished portrait of the good in figure B.3 on page 189.)

Question 1. Self-Interest: What Do You Ultimately Want?

In the upper-left corner of your paper write the title: "My Goal" and underline it. Then, from among the six potential personal goals listed below, choose the answer that best describes what you are most interested in achieving in life. Even though you may desire all of these ends, this question asks you to choose the life goal that appeals to you most. Write your answer in the upper-left corner of your paper underneath the "My Goal" title.

A) Happiness

B) Success

C) Respect and Recognition

D) Peace of Mind

E) Self-actualization

F) Self-transcendence

Question 2. Other-Interest: Who Are the Others You Care Most About?

Below your answer to question 1, on the left hand margin of your paper write the title: "My People" and underline it. This three-part question asks you to visualize some of the significant others in your life. In short, who are "your people?" Underneath the "My People" title, answer questions A, B, and C below by writing the names of the people and groups you care most about. Try to limit your responses to a single column on the left.

A) Who are your closest loved ones?

B) Who are your most significant friends and colleagues?

C) What groups do you identify with? For instance, this list might include humanity, your gender, your nationality, your political affiliation, and perhaps your race, and your common interest and affinity groups. Limit your answers to only the groups that help define your personal identity.

Question 3. Greater-Than-Self Interest: What Qualifies as Authentically Transcendent for You?

In the upper-right corner of your paper write the title: "The Transcendent" and underline it. This question asks you to consider who and what is ultimately more important than you. Underneath "The Transcendent" title, list some of the people and things on whose behalf you would readily sacrifice your own self-interest. This list should include things you are dedicated to, and perhaps even people and things for which you would lay down your life, if it became necessary. Possible answers could include: Your family, your country, humanity, God, your deepest convictions, animals, the environment, freedom, adventure, art, science, a better world, or anything you consider authentically transcendent. There will likely be some overlap between your answers to question 2, which is fine.

STEP 2: DISCERN YOUR MOST IMPORTANT VIRTUES (SEVEN QUESTIONS)

The following questions help you identify seven specific "core virtues" (from a list of forty-nine potential choices) that best describe your ideal character strengths. These core virtues are discovered through the process of reflecting on the sense of obligation you have to yourself, to others, and to that which you recognize as transcendent. The relationship between your core virtues and these moral obligations—to self, to others, and to the transcendent—are discussed in chapter 8 (pages 137-141). Figure B.1 uses the seven fundamental virtues to illustrate this relationship of virtues and obligations, but the core virtues you choose may differ from these classical seven.

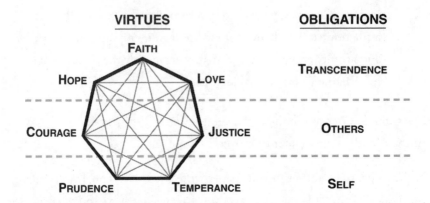

Figure B.1. *The seven fundamental virtues and their corresponding obligations (figure 8.4, reproduced)*

To begin Step 2, draw the seven-pointed heptagon shown in figure B.2 in the middle of your paper (or just draw a circle if that's easier). As you draw your heptagon, make it small enough to allow room to write a virtue term for each of the seven positions, which you will fill-in as you answer the seven questions in Step 2. Then above your heptagon, write and underline the title: "Virtues" (leaving room for position 6 as shown).

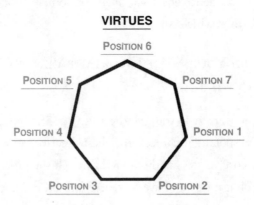

Figure B.2. *The seven virtue positions for your portrait of the good*

Contemplating and choosing the seven specific virtues that are most meaningful to you can be compared to composing music—the virtues you select are like the musical tones that comprise the composition of your character.

Question 1. What Do You Owe to Others?

Starting with position 1 on the middle-right side of your heptagon, write the virtue term that best describes the basic standard of care or conduct that you owe to the other people and groups you identified in Step 1. In other words, what is the best way to treat the people who are in your life, and the groups you're most concerned about? For position 1, the fundamental root virtue is *Justice*. You may choose justice for your answer, or any of the other six virtues listed below:

A) Justice

B) Fairness

C) Respect

D) Honesty

E) Decency

F) Cooperation

G) Generosity

Question 2. What Do You Owe to Yourself?

Moving to position 2 at the bottom right of your heptagon, select the term that best describes the standard of goodness, or right action, that you try to hold *yourself* to. For position 2, the fundamental root virtue is *Temperance*. You may choose temperance for your answer, or any of the other six virtues listed below:

A) Temperance

B) Dignity

C) Honor

D) Reliability

E) Humility

F) Righteousness

G) Integrity

Question 3. What Do You Owe to Your Plans and Dreams?

For position 3, select the term that best describes the standard of care that you owe to your life plans and projects. In other words, what guiding principle of action should you proceed by in your endeavors? For position 3, the fundamental root virtue is *Prudence*. You may choose prudence for your answer, or any of the other six virtues listed below:

A) Prudence

B) Common Sense

C) Practical Wisdom

D) Foresight

E) Reason

F) Industry

G) Creativity

Question 4. How Do You Face Your Fears and Respond to Difficulties?

Moving to position 4 on the middle left side your heptagon, select the term that describes your best possible stance when faced with challenges or threats from others. In other words, what allows you to stand your ground and live-up to the best you can be? For position 4, the fundamental root virtue is *Courage*. You may choose courage for your answer, or any of the other six virtues listed below:

A) Courage

B) Confidence

C) Determination

D) Conviction

E) Patience

F) Passion

G) Sincerity

Question 5. What Is Your Best Stance Toward the Future?

The final three virtue positions help identify the duties you owe to your greater-than-self-interests, as identified in Step 1. For position 5 select the term that describes how you relate to your highest expectations for this life, and potentially beyond this life. For position 5, the fundamental root virtue is *Hope*. You may choose hope for your answer, or any of the other six virtues listed below:

A) Hope

B) Optimism

C) Enthusiasm

D) Humor

E) Grace

F) Trust

G) Realization

Question 6. How Do You Relate to What Is Ultimately Real?

For position 6 choose the term that best describes your relationship to what you really believe deep down. In other words, how do you relate to your ideals of goodness, truth, and beauty, or your chosen higher purpose? For position 6, the fundamental root virtue is *Faith*. You may choose faith for your answer, or any of the other six virtues listed below:

A) Faith

B) Acceptance

C) Open-Minded Uncertainty

D) Delight

E) Loyalty

F) Gratitude

G) Devotion

Question 7. What Is the Best You Can Be, Do, or Give in This World?

Finally, in position 7 write the word that describes the highest good you are capable of expressing, or the best person you are capable of being. In other words, what personal quality are you the most proud of? For position 6, the fundamental root virtue is *Love*. You may choose love for your answer, or any of the other six virtues listed below:

A) Love

B) Kindness

C) Tenderness

D) Forgiveness

E) Care

F) Goodwill

G) Compassion

Complete Step 2 By Reviewing Your Finished Portrait of the Good

Once all seven positions have been filled in, you have your personal portrait of the good. As you review your portrait (which should look roughly similar to the example shown in figure B.3), consider how practicing these virtues will make you a better person, and anticipate the sense of satisfaction that will accompany this personal growth. As Aristotle understood, pursuing personal excellence through the practice of virtues is the key to happiness. The practice of these virtues can accordingly fulfill your ultimate self-interest, which you identified in Step 1 and wrote in the top left of your paper.

Beyond your self-interest, living ethically according to these virtues can also help fulfill your duty to the others listed on the left side of your paper. Living your chosen virtues assures that you will be the kind of person that these people can count on and admire.

And finally, as also explained in chapter 8, the practice of virtues can connect you with the energy of transcendence, giving you the power that only an authentic higher purpose can supply. The higher purposes and significant others listed on the right and left sides of your portrait of the good thus provide the intrinsic reasons—the *why*—that can help you fully engage the practice of virtues and thereby fulfill both your self-interest and your greater-than-self-interest simultaneously.

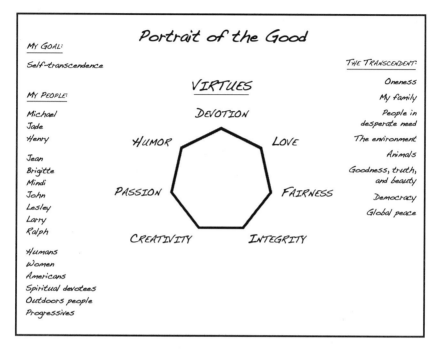

Figure B.3. An example of a completed portrait of the good

Now with your completed portrait of the good in hand, you are ready to move to Step 3.

STEP 3: LIVE WITH YOUR PORTRAIT OF THE GOOD—WORK TO MAKE IT A PORTRAIT OF WHO YOU REALLY ARE

For the following ten suggested practices, pursue as many of these as reasonably possible:

1. Place your finished portrait of the good in a prominent place in your personal space where you can review it regularly.

2. Memorize your seven chosen virtues. Repeat them out loud to yourself, tell your companions about them over a meal, and do your best to keep them in mind as you go through life.

3. Create a weekly ritual to chart the progress of your virtue practice. This was the technique Benjamin Franklin used to practice his famous list of thirteen virtues.[1] Franklin focused on one virtue a week for thirteen weeks. At the end of each week he assessed his performance for that week's virtue and recorded it in his journal.

4. Write a short essay or blog post about what your chosen virtues mean to you, and what your practice commitment is. Explain, for example, which of your chosen virtues is the strongest and which needs the most work.

5. Write a "Future Me" email (www.futureme.org) to yourself that will prompt you to check in on how you're doing with your virtue practice after some time has passed. Write either a single future email to yourself that will come back to you in a month, or write a series of future emails that will be delivered once a week for seven weeks.

6. Draw a symbolic picture of each of your seven virtues. Hand drawing each of your chosen virtues will help you keep them in mind. Even if you are not a good artist, or the pictures you draw are goofy or cliché (like my examples below), this process is proven to work as a mnemonic device.[2] Examples of simple drawings that could represent the seven fundamental virtues include: a balance scale for justice, a circle with a backslash "no symbol" for temperance, an owl for prudence, a sword and shield for courage, praying hands for hope, a religious symbol such as a cross or a sitting Buddha for faith, and a valentine heart for love. Thinking of similar symbolic pictures to represent the specific virtues you selected is part of the exercise. You can even draw your pictures on the back of your portrait of the good.

7. Combine your virtue practice with a mindfulness practice by repeating your specific list of virtues to yourself just prior to bringing your awareness into the present moment.

8. Start an affinity group or mutual improvement club, and meet

once a month to discuss the practice of virtues and related topics.

9. Create a "habit loop" by using a cue from something you see daily to remind you of your commitment to being virtuous. For example, when you look at yourself in the mirror, use that moment to remember the virtues that define who you want to be. Just as the mirror reflects your face, affirm your conviction that your character will reflect your virtues. And when you subsequently act in a virtuous way, reward yourself with a treat, or draw a small star on your portrait of the good. Celebrate your success!

10. Read more about the power of virtues in one or more of these noteworthy books: The *Nicomachean Ethics* by Aristotle, *Dependent Rational Animals: Why Human Beings Need the Virtues* by Alasdair MacIntyre, *Natural Goodness* by Philippa Foot, *The Bourgeois Virtues* by Deidre McCloskey, *Ethics and Excellence* by Robert Solomon, *Virtuous Leadership* by Alexandre Havard, and *Varieties of Virtue Ethics* edited by Carr and Kristjánsson. All of these books are included in the selected bibliography.

* * *

Remember, living with your virtues is a life-long practice that takes time to develop. As the ancient Greek philosopher Heraclitus wrote: "Good character is not formed in a week or month. It is created little by little, day by day. Protracted and patient effort is needed to develop good character."[3]

NOTES

PREFACE

1. Integral philosophy is a broad philosophy of evolution that focuses on the structures and larger meanings behind the evolutionary development of humanity. This philosophy of evolution begins with G.W.F. Hegel, but it is not a strictly Hegelian philosophy. Other notable philosophers who have attempted to understand the evolution of consciousness and culture, and have thus contributed to integral philosophy, include Henri Bergson, Alfred North Whitehead, Pierre Teilhard de Chardin, Sri Aurobindo, Jean Gebser, Jürgen Habermas, and Ken Wilber. Although the word "integral" is often associated specifically with the work of Wilber, this body of thought is much larger than Wilber's philosophy alone. The use of the term "integral" to refer to this larger philosophy of evolution can be traced back to the first half of the twentieth century in the work of Gebser, Aurobindo, and in the writing of Harvard sociologist Pitirim Sorokin. And interestingly, although there is a remarkable degree of overlap among these three early integral philosophers, each of these authors independently chose to label their thinking "integral" even though they were not aware of each other's work. Then later in the 1980s, Wilber adopted this term to refer to his work as well. Overall, I respect Wilber and have benefited from his writing but, as explained in note 9 to chapter 4, and further in appendix A, my interpretation of integral philosophy differs from his. While I too describe my thinking as "integral," I am not a "Wilberian." For an intellectual history of integral philosophy see: Steve McIntosh, *Integral Consciousness and the Future of Evolution* (St Paul, MN: Paragon House, 2007), chapter 7, "The Founders of Integral Philosophy," pp. 153-197.

CHAPTER 1

1. The proposition that since the 1950s the culture of the developed world has moved from "allegiance values" to "assertive values" comes primarily from political scientist Christian Welzel's analysis of data from the World Values Survey. See *Freedom Rising: Human Empowerment and the Quest for Emancipation*, (Cambridge University Press, 2013).

2. My definition of the word "culture" includes the following three meanings from Dictionary.com:

"1. The quality in a person or society that arises from a concern for what is regarded as excellent in arts, letters, manners, scholarly pursuits, etc.

2. A particular form or stage of civilization, as that of a certain nation or period.

3. Development or improvement of the mind by education or training."

In *The New Yorker Magazine* Joshua Rothman writes about the meaning of the word "culture," citing Raymond Williams' observation that "many people ... have called 'culture' a 'loose or confused' term. It's possible to imagine a more rational system, in which one word describes the activities of artistic and intellectual life, another our group identity, and a third our implicit norms and ways of living. Those terms, whatever they might be, would be narrower and simpler—but they'd also be less accurate. They would obscure the overlap between life, art, and politics." https://www.newyorker.com/books/joshua-rothman/meaning-culture

3. To prevent any possible confusion here at the beginning, unlike my use of the phrase "values system," which refers to all worldviews in general, the phrase "moral system" refers specifically to America's two major communitarian worldviews: traditionalism and progressive postmodernism. As explained in chapter 2: "Moral systems are the product of collective agreements enforced through social norms, peer pressure, and the expectations of the larger community. And the effectiveness of these cultural agreements depends on a *communitarian ethos*—a binding sense of solidarity that emphasizes the sacrifice of the self for the sake of the larger group. This communitarian ethos or ethic is strongly present in both the traditional worldview and the progressive postmodern worldview, which is why each of these worldviews give rise to strong moral systems of their own. Conversely, the absence of a strong communal ethos within modernity helps explain why the modernist worldview [or 'values system'], with its contrasting individualistic ethos emphasizing the sovereign expression of the self, cannot supply the communitarian expectations and compelling group norms that are necessary for the functioning of a robust moral system."

CHAPTER 2

1. See Ronald Inglehart, *Cultural Evolution: People's Motivations are Changing, and Reshaping the World* (Cambridge University Press, 2018), Ronald Inglehart, Ed., *Human Values and Social Change* (New York: Brill, 2003); Christian Welzel, *Freedom Rising: Human Empowerment and the Quest for Emancipation*, (Cambridge University Press, 2013); Paul Ray and Sherry Anderson, *The Cultural Creatives: How 50 Million People Are Changing the World* (New York: Harmony Books, 2000). See also,

Jean Piaget, *The Child's Conception of the World* (New York: Routledge, 1928); Lawrence Kohlberg, *From Is to Ought* (New York: Academic Press, 1971); Robert Kegan, *The Evolving Self: Problem and Process in Human Development* (Cambridge: Harvard, 1982); M. Commons, F. A. Richards, & C. Armon (Eds.), *Beyond formal operations: Vol. 1. Late adolescent and adult cognitive development*, (New York: Praeger 1984); Clare W. Graves, "Levels of Existence: An Open System Theory of Values," *Journal of Humanistic Psychology* (November 1970); Don Beck and Chris Cowan, *Spiral Dynamics* (New York: Blackwell, 1995); Jenny Wade, *Changes of Mind: A Holonomic Theory of the Evolution of Consciousness* (Albany, NY: SUNY Press, 1996); and Jeremy Rifkin, *The Empathic Civilization* (New York: Tarcher Putnam, 2009).

2. Christopher Lasch, *The Revolt of the Elites and the Betrayal of Democracy* (W. W. Norton & Co, 1995), p. 93.

3. John Tomasi, *Free Market Fairness* (Princeton University Press, 2012), p. 32.

4. Deidre McCloskey, *The Bourgeois Virtues: Ethics for an Age of Commerce* (University of Chicago Press, 2007), p. 16.

5. H. L. Mencken, *A Book of Prefaces* (Pinnacle Press 2017), p. 110.

6. Christopher Lasch, *The Revolt of the Elites and the Betrayal of Democracy* (W. W. Norton & Co, 1995), p. 86.

7. Note the ascending spiral or "logarithmic helix" used in figure 2.3 to illustrate the sequence of worldview emergence in history. This developmental geometry results from evolution's evident dialectical progression, which has been conceived of as a spiral by most commentators. The vertical hierarchy of development implied by this figure is explained and justified in chapters 7 and 9.

Note further that figure 2.3 shows two additional worldviews, labeled "tribal" and "pretraditional," both of which precede the traditional worldview in the timeline of history. The tribal worldview is a stage of culture that has been clearly identified as a distinct level of development by almost every researcher who has studied the growth of consciousness and culture, so there is strong mainstream agreement regarding the existence of this tribal stage. The pretradtional or "warrior" stage of cultural development, although less familiar, is also well-documented by the research of developmental psychology, where it is sometimes called the "preconventional" or "egocentric" form of consciousness, which prevails prior to the emergence of the ethnocentric traditional stage. Although authentic tribal culture continues to exist in very few places, such as isolated pockets of the Amazon rain forest, pretradtional culture is still fairly ubiquitous, even in the developed world. The egocentric consciousness of this pretraditional "warrior worldview" is clearly evident in America. It can be recognized, for example, in street gangs and prison culture. For a detailed description of the tribal and warrior worldviews, see McIntosh, *Integral Consciousness and the Future of Evolution*, pp. 37-42.

8. This idea of the "developmental logic" of cultural evolution comes from the social theory of Jürgen Habermas, who is careful to distinguish this pattern of development from the totalizing universal histories of the nineteenth century. Habermas scholar David S. Owens compares this developmental logic to a staircase: "When an individual steps up to a higher stair, she can see for a greater distance, and when she steps down, the distance of her vision is reduced. The same can be said of societies that develop. When they 'step up' to a higher level of development, they have expanded their consciousness, in the sense of an expansion of learning capacity; and when they step down, they constrict their consciousness or learning capacity. On this model of social evolution, then, the developmental logic is constituted in a hierarchical series of levels of learning that manifest themselves as horizons of consciousness. And within each learning level, or collective horizon of consciousness, many different social formations are possible. So while two determinate societies may occupy the same learning level, they may appear on the surface to be significantly different." David S. Owens, *Between Reason and History: Habermas and the Idea of Progress* (Albany, NY: SUNY Press, 2002), p. 3.

CHAPTER 3

1. Quoted in: Deirdre McCloskey, *The Bourgeois Virtues*, p. 511.

2. Ibid, p. 57.

3. Ibid, p. 173.

4. It should be acknowledged in this context that a common characteristic of postmodern consciousness, which goes against the grain of its communitarian ethos, is the narcissism that inflicts many of its most privileged members. As discussed in chapter 4, as with all worldviews, the positive values of postmodernism have a shadow. The shadow of postmodernism's welcoming pluralism and emphasis on racial and ethnic diversity can be seen in the alienating aspects of its identity politics. And similarly, the shadow of postmodernism's quest for ideological moral purity shows up in its narcissism. However, despite the narcissistic strain within this culture, its primary norm of communitarianism remains postmodernism's defining ethos.

CHAPTER 4

1. The "National Institute for Civil Discourse" is probably the most established organization seeking to overcome hyperpolarization through the process of more respectful dialogue. But many similar organizations can be found within the "Bridge Alliance" network of nonprofits, which all focus on some kind of political reform or civic renewal. See https://www.bridgealliance.us

2. See George Lakoff, "In Politics, Progressives Need to Frame Their Values" https//georgelakoff.com/2014/11/29/george-lakoff-in-politics-progressives-need-to-frame-their-values; Dan Kahan, "The Politically Motivated Reasoning Paradigm" https://papers.ssrn.com/sol3/papers.cfm?abstract_id=2703011; and Richard H. Thaler and Cass R. Sunstein, "Libertarian Paternalism Is Not an Oxymoron" https://chicagounbound.uchicago.edu/cgi/viewcontent.cgi?article=1184&context=public_law_and_legal_theory

3. Plato, *The Republic* (New York: Penguin Classics, 2007), p. 468.

4. A number of recent surveys purporting to map "America's tribes" reveal cultural categories that are very similar to the four basic positions charted by figure 4.3. These surveys, however, also detect a demographic segment of Americans who are "politically disengaged." This disaffected demographic group is not included in figure 4.3 because this figure is a map of value structures. Those who give little thought to their values, or who are otherwise apathetic or alienated from American culture, are largely disengaged from cultural worldviews. And because these disengaged citizens have little impact on American politics, they are not included in this chart. See "Hidden Tribes: A Study of America's Polarized Landscape" https://hiddentribes.us/pdf/hidden_tribes_report.pdf and "Five Tribes of American Voters"

https://www.realclearpolitics.com/articles/2018/10/18/five_tribes_of_american_voters_138390.html; see also Lee Drutman's chart of factions in: "How to build a new majority in American politics" https://www.vox.com/polyarchy/2016/12/6/13854668/six-factions-us-politics

5. Notwithstanding the research on "America's tribes" cited in the note directly above, data on the demographics of worldviews per se is fairly scant, and ultimately difficult to research given that the same person can use a different cultural worldview in different circumstances. Nevertheless, as a point of clarification, the left-right split within modernism is probably more like 55% liberal and 45% fiscally conservative, rather than a 50-50 split, as shown in figure 4.3. However, for purposes of graphical clarity and simplicity, this nuance is omitted. It should also be mentioned in this context that there are some traditionalists who remain registered Democrats, and there are even a few postmodernists who vote Republican. But these relatively small demographic segments have little current impact on American politics.

6. See e.g. The Pew Research Center's 2016 report, "5 facts about America's political independents" http://www.pewresearch.org/fact-tank/2016/07/05/5-facts-about-americas-political-independents; and Alan I. Abramowitz, *The Great Alignment: Race, Party Transformation, and the Rise of Donald Trump* (Yale University Press, 2018). According to E.J. Dionne, "As Abramowitz shows, most people who identify as independents lean toward one party or the other. When it comes to

casting ballots, 'leaning independents as well as strong and weak party identifiers are voting more along party lines than at any time in the past half century.'" See also Klar and Krupnikov, "Swing Voters Exist. Here's How to Scare Them Off (and How Not To)" https://www.nytimes.com/2018/10/17/opinion/midterms-independents-swing-voters-.html?action=click&module=Opinion&pgtype=Homepage

7. The coevolution of human culture and consciousness is described by neuropsychologist Merlin Donald: "Human beings are cognitive hybrids, tethered to both biology and cultural environment. Another way of phrasing this is that humans were the first species to evolve a truly 'distributed' cognitive system, that is, a system in which thought and memory are carried out in a community of minds. In a network, individuals are joined to a larger cognitive architecture that can have powers (e.g., deep memory resources and diverse expertise) that are not available to single individuals. Networks can also serve as generators of novel and powerful cognitive tools (e.g., languages, instruments, and symbolic notations). Languages in particular are network-level phenomena." Merlin Donald, "The Virtues of Rigorous Interdisciplinarity," in Joan M. Lucariello et al, Eds. *The Development of the Mediated Mind* (London: Psychology Press, 2004), p. 254. See also: Cecilia Heyes, *Cognitive Gadgets: The Cultural Evolution of Thinking* (Cambridge, MA: Harvard Belknap Press, 2018). Further, see the research cited in note 1 for chapter 2, above.

8. The idea that human conditions are genuinely improved through cultural evolution has been critiqued as a "growth-to-goodness fallacy." This criticism, however, is part of the larger critique of evolutionary progress, which is discussed at length in chapters 7 and 9. But as a preview of those arguments, I will acknowledge that the process of worldview development has not only made things better, it has also brought about unprecedented threats to humanity. For example, despite its oppression, the traditional stage of development never threatened the biosphere with catastrophic climate change or the proliferation of nuclear weapons, as the modernist stage has done. And these emergent pathologies of modernity have been frequently cited in the attempt to discredit its progress narrative. Yet even though the evolution of consciousness and culture results in the rise of new threats and potential pathologies, it is these very pathologies that spur us to keep going in our quest for a better world. Indeed, the emergence of new pathologies, as well as periodic regressions, are inevitable aspects of the process of growth itself. But as discussed in the main text, the fact that worldview development results in an increase of the scope of those deemed worthy of moral consideration is itself strong evidence that our attempts to improve our conditions are not in vain, and despite the inevitability of new threats and problems, humanity's ongoing growth toward greater goodness is not a fallacy.

9. Business consultant Barry Johnson is the most prominent popularizer of polarity theory. See Barry Johnson, *Polarity Management* (Amherst, MA: HRD Press, 1996). The theory itself, however, can be traced back to these sources: Charles

M. Hampden-Turner and Fons Trompenaars, *Building Cross-Cultural Competence: How to Create Wealth from Conflicting Values* (Yale University Press, 2000), Charles Handy, *The Age of Paradox* (Cambridge, MA: Harvard Business Review Press, 1995), Charles Johnston, *Necessary Wisdom: Meeting the Challenge of a New Cultural Maturity* (Berkeley: Ten Speed Press, 1991), Robert E. Quinn and Kim S. Cameron, *Paradox and Transformation: Toward a Theory of Change in Organization and Management* (Cambridge, MA: Ballinger, 1988), Bob de Wit and Ron Meyer, *Strategy: Process, Content, Context: an International Perspective* (Boston, MA: Cengage Learning Business Press, 1998), and Archie J. Baum, *Philosophy: An Introduction* (Hoboken: Wiley, 1953).

10. Niels Bohr, quoted in: Kathleen M. Higgins, Robert C. Solomon (Eds) *The Age of German Idealism: Routledge History of Philosophy, Volume 6* (Routledge 2003), p. 259.

11. See the Institute for Cultural Evolution's 2013 paper: "Campaign Plan for Climate Change Amelioration," https://www.culturalevolution.org/docs/ICE-Climate-Plan.pdf

12. As originally discussed in note 1 to the preface, some readers may associate the label "integral" primarily with the work of American philosopher Ken Wilber. However, while I respect Wilber and have personally benefited from his work, my interpretation of integral philosophy differs from his. For instance, Wilber's book, *Trump and a Post-Truth World* (Boston, MA: Shambhala, 2017) discusses some of the political challenges associated with the rise of the postmodern worldview. But even though I agree with Wilber on numerous points, I disagree with his main thesis that "[postmodernism], as a leading-edge, has collapsed," p. 19. On the contrary, I think the postmodern worldview is in fact succeeding by serving as an antithesis to the established order that is leading to further growth. By declaring postmodernism a "failure," Wilber is not adequately acknowledging the increasing cultural influence of postmodernism's *new layer of care*. Wilber's thesis in *Trump and a Post-Truth World* is that the failure of postmodernism caused Donald Trump to be elected. The American electorate's political backlash against postmodernism, however, did not result from postmodernism's failure. The pushback that Trump's election represented was rather the result of postmodernism's cultural success. This backlash against postmodernism can thus be seen as a natural and predictable part of the ongoing evolutionary process. Some of my additional disagreements with Wilber are discussed in appendix A, and in my books: *Integral Consciousness and the Future of Evolution*, and *The Presence of the Infinite* (Wheaton, IL: Quest Books 2015). For more on the current state of the integral movement as a whole, see chapter 7, page 125.

13. I use the term "dialectical" here and elsewhere in the book to indicate a partially opposing relationship characterized by both tension and interdependence. Within dialectical philosophy this relationship is recognized in practically all forms of mutually co-creating opposites, and indeed in all detectible forms of "identity

and difference." Polarity theory, however, is focused exclusively on positive-positive dialectical relationships, which are only a subset of the larger category of relations analyzed by dialectical philosophy overall. Nevertheless, I think positive-positive polarities demonstrate the "upward flow" of dialectical development most distinctly in the way they function "procreatively" to maximize the value generating capacity of each value pole by turns. See also, note 7 for chapter 7 below.

14. Robert Kegan, *In Over Our Heads* (Cambridge, MA: Harvard University Press, 1994), p. 351.

CHAPTER 5

1. Even though the human body is continuing to evolve in some respects, the physical structures of the human brain have changed very little since prehistoric times. Yet although every human infant begins life with the same basic biological consciousness as her ancient forebears, as a result of the evolution of culture the average level of adult human consciousness has nevertheless evolved considerably since the stone age in most parts of the world. Our proclivity to evolve our culture (and hence our consciousness) can thus be seen as an essential part of our "nature." We are deeply cultural creatures and as we evolve our civilization, we arguably evolve our essential human nature along with it. While consciousness can sometimes regress when subjected to severe survival pressures, or when civilizing cultural restraints become removed, the character of most twenty-first century Americans has clearly grown beyond our original "state of nature."

2. Pierre Teilhard de Chardin, *The Phenomenon of Man* (Harper & Row, 1955), p. 219.

3. See e.g. Thomas R. Rochon, *Culture Moves: Ideas, Activism, and Changing Values* (Princeton University Press 2018). See also the discussion of value frames and persuasion strategies in: "The Common Cause Report: The Case for Working with our Cultural Values," published September 2010, by The World Wildlife Fund: https://assets.wwf.org.uk/downloads/common_cause_report.pdf.

4. Quote on Pirsig from: https://en.wikipedia.org/wiki/Pirsig%27s_Metaphysics_of_Quality.

5. Iris Murdoch, *The Sovereignty of the Good* (New York: Routledge and Kegan Paul, London, 1970), p. 103.

CHAPTER 6

1. Iris Murdoch, *The Sovereignty of the Good* (New York: Routledge and Kegan Paul, 1970), p. 97.

2. I heard Dr. Margolis make this statement at a scholarly conference on evolution and religion held at the Claremont Graduate School of Theology, in October 2004. I do not know if this idea has been articulated in any of Dr. Margolis's many books, but the profundity of this simple statement was not lost on the conference participants.

3. Stuart Kauffman, *Reinventing the Sacred* (New York: Basic Books, 2008), pp. 86-87.

4. Charles Darwin, *The Origin of Species* (New York: Mentor Books, 1958), p. 171.

5. Holmes Rolston III, *Environmental Ethics, Duties to and Values in the Natural World* (Philadelphia, PA: Temple University Press, 1988), p. 187.

6. See *Stanford Encyclopedia of Philosophy*, "Biological Altruism," https://plato. stanford.edu/entries/altruism-biological; see also Brethel-Haurwitz and Marsh; and "Animal Altruism? New research describes how humpback whales protect seals from harm," https://www.psychologytoday.com/us/blog/goodness-sake/201610/animal-altruism

7. Viktor E. Frankl, *Man's Search for Meaning* (Boston, MA: Beacon Press, 2006), p. 175.

8. Candace Vogler, "Virtue, the Common Good and Self-Transcendence," in: Carr D., Arthur J., and Kristjánsson K. (Eds.) *Varieties of Virtue Ethics* (London: Palgrave Macmillan, 2017).

9. See the explanation of "warrior consciousness" in note 4 to chapter 2, above. See also, chapter 3 of McIntosh, *Integral Consciousness and the Future of Evolution*, pp. 39-42.

10. Charles Taylor, *A Secular Age* (Cambridge, MA: Harvard Belknap Press, 2007), p. 768.

11. Ibid., p. 727.

CHAPTER 7

1. Charles Taylor, *A Secular Age* (Cambridge, MA: Harvard Belknap Press, 2007), p.768.

2. Physicist and militant atheist Lawrence Krause proposes a speculative material explanation of the big bang, contending that this primordial emergence was merely the result of gravity. See Lawrence Krause, *A Universe from Nothing: Why There Is Something Rather than Nothing* (New York: Atria Books, 2013). However, Krause's "explanation" that gravity is the physical cause of the universe only begs the question: Why is gravity so marvelously creative, and what caused gravity to come into existence in the first place?

3. Arthur Koestler, *Janus: A Summing Up* (New York: Random House, 1978), p. 275.

4. Quoted in Holmes Rolston, *Three Big Bangs* (New York: Columbia University Press), p. 105.

5. Building on the work of developmental psychologists Jean Piaget and Lawrence Kohlberg, social philosopher Jürgen Habermas has used the evident "homologies" between individual psychological development and humanity's overall historical development as the basis for his moral philosophy. Habermas takes great care in distinguishing his understanding of these homologies from a literal interpretation of the idea that "ontogeny recapitulates phylogeny." But he nonetheless finds that culture and consciousness do generally progress by employing what he calls the same "developmental logic." According to Habermas, "If one examines social institutions and the action competencies of socialized individuals for general characteristics, one encounters the same structures of consciousness. ... All provisos notwithstanding, certain homologies can be found." Jürgen Habermas, *Communication and the Evolution of Society* (Boston, MA: Beacon Press, 1979), pp. 98-99. See also the discussion of developmental logic in note 5 to chapter 2 above.

6. Figure 7.1's simplified illustration of the structure of evolutionary emergence provides a good place to comment about the role of technology in the future of human evolution. The macro-layers of evolutionary emergence shown in this figure—physiosphere, biosphere, and noosphere—may raise questions about the possible future emergence of a fourth layer of evolution, which may come to transcend and envelop these three previous domains of evolution. This idea of a new layer of evolution is most frequently imagined as the emergence of the "technosphere"—a realm of development in which artificial intelligence begins to initiate its own growth, and then accelerates in a way that subordinates humanity, making us subservient or obsolete. This dystopian scenario is currently being promoted by techno-utopians such as Ray Kurzweil, and has become fashionable in places like Silicon Valley. However, I think the idea of the "coming singularity," as it is often called, is a science fiction fantasy that fundamentally misunderstands the nature of consciousness. While future technological developments will certainly continue to have a profound effect on human culture and consciousness throughout the twenty-first century and beyond, I do not think the technosphere represents the future of evolution.

Separately, but also regarding figure 7.1, the large-scale structure of evolutionary emergence demonstrates two parallel yet opposite patterns. First, as illustrated in figure 7.1, each emerging layer of evolution transcends and includes previous levels of development, "enveloping them" so to speak, like Russian dolls. And second, simultaneously and inversely, the emergent evolutionary realms of the biosphere and the noosphere can also be alternatively conceived as "arising within" their antecedent evolutionary domains. In other words, life emerges *within* the larger physical cosmos, and subjective consciousness and intersubjective culture likewise emerge *within* a biological context. This means that the nested sequence of emergence depicted in figure 7.1 can also be accurately represented in the inverse, with the noosphere as the innermost layer and the physiosphere as the outermost, as shown in the diagram below.

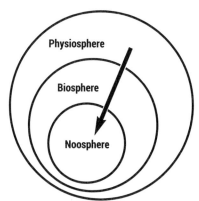

When considered together with figure 7.1, these two concentric circle diagrams illustrate opposite, yet mutually reinforcing, conceptions of the structural relationship of evolutionary emergence. The "arising within" conception shown in the diagram above is also echoed in figure A.1 in appendix A. For more on these inverse parallels, see Steve McIntosh, *Evolution's Purpose* (New York: Select Books, 2012), pp. 134-137. Further, it should be mentioned in this context that evolution's emergent structure reveals more than a linear sequence of transcendence and inclusion. As Ken Wilber has shown in his four-quadrant model of evolution (also discussed in appendix A), emergence unfolds simultaneously in both individual and collective dimensions, and not only externally and physically, but also within the interiors of consciousness and culture. See Ken Wilber, *Sex Ecology, Spirituality,* (Boston, MA: Shambhala, 1995), chapters 4 and 5.

7. Beyond the confines of neo-Platonic philosophy, the special significance of the value triad of goodness, truth, and beauty has also been recognized by a wide diversity of significant writers such as Aquinas, Kant, Diderot, Rousseau, Schelling, Tolstoy, Whitehead, Freud, Gandhi, Sorokin, and Einstein, to name a few. Many spiritual teachers, in both the East and the West, have also extolled this triad of values, including Sri Aurobindo, Rudolf Steiner, Thich Nhat Hanh, Cardinal Newman, and Osho Rajneesh. Sri Aurobindo, for example, describes goodness, truth, and beauty as the "three dynamic images" through which one makes contact with "supreme Reality." The leading secular writer currently championing this triad is Howard Gardner, whose book, *Truth, Beauty, and Goodness Reframed* (New York: Basic Books, 2012) is mentioned in the main text.

202 | *Developmental Politics*

8. This interpretation of Whitehead's philosophy comes from eminent process theologian David Ray Griffin, who writes: "This Whiteheadian criterion for judging evolutionary progress—greater capacity for experience that is intrinsically valuable—is positively correlated with greater capacity to include more feelings and objective data from the environment in one's experience." David Ray Griffin, *Religion and Scientific Naturalism: Overcoming the Conflicts* (Albany, NY: State University of New York Press, 2000), p. 301.

9. See McIntosh, *The Presence of the Infinite*, pp. 125-128.

10. Many readers will have some familiarity with the "Hegelian Dialectic," which is often simplified through the three-term construct of *thesis-antithesis-synthesis*. It should be noted in this context, however, that some dialectical philosophers reject this description. For example, French social theorist Georges Gurvitch argued that dialectical thinking is: "The destruction of all rigid, objectifying, reductionist thought—the kind of thinking that is exemplified quite precisely by stereotyped ... thesis-antithesis-synthesis explanations ... [D]ialectic is 'essentially anti-dogmatic,' consisting of 'the demolition of all acquired and crystallized concepts.' ... it must 'eliminate any pregiven philosophical or scientific point of view,' and remain open to 'ever-renewed experiences that do not allow themselves to be trapped in any immobilized operational framework.' ... it 'refrains from annihilating the unity within the multiplicity or the multiplicity within the unity, the simultaneous movement of wholes and their parts.'" According to contemporary dialectician John P. Clark, "Gurvitch warns in particular against the 'fetishism of the antinomy,' by which he means the tendency to reduce dialectic to the interaction between polarized contradictories. In other words, he warns specifically against the error of most critics of dialectic, and of numerous inept amateur dialecticians, both of whom latch on to the stereotyped dialectical template of 'thesis versus antithesis' to disguise the fundamentally anti-dialectical content of their thinking." All quotes above are from: http://review31.co.uk/essay/view/7/it-is-what-it-isn%27t-a-defence-of-the-dialectic. As these quotations indicate, dialectical philosophy is highly nuanced and even somewhat slippery. But while I agree with Gurvitch that authentic dialectical thinking breaks out of preconceived mechanical categories, this point should not prevent us from recognizing how the antithetical character of postmodernism needs to be transcended and included by a more "synthetic" political perspective. See also, the definition of "dialectical relationship" in note 10 for chapter 4 above.

11. See McIntosh, *The Presence of the Infinite*, chapter 8: "Toward a Method for Evolving Consciousness," pp. 221-246.

12. As of this writing the most visible proponent of integral philosophy continues to be Ken Wilber, although as noted in note 9 for chapter 4 above, my interpretation of integral philosophy differs from his. Wilber has certainly shown leadership through his writing, but his attempts to lead a social movement have

failed. Other leaders in the integral intellectual community have been brought low by a variety of missteps, including sexual impropriety and abuse of authority. The integral movement has also been hampered by conflicts between Wilber and the followers of Clare Graves' "Spiral Dynamics" theory, as well as by the attacks of vocal materialists who object to the spiritual component of integral philosophy. But the fact that the integral movement's time has not yet come does not diminish the power of its insights regarding the evolution of consciousness and culture.

CHAPTER 8

1. Researchers in the field of developmental psychology have identified numerous "lines of development" within the human mind, including cognitive lines, emotional lines, and moral lines. See e.g. Howard Gardner, *Intelligence Reframed* (New York: Basic Books, 1999). For an integral interpretation of developmental lines, see McIntosh, *Integral Consciousness and the Future of Evolution*, chapter 9; and Ken Wilber, *Integral Spirituality* (Boston, MA: Shambhala, 2006), pp. 58-60. See also, the discussion in appendix A.

2. Blaise Pascal, quoted in *The University Record*, vol. 1 (Chicago: University of Chicago Press, 1897), p. 112.

3. Although Saint Paul's theological virtues are traditionally named "faith, hope, and charity," the original Latin word for "charity" is *caritas*, which is more accurately translated in modern English as "love." The word love is thus now used more frequently by scholars in this context.

4. Alasdair MacIntyre, *Dependent Rational Animals: Why Human Beings Need the Virtues* (Chicago, IL: Open Court, 1999), p. 5. As quoted in McCloskey, *The Bourgeois Virtues*, p. 307.

5. Christopher Peterson, Martin E. P. Seligman, *Character Strengths and Virtues: A Handbook and Classification* (Oxford University, 2004), p. 36.

6. McCloskey, *The Bourgeois Virtues*, p. 319.

7. Ibid, p. 308.

8. Thomas Aquinas, *Summa Theologica* (Christian Classics; English Dominican Province Translation edition 1981), Ia IIae, question 73.

9. Deirdre McCloskey. This quotation is from the article: "The Faithful and Hopeful Economic Agent," p. 20, https://www.deirdremccloskey.com/docs/faithful.doc.

10. The idea of "perfecting the universe" is not meant as an endorsement of either social perfectionism or utopianism. Humans may not be "perfectible," but we nevertheless have the power to make the world incrementally more perfect by

contributing to the evolution of consciousness and culture. Perfecting the universe is therefore an evolutionary idea that entails gradual improvement into what systems scientist Stuart Kauffman calls the "adjacent possible." The spiritual connotations of this idea were articulated by Rabbi Abraham Joshua Heschel, who wrote: "The measure of man's life lies in perfecting the universe," quoted in: Krista Tippett's blog: "On Being" https://blog.onbeing.org/page/169. For a fuller discussion of the theology of perfecting the universe see passim: McIntosh, *The Presence of the Infinite*, and *Evolution's Purpose*.

11. See Ryan Niemiec, *Mindfulness and Character Strengths*, (Boston, MA: Hogrefe Publishing, 2013). This book is tied-in with positive psychology's promotion of the practice of virtues. See https://www.viacharacter.org/www/Mindfulness.

CHAPTER 9

1. David Brooks, *New York Times* op-ed, "The Virtue of Radical Honesty," Feb. 22, 2018, https://www.nytimes.com/2018/02/22/opinion/steven-pinker-radical-honesty.html.

2. Proverbs 29:18, *Holy Bible: King James Version* (Nashville, TN: Christian Art Publishers 2013).

3. Amartya Sen, *Development as Freedom* (New York: Anchor, 2000), p. 18.

4. See The Social Progress Index's website: https://www.socialprogress.org.

5. Taylor, *A Secular Age*, pp. 626-631.

6. Michael Polanyi, *Personal Knowledge: Towards a Post-Critical Philosophy* (New York: Routledge and Kegan Paul, 1962), p. 404.

APPENDIX A

1. *The Stanford Encyclopedia of Philosophy*, "Social Ontology," https://plato.stanford.edu/entries/social-ontology.

2. Ibid.

3. See Wilber, *Sex Ecology, Spirituality*, pp. 40-198. For a simplified explanation of the quadrant model, see the article: "What Are the Four Quadrants?" on the Integral Life website: https://integrallife.com/four-quadrants

4. For those familiar with Wilber's four-quadrant model, the problems it encounters at the level of noosphere evolution include the following: Contrary to the mind-body (interior-exterior) relationship implied by the upper individual quadrants, human consciousness can evolve in ways that do not depend on the

underlying evolution of human biology. Even though some simple forms of consciousness have clear neural correlates, and even though the activity of all forms of consciousness leaves traces in the physical brain, there is not a one-to-one correspondence between brain activity and conscious states and stages, as Wilber's model indicates. A similar problem can be seen in the implied relationship between the lower collective quadrants. Not all intersubjective structures are dependent on, or otherwise bound by, the evolution of physical human artifacts, or "Its." As with consciousness, interior systems of culture extend partially into the physical world, but worldviews do not evolve in lock-step with economic systems or other "interobjective" structures. While newly emerging worldviews do eventually give rise to physically observable political, economic, and technological systems, the emergence of new levels of interior culture generally precedes the appearance of more evolved exterior systems and institutions. Like consciousness, the interior evolution of culture enjoys degrees of freedom from the physical world and its material determinism. In fact, it is the partial freeing of interior development overall (individual and collective) from the physical constraints of biological evolution that ultimately makes noosphere evolution a unique and vitally important kind of evolution. As noted, Wilber's quadrants accurately chart evolution in the biosphere, where the quadrants are indeed symmetrical in their development. And these biospheric relationships continue to configure the noosphere to some extent, which makes the quadrant model "true but partial." However, trying to frame noosphere evolution by using the developmental parameters of the biosphere is ultimately reductionistic and does not accurately chart the unique features of noosphere evolution.

5. In addition to the objections discussed in the note directly above, see also: McIntosh, "Problematizing Interobjectivity: A Response to Edwards," originally published in *The Journal of Integral Theory and Practice*, vol 3, no. 4 (Winter 2008), and now available online at: https://www.stevemcintosh.com/articles/ problematizing-interobjectivity-a-response-to-edwards. See also McIntosh, *Integral Consciousness and the Future of Evolution*, "Appendix B," pp. 324-42.

6. As a remedy for developmental psychology's lack of consensus regarding the stages that define a person's overall level of psychological development, Ken Wilber has proposed a theory of "altitude" within consciousness, which is intended to be a neutral measure, like inches or meters. According to this theory, within the overall "opening of consciousness," *altitude* refers to "general similarities across the various lines, yet ... itself has no content." (*Integral Spirituality*, p. 68.) However, regardless of Wilber's dictum that "all holons have four quadrants," his theorizing in this area remains embedded in the psychological "upper-left quadrant" of his model. This results in an analysis that treats subjective structures of consciousness and intersubjective structures of culture as though they are essentially identical. But according to the argument I'm making in appendix A's main text, notwithstanding the evident

206 | *Developmental Politics*

"homologies" between the individual and collective structures of development in these two domains, and notwithstanding the obvious overlap between consciousness and culture, intersubjective structures of culture have a degree of systemic independence from subjective structures of consciousness (and vice versa). Which means that structural similarities between the multiple lines of subjective psychological development can be best explained, not by a theory of interior altitude, but by the imprint of historical cultural development, which influences these psychological lines by varying degrees. Simply put, the stages of development demonstrated by subjective lines of growth are evidently shaped by the stage-wise development of human history.

7. For the direct quote and citation for Habermas' thinking in this area, see note 2 to chapter 7.

8. See e.g. the Wikipedia article: "The Replication crisis" https://en.wikipedia.org/wiki/Replication_crisis. See also The New York Times article: "Psychology Itself Is Under Scrutiny" July 16, 2018, https://www.nytimes.com/2018/07/16/health/psychology-studies-stanford-prison.html

9. Types of intersubjectivity range from small-scale agreements, such as the meanings of words, to large-scale agreements, such as money, law, and the value agreements that cohere into major worldviews. The realm of intersubjectivity also encompasses feelings that bind families, friends, and larger communities. As a starting place for further research into the field, this Wikipedia article on intersubjectivity is helpful: https://en.wikipedia.org/wiki/Intersubjectivity.

10. Please note that figure A.1 is not intended as a replacement or substitute for Wilber's quadrant model. The four-quadrant model ambitiously attempts to chart the entire structure of evolutionary emergence since the big bang. Charting the structure of emergence is an important project, and the quadrants provide a "true but partial" beginning to this mapping process. Even though figure A.1 does not include a timeline of development, it does more accurately show how the subjective and intersubjective interiors of the noosphere fit together with the objective exteriors of nature and biology. Figure A.1 also shows the crucial evolutionary role played by manmade artifacts. This figure thus avoids the distortion created by a chart that shows "four quadrants" placed next to each other as symmetrical equivalents. As I am arguing, in the noosphere, the interior universe interpenetrates the exterior universe, but it is not completely bound by it, or otherwise symmetrical in its development. Figure A.1 accordingly provides a more accurate "snapshot" of the noosphere relationships of "I, We, and It."

APPENDIX B

1. The thirteen virtues recommended by Benjamin Franklin were: "Temperance, Silence, Order, Resolution, Frugality, Industry, Sincerity, Justice, Moderation, Cleanliness, Tranquility, Chastity, and Humility." See *The Autobiography of Benjamin Franklin* (Seattle, WA: CreateSpace Independent Publishing, 2019), p. 38 forward.

2. See the *New York Times* article "A Simple Way to Better Remember Things: Draw a Picture—Activating more parts of your brain helps stuff stick," January 6, 2019, https://www.nytimes.com/2019/01/06/smarter-living/memory-tricks-mnemonics.html.

3. Heraclitus, quoted in: Wayne Hogue, *Elements of Leaders of Character* (Nashville, TN: Westbow Press 2013), p. 34.

SELECTED BIBLIOGRAPHY

Abramowitz, A., *The Great Alignment: Race, Party Transformation, and the Rise of Donald Trump* (Yale University Press, 2018).

Aquinas, T. *Summa Theologica* (Coyote Canyon Press, 2018).

Aristotle. *The Nicomachean Ethics* (Oxford University Press, 2009).

Aurobindo, G. *The Future Evolution of Man: The Divine Life upon Earth.* (Wheaton, IL: Quest Books, 1974).

Basseches, M. *Dialectical Thinking and Adult Development* (New York: Ablex Pub. Corp., 1984).

Baum, A. J. *Philosophy: An Introduction* (Hoboken: Wiley, 1953).

_____. *Polarity, Dialectic, and Organicity* (Thomas, 1970).

Beck, D. & Cowan, C. *Spiral Dynamics: Mastering Values, Leadership and Change* (Blackwell, 1996).

Bell, D. *Cultural Contradictions of Capitalism* (Basic Books, 1976).

Bergson, H. *Creative Evolution.* Mineola, (NY: Dover Publications, 1998).

Bohman, J. & Rehg, W. (Eds.) *Deliberative Democracy Essays on Reason and Politics* (MIT, 1997).

Boyd R. and Richerson P. *Culture and the Evolutionary Process* (University of Chicago Press, 1985).

Carr, D., Arthur, J. & Kristjánsson, K. (Eds.) *Varieties of Virtue Ethics* (Palgrave Macmillan, 2017).

Commons, M., Richards, F. A. & Armon C. (Eds.), *Beyond Formal Operations: Vol. 1. Late adolescent and adult cognitive development,* (New York: Praeger, 1984).

Courser, Z., Helland, E., & Miller, K. (Eds.) *Parchment Barriers: Political Polarization and the Limits of Constitutional Order* (University Press of Kansas, 2018).

Crowder, G. *Liberalism and Value Pluralism* (Continuum, 2001).

Dalton, R. J. & Welzel, C. *The Civic Culture Transformed: from allegiant to assertive citizens* (Cambridge University Press, 2014).

Deneen, P. *Why Liberalism Failed* (Yale University Press, 2018).

De Wit, B. & Meyer, R. Strategy: *Process, Content, Context: an International Perspective* (Cengage Learning Business Press, 1998).

Donald, M. "The Virtues of Rigorous Interdisciplinarity," in Lucariello, J. et al, (Eds.) *The Development of the Mediated Mind* (London: Psychology Press, 2004).

Feuerstein, G. *Structures of Consciousness: The Genius of Jean Gebser, an Introduction and Critique* (Integral Publishing, 1987).

Foot, P. *Natural Goodness* (Oxford University Press, 2001).

Frankl, V. *Man's Search for Meaning* (Beacon Press, 2006).

Franklin, B. *The Autobiography of Benjamin Franklin* (CreateSpace Independent Publishing 2019).

Freinacht, H. *The Listening Society* (Metamoderna, 2017).

Frey, J. and Vogler, C. (Eds.) *Self-Transcendence and Virtue: Perspectives from Philosophy, Psychology, and Theology* (Routledge, 2018).

Friedman, T. *The Lexus and the Olive Tree* (Farrar, Straus and Giroux, 1999).

Fukuyama, F. *Political Order and Political Decay* (Farrar, Straus and Giroux, 2014).

_____. *Identity: The Demand for Dignity and the Politics of Resentment* (Farrar, Straus and Giroux, 2018).

Gardner, H. *Intelligence Reframed* (Basic Books, 1999).

_____. *Truth, Beauty, and Goodness Reframed* (Basic Books, 2012).

Gaus, G. F. *Contemporary Theories of Liberalism* (SAGE Publications, 2003).

Gebser, J. *The Ever-Present Origin* (Ohio University Press, 1985).

Gilbert, M. *Joint Commitment: How We Make the Social World* (Oxford University Press, 2015).

Goldberg, J. *Suicide of the West* (Crown Forum, 2018).

Goodin, R. E. (Ed.), *Oxford Handbook of Political Science* (Oxford University Press, 2011).

Gorski, P. *American Covenant* (Princeton University Press, 2017).

Graves, C. W. *Levels of Human Existence* (Example Product Manufacturer, 2004).

Griffin, D. R. *Religion and Scientific Naturalism: Overcoming the Conflicts* (Albany, NY: State University of New York Press, 2000).

Habermas, J. *Communication and the Evolution of Society* (Beacon Press, 1979).

_____. *The Philosophical Discourse of Modernity* (MIT Press, 1987).

Haferkamp, H. & Smelser, N. J. (Eds.) *Social Change and Modernity* (U.C. Berkeley Press, 1992).

Haidt, J. *The Righteous Mind: Why Good People Are Divided by Politics and Religion* (Pantheon, 2012).

Hampden-Turner, C. M. & Trompenaars, F. *Building Cross-Cultural Competence: How to Create Wealth from Conflicting Values* (Yale University Press, 2000).

Handy, C. *The Age of Paradox* (Harvard Business Review Press, 1995).

Havard, A. *Virtuous Leadership: An Agenda for Personal Excellence* (Scepter Publishers, 2007).

Hegel, G. W. F. *The Phenomenology of Spirit* (Oxford University Press, 1979).

Herman, A. *The Idea of Decline in Western History* (Free Press, 1997).

Heyes, C. *Cognitive Gadgets: The Cultural Evolution of Thinking* (Harvard, Belknap Press, 2018).

Hiebert, P. *Transforming Worldviews* (Baker Academic, 2008).

Huntington, S. *The Clash of Civilizations and the Remaking of World Order* (Simon & Schuster, 1996).

Inglehart, R. *Modernization and Postmodernization: Cultural, Economic, and Political Change in 43 Societies.* (Princeton University Press, 1997).

_____. *Human Values and Social Change* (New York: Brill, 2003).

_____. *Cultural Evolution: People's Motivations are Changing, and Reshaping the World* (Cambridge University Press, 2018).

Israel, J. *Radical Enlightenment: Philosophy and the Making of Modernity, 1650–1750* (Oxford University Press, 2001).

Jantsch, E. *The Self-Organizing Universe* (Pergamon Press, 1980).

Johnson, B. *Polarity Management* (Amherst: HRD Press, 1996).

Johnston, C. *Necessary Wisdom: Meeting the Challenge of a New Cultural Maturity* (Berkeley: Ten Speed Press, 1991).

Kahan, A. S. *Mind vs. Money: The War between Intellectuals and Capitalism* (Transaction Publishers, 2010).

Kauffman, S. *Reinventing the Sacred* (Basic Books, 2008).

Kegan, R. *The Evolving Self: Problem and Process in Human Development* (Harvard University Press, 1982).

_____. *In Over Our Heads* (Harvard University Press, 1994).

Koestler, A. *The Act of Creation* (The Macmillan Company, 1964).

Kohlberg, L. *From Is to Ought* (New York: Academic Press, 1971).

Lasch, C. *The Revolt of the Elites and the Betrayal of Democracy* (W. W. Norton & Co, 1995).

Lane, J. & Wagschal, U. *Culture and Politics* (Routledge, 2012).

Lichbach, M.I. & Zuckerman A. S. (Eds.) *Comparative Politics: Rationality, Culture, and Structure* (Cambridge University Press, 2009).

MacIntyre, A. *Dependent Rational Animals: Why Human Beings Need the Virtues* (Chicago, IL: Open Court, 1999).

_____. *After Virtue: A Study in Moral Theory* (University of Notre Dame Press, 2007).

Mackey, J. & Sisodia, R. *Conscious Capitalism: Liberating the Heroic Spirit of Business* (Harvard Business Review Press, 2012).

Maslow, A. *Motivation and Personality* (HarperCollins, 1987).

McCloskey, D. N., *The Bourgeois Virtues: Ethics for an Age of Commerce* (University of Chicago Press, 2007).

_____. *Bourgeois Dignity: Why Economics Can't Explain the Modern World* (University of Chicago Press, 2010).

_____. *Bourgeois Equality: How Ideas, Not Capital or Institutions, Enriched the World* (University of Chicago Press, 2016).

McIntosh, S. *Integral Consciousness and the Future of Evolution: How the Integral Worldview Is Transforming Politics, Culture and Spirituality* (St. Paul, MN: Paragon House, 2007).

_____. *Evolution's Purpose: An Integral Interpretation of the Scientific Story of Our Origins* (New York: SelectBooks, 2012).

_____. *The Presence of the Infinite: The Spiritual Experience of Beauty, Truth, and Goodness* (Wheaton, IL Quest Books, 2015).

Mounk, Y. *The People vs. Democracy: Why Our Freedom Is in Danger and How to Save It* (Harvard University Press, 2018).

Murdoch, I. *The Sovereignty of the Good.* (New York: Routledge and Kegan Paul, 1970).

Murray, C. *Coming Apart: The State of White America, 1960-2010* (Crown Forum, 2013).

Nicholls, A., Simon, J., & Madeleine, G. (Eds.) *New Frontiers in Social Innovation Research* (Palgrave Macmillan, 2015).

Niemiec, R. *Mindfulness and Character Strengths* (Boston, MA: Hogrefe Publishing, 2013).

Niemiec, R. M., & McGrath, R. E., *The Power of Character Strengths: Appreciate and Ignite Your Positive Personality* (VIA Institute on Character, 2019).

Owen, D. S. *Between Reason and History: Habermas and the Idea of Progress* (Albany, NY: State University of New York Press, 2002).

Peterson, C. & Seligman, M. *Character Strengths and Virtues: A Handbook and Classification* (Oxford University, 2004).

Phipps, C. *Evolutionaries: Unlocking the Spiritual and Cultural Potential of Science's Greatest Idea.* (Harper Perennial, 2012).

Piaget, J. *The Child's Conception of the World* (New York: Routledge, 1928).

Pieper, J. *The Four Cardinal Virtues* (University of Notre Dame Press, 1967).

Pinker, S. *Enlightenment Now: The Case for Reason, Science, Humanism, and Progress* (Viking, 2018).

Pirsig, R. *Lila: An Inquiry Into Morals* (Bantam, 1992).

Plato. *The Republic* (Capstone, 2012).

Quinn, R. E. & Cameron, K. S. *Paradox and Transformation: Toward a Theory of Change in Organization and Management* (Cambridge, MA: Ballinger, 1988).

Rawls, J. *Justice as Fairness: A Restatement* (Harvard, Belknap Press, 2001).

Ray, P. & Anderson, S. *The Cultural Creatives: How 50 Million People Are Changing the World* (New York: Harmony Books, 2000).

Raz, J. *The Practice of Value* (Clarendon Press, 2003).

Rifkin, J. *The Empathic Civilization* (New York: Tarcher Putnam, 2009).

Rochon, T. R. *Culture Moves: Ideas, Activism, and Changing Values* (Princeton University Press, 2018).

Rokeach, M. *The Nature of Human Values* (Free Press, 1973).

Rolston, H. *Environmental Ethics: Duties to and Values in the Natural World.* (Temple University Press, 1988).

_____. *Science and Religion: A Critical Survey* (Templeton Foundation Press, 2006).

_____. *Three Big Bangs* (Columbia University Press, 2011).

Rubin, E. L. *Soul, Self, and Society: The New Morality and the Modern State* (Oxford University Press, 2015).

Schuck, P. H. *Why Government Fails So Often: And How It Can Do Better* (Princeton University Press, 2014).

Solomon, R. *Ethics and Excellence* (Oxford University Press, 1993).

Strauss, W., & Howe, N. *The Fourth Turning: An American Prophecy* (Broadway Books, 1997).

Talisse, R. B. *Democracy and Moral Conflict* (Cambridge University Press, 2011).

_____. *Pluralism and Liberal Politics* (Routledge, 2012).

Taylor, C. *Sources of the Self* (Harvard University Press, 1989).

_____. *A Secular Age* (Harvard, Belknap Press, 2007).

Teilhard de Chardin, P. *The Phenomenon of Man* (Harper & Row, 1955).

Tepperman, J. *The Fix* (Crown, 2016).

Tomasi, J. *Free Market Fairness* (Princeton University Press, 2012).

Vance, J. D. *Hillbilly Elegy: A Memoir of a Family and Culture in Crisis* (Harper, 2016).

Volk, T. *Quarks to Culture: How We Came to Be* (Columbia University Press, 2017).

Wade, Jenny, *Changes of Mind: A Holonomic Theory of the Evolution of Consciousness* (Albany, NY: SUNY Press, 1996).

Welzel, Christian, *Freedom Rising: Human Empowerment and the Quest for Emancipation* (Cambridge University Press, 2013).

Westover, T. *Educated: A Memoir* (Random House, 2018).

Whitehead, A. N. *Adventures of Ideas*. New York: Free Press, 1967.

_____. *Process and Reality* (Free Press, 1978).

Wilber, K. *Sex, Ecology, Spirituality* (Boston, MA: Shambhala, 1995).

_____. *Integral Spirituality* (Boston, MA: Shambhala, 2006).

_____. *Trump and a Post-Truth World* (Boston, MA: Shambhala, 2017).

Wilson, D. S. *Does Altruism Exist?: Culture, Genes, and the Welfare of Others* (Yale University Press, 2015).

Woodard, C. *American Nations* (Viking, 2011).

Wolin, S. *Politics and Vision: Continuity and Innovation in Western Political Thought* (Princeton University Press, 2004).

Wydra, H. *Politics and the Sacred* (Cambridge University Press, 2015).

Zak, P. J. and Jensen, M. C. *Moral Markets: The Critical Role of Values* (Princeton University Press, 2008).

ACKNOWLEDGMENTS

First, I am deeply indebted to my wife, Tehya McIntosh, whose encouragement, patience, and support helped make the writing of this book possible. Thanks also to my two sons, Ian and Peter, who forgave me for the long hours I spent in my "writer's cave."

Special thanks to my close friend and neighbor, Jeff Salzman, whose integral wisdom and good advice made a significant contribution to this book. I am also grateful for the encouragement and support of my other friends and colleagues at the Institute for Cultural Evolution: John Mackey, Carter Phipps, John Street, Michael Zimmerman, and Elizabeth Debold. Thanks also to the additional readers of my earlier drafts: Tony Schwartz, Ron Meyer, Pat Trahan, Karen Everett, and Gary Sheng. And thanks to the other kind folks who have supported the work of the Institute: Craig Hamilton, Ann Drum, David Drum, Verona Rylander, Margo Yoder, Tom Curren, Luke Comer, Susan Cannon, Ted Nordhaus, Bert Parlee, and Annick de Witt.

Thanks to my publishers at Paragon House, Gordon Anderson and Rosemary Yokoi, my agent John White, my editor Byron Belitsos, my publicist Ileana Wachtel, and my webmaster Andy Schwarz.

Finally, I wish to acknowledge the living authors whose ideas have had a significant impact on *Developmental Politics*: Charles Taylor, Robert Kegan, Jürgen Habermas, Holmes Rolston III, Ken Wilber, Jonathan Haidt, Ronald Inglehart, Christian Welzel, Charles Johnston, Candace Vogler, Francis Fukuyama, Deirdre McCloskey, and David S. Owen. And thanks also to the many deceased authors, too numerous to name, whose wisdom informs my perspective.

INDEX

ABOUT THE AUTHOR

STEVE MCINTOSH is president of the Institute for Cultural Evolution think tank, which focuses on the cultural roots of America's political problems. He has authored three previous books on integral philosophy: *The Presence of the Infinite* (Quest, 2015), *Evolution's Purpose* (Select Books, 2012), and *Integral Consciousness and the Future of Evolution* (Paragon House, 2007). McIntosh is also coauthor, with John Mackey and Carter Phipps, of the book: *Conscious Leadership* (Penguin, 2020). Before becoming a writer and social entrepreneur, McIntosh had a variety of other successful careers, including founding the consumer products company Now & Zen, and practicing law with one of America's largest firms. His innovative political thinking has been featured on *NPR*, *The Daily Beast*, *The National Journal*, and in a wide variety of other media. He is an honors graduate of the University of Virginia Law School, and the University of Southern California Business School. McIntosh grew up in Los Angeles and now lives in Boulder, Colorado with his wife and two sons. For more on his work visit: stevemcintosh.com.